Russia's Future

Published in cooperation with
the Center for Foreign Policy Development
of the Thomas J. Watson Jr. Institute for
International Studies, Brown University

Russia's Future

Consolidation or Disintegration?

EDITED BY

Douglas W. Blum

Westview Press

BOULDER • SAN FRANCISCO • OXFORD

Copyright © 1994 by Westview Press, Inc.

Published in 1994 in the United States of America by Westview Press, Inc., 5500 Central Avenue, Boulder, Colorado 80301-2877, and in the United Kingdom by Westview Press, 36 Lonsdale Road, Summertown, Oxford OX2 7EW

A CIP catalog record for this book is available from the Library of Congress.
ISBN 0-8133-2201-4 — ISBN 0-8133-2202-2 (pbk.)

Printed and bound in the United States of America

The paper used in this publication meets the requirements
of the American National Standard for Permanence of Paper
for Printed Library Materials Z39.48-1984.

10   9   8   7   6   5   4   3   2   1

To my friend, Jo-Anne Hart,
for suggesting the project,
and
my wife, Jessica Regelson,
for her love and encouragement

Contents

Acknowledgments

The editor would like to express thanks to the authors who contributed to this book and who were asked to make revisions under severe deadline pressure. The editor also gratefully acknowledges Mary Lhowe, assistant editor, for her work in preparing the manuscript. Given the need for ongoing revisions and the demanding publication schedule, this was an unusually difficult job, yet it was always done with professionalism and good humor. Amy Langlais also provided valuable assistance in preparing the final draft. Mary Rhodes of the Department of Political Science at Providence College and Brenda Menard at the Center for Foreign Policy Development of the Thomas J. Watson Jr. Institute for International Studies were also very helpful in providing technical and secretarial support at various stages of the project. Finally, thanks go to the center for supporting a conference on Russia's future in October 1992, from which this book evolved.

Douglas W. Blum

Introduction

Douglas W. Blum

In what direction is Russia heading? Is it likely to disintegrate into territorial sub-units or dissolve into social and political anarchy? What prospects does it have for reemerging as a consolidated nation-state? What forces or trends are likely to influence either outcome? The following chapters present a number of findings and arguments that carry important implications for Russia's future.

Because edited volumes can be weakened by a lack of internal cohesion, a concerted effort has been made here to focus on a consistent theme and to connect the findings in each chapter. The contributors were asked to consider developments in their areas of expertise from the standpoint of their implications for the overall prospects of consolidation versus disintegration in Russia. There is no attempt to provide exhaustive descriptions in each area of inquiry. Instead, the emphasis is on analysis, and the thrust of each chapter is to elucidate the causes and effects of change.

Fundamental issues are at stake in Russia regarding the nature of the evolving political and economic order. At the most basic level is the question of how Russia defines itself as a society, and how it conceives of its place in relation to other states in the international system. Such essential values and self-definitions are likely to have an important influence on patterns of institution-building and to impart a general direction to domestic and foreign policy.

This issue is addressed in Chapter 1, as Stephen Shenfield sets a provocative tone for the volume by exploring the possible ideological bases for social and political cohesion. As he observes, consolidation of the Russian state requires broad popular agreement about a range of practical and abstract questions relating to national identity, including demarcation of borders, constitutional structure, ethnic character, and cultural orientation. At present there is a great deal of uncertainty about the answer to these questions, and this raises fundamental doubts about the legitimacy of the state. Shenfield considers various sources for creating a viable self-identity, including pragmatic accomplishments, ideals of the Russian revolution, prevailing international norms of human rights and democracy, and historical traditions of the recent or distant past. He considers several alternative "ideal types" of historical self-identification, including neo-Soviet, archaic, liberal, and statist, but concludes that none of them is likely to provide the necessary degree of ideological cohesion in the foreseeable future.

In Chapter 2, Eric Rudenshiold and N. Catherine Barnes examine the complexities of local politics in Russia, and highlight the divergent forces that may determine the prospects for national cohesion from the grassroots up. Since the collapse of communism there has been a tremendous proliferation of political parties. Yet, as the authors point out, many of them lack clear goals, and many have been crippled by infighting and fragmentation. Most parties are severely hampered by the economic crisis, and they often lack even the most basic resources. Furthermore, many local political apparatuses are still controlled by communists, and therefore in many areas there is a tug-of-war between elected officials, central appointees, and holdovers from the Soviet regime. In all of these ways the chaotic condition of Russian society impedes the emergence of functional pluralism and contributes to centrifugal tendencies.

A crucial arena for working out a post-Soviet national identity and system of governance is the elite level of politics. In Chapter 3, Regina Smyth considers the evolution and political dynamics of the Russian parliament, including the emergence of internal institutions and procedures, as well as the interaction between parliament and external actors such as the executive and various organized interest groups. Smyth analyzes the nature of political struggles for the development of stable mechanisms of governance and for control over information relevant to key issue areas. She also assesses the carryover of old structures and personnel, and the problems involved in building a majority coalition, both from the standpoint of individual deputies and the institution as a whole. While most (though not all) participants favor "democracy," this concept may be construed in quite different ways, each of which suggests disparate forms of political organization at the central and local levels.

Such basic political questions are inseparable from the roiling debate about the trajectory of economic development. Advocates of capitalism, socialism, command-control, and mixed economies all clamor for attention. Clearly the choice that is made will affect the prospects for internal growth and stability. The issues of economic orientation and investment philosophy are addressed by Michael Spagat in Chapter 4, and the issue of labor relations is examined by Linda Cook in Chapter 5.

Spagat focuses on the structural imbalance that underlies the disintegration of the Russian economy. He argues that investment decisions in the USSR were highly irrational from an economic point of view, which means that a high percentage of Russian firms would be likely to fail if they were exposed to world market conditions. Indeed, the collapse of the economy following the reforms of January 1992 was partly a response to the imposition of financial discipline and higher prices. Firms that heeded the government's threats to drive them into bankruptcy if they were unprofitable were forced to cut back their output dramatically in order to reduce their losses. However, many firms correctly assumed that the government would ultimately bail out lossmakers, as it had always done in the past. Spagat suggests that such tendencies may continue to operate in the foreseeable future, as powerful political pressures act to retard the process of privatization and to subsidize state industry. At the same time, he analyzes the prerequisites of efficiency, and assesses the factors conducive to reform in the economic and political spheres.

This same theme is taken up by Cook in her chapter on labor relations. Cook explores Yeltsin's policy of "social partnership," in which representatives of organized labor, management, and government were brought together to reach workable compromises. She contends that this approach reduced labor unrest, but at an unacceptably high economic and political cost. Here again, as in the case of firm insolvency, the government consistently compromised in order to prevent worker unrest by increasing wages and thereby contributing to the inflationary spiral. By accommodating labor's demands it impeded recognition of the need for structural adjustment, and at the same time the situation failed to produce a stable institutional mechanism for arbitration among the three sectors. Cook also evaluates the significance of the official union's collapse, and examines the most important avenues of change within the labor movement, as well as their relationship to the larger problem of Russian disintegration.

In addition to questions about the overall content of Russia's political and economic development, there remains the question of interregional relations. In Chapter 6, Sergei Khrushchev considers whether separate local economies, rather than an integrated national economy, are emerging. Russia and the Soviet Union were held together by the dependence of enterprises and regions on the centrally planned economy, which was upheld by the existing legal and institutional framework. In the post-Soviet period, every locality is able to assert its own prerogatives. The result of this situation has been the emergence of independent or even autarkic regional economic development, often coupled with non-payment of taxes.

Given these disturbing trends, many commentators have expressed concerns about the possibility of civil upheaval or ethnic wars. Equally realistic fears have been voiced about the danger of an expansionist or militaristic Russia asserting its will throughout the former Soviet Union, or perhaps exerting a destabilizing influence on regional conflicts. Given Russia's size, geographical situation, and military power, any factors likely to affect Russia's international orientation or domestic cohesion are worthy of our attention. Whatever the specific outcome may be, it is certain to have a major impact on international security—on regional conflict management, arms control, environmental regulation, and social stability—throughout Europe, Asia, and the Middle East.

In Chapter 7, John Lepingwell focuses on one aspect of this problem by considering the process whereby a new relationship between military and civilian authorities is evolving. Several quite different platforms are currently competing for power, and this struggle has important implications for the nature of civil-military relations. Should an authoritarian platform emerge, military power might play a dominant role in the bid to achieve consolidation. Conversely, in order to prevent massive use of military power, a democratically oriented platform must emerge to guarantee civilian control over the military. As a way of gauging possible developments, Lepingwell examines trends in five key areas, including: (1) the need to restructure the military while ensuring adequate command and control; (2) the problem of maintaining professionalism; (3) the battle against corruption; (4) the strength of nationalism and regionalism; and (5) the creation of new institutions of civilian oversight. He argues that important problems in each area must be resolved if stable civil-military relations are to emerge in Russia.

In Chapter 8, Douglas W. Blum discusses the complex relationship between foreign policy and the forces that are holding Russia together or tearing it apart. The author identifies four tendencies toward disintegration that affect Russian foreign policy: (1) ethnic separatism; (2) Islamic fundamentalism; (3) outside territorial claims; and (4) local economic particularism or territorial secession. At the same time, Blum emphasizes that there are divergent approaches for addressing these problems. Three major orientations—liberal, statist, and national-patriotic—are currently competing for influence. Each has a quite different perception of international politics, and this has a direct bearing on prescriptions for managing instability at home. Here again, as with civil-military relations, there are important connections between Russian disintegration, domestic politics, and foreign affairs.

It should be stressed that the contributors to this volume are aware of the tentative nature of their conclusions. As these chapters were being written, important developments were taking place in Russia, and the foreseeable period is certain to remain fluid in many essential respects. Indeed, the purpose of this work is not to engage in specific prognostication, but rather to understand better the scope of possible outcomes, the nature of indigenous political and economic forces, and the combined sources of change that may push developments in one or another direction. Without pretending to read the future, a cautious prospective analysis may be helpful in alerting us to tendencies at work and the factors affecting them. This, in turn, can facilitate our ability to exert an influence on developments or, at least, to better prepare for their coming.

1

Post-Soviet Russia in Search of Identity

Stephen D. Shenfield

Introduction

When we look back at our state as it existed in the past, do we recognize the links between its present existence and its earlier forms? Do we identify ourselves psychologically with its citizens, feel proud of their accomplishments and ashamed of their misdeeds? Do we conceive of them and ourselves as belonging to a single community linking past, present, and future? Are we inclined to refer to our predecessors as "we" or as "they"? This chapter addresses the problem of historical self-identification in general, and its special pertinence to post-Soviet Russia.

This problem of historical self-identification is salient in the political and cultural controversies even of those countries that have enjoyed a fairly smooth and continuous historical evolution. Even now a significant fault line divides Britons who recall the days of the British Empire with nostalgia from those for whom reminders of the imperial heritage evoke embarrassed unease. It is often said that Americans care little for history; yet even in the United States passions can be ignited by such issues as how the anniversary of Columbus's arrival in America should be commemorated, or how school textbooks should handle the fact that George Washington was a slave holder.

How much more vital and sensitive, then, is the problem of historical self-identification in national societies that bear the legacy of sharp discontinuities in their development, especially if a lively historical consciousness also prevails! For example, it still matters a great deal in France whether one is "for" or "against" the Revolution of 1789; and the relationship of present-day Germany and Japan to their predecessor states defeated in 1945 is still an extremely painful and divisive question.[1]

When we turn to today's Russia, however, the problem of historical self-identification reaches a level of acuity perhaps unparalleled elsewhere. Russians have always had a very strong sense of their history, vividly encapsulated in the Russian expression *sviaz vremen* (the tie of ages). And contemporary Russians must reorient themselves again in the wake of two sharp breaks in the development of the Russian state that have occurred within the space of a single life span—that is, the dual revolution of February and October 1917, and the transformation that culminated in the collapse of the USSR in December 1991.

It is not surprising, therefore, that the contemporary politics of Russia is defined to a large extent by the divergent answers that its citizens give to the question of the place that the "new Russia" (or is it a reborn "old Russia"?) should strive to occupy in the history of the Russian state. Do they perceive the Russia of 1993—or the future Russia of 2003 that they hope to shape—as basically a successor to and continuation of Soviet Russia? Or as a successor to Tsarist Russia, the evolution of which was so rudely interrupted? As both? Neither?

The answer to this question is a crucial factor in determining the institutions that Russia seeks to build and upon which the country's future and its domestic and foreign policies depend. Whether a sufficiently broad and firm consensus can be established among Russia's citizens on how to answer this question is a critical element in determining whether Russia will acquire the social cohesion and psychic (Russians prefer to say "spiritual") coherence necessary for its consolidation as a state, or whether it will disintegrate.[2]

The argument of this chapter is organized as follows. I first consider how to structure the history of the Russian state in order to define the four main ideal types of historical self-identification that are reflected in the politics and culture of today's post-Soviet Russia. I characterize these ideal types and illustrate how each manifests itself in contemporary Russian life. I then proceed to assess the likely potential effect of each type upon the consolidation or disintegration of Russia. In conclusion, I consider the likely fate of post-Soviet Russia insofar as this is determined by the nature of its people's historical self-identification.

Russian History and the "Ideal Types" of Historical Self-Identification

In considering Russia's historical heritage as it is reflected in the thinking of contemporary citizens of Russia, it is useful initially to distinguish the following three periods in the development of the Russian state: (1) the period of the Tsarist empire; (2) the democratic republic of February 1917 to October 1917; and (3) the period from 1917 to 1991. The following discussion characterizes these periods and illustrates how awareness of them manifests itself in contemporary Russian life. This, in turn, makes it possible to identify four distinct ideal types of self-identification that are likely to be influential in shaping the development of post-Soviet Russia.

1. Tsarist: In the period before Peter the Great, Russia existed as a fairly homogeneous (in the ethnic and cultural sense), landlocked kingdom within borders much narrower than those it would later acquire, centered at various times around either Kiev (the early Kievan Rus) or Moscow (Muscovy). A few Russian observers have attempted to reconcile their fellow countrymen to Russia's loss (to the other post-Soviet states) of "historical Russian lands" that once were part of both the imperial Tsarist and the Soviet empires by drawing a parallel between pre-Petrine Russia and today's Russia.[3] Nevertheless, it is primarily those who welcome the disintegration of Russia and the rise of new regional states, rather than those who wish to consolidate Russia as a historically recognizable entity, who draw inspiration from the pre-imperial period.[4]

The majority focus on the imperial period, which lasted from the reign of Peter the Great to the collapse of Tsarism in February 1917. At present, the idea of partially or completely restoring the traditions of the Tsarist empire is the most obvious and widely understood alternative to continued reliance upon an adapted and reformed Soviet heritage. The key elements of the Tsarist mode of self-identification include Orthodoxy as the ideological foundation of the state, autocracy, and Great Russian nationalism, in addition to other auxiliary elements such as Cossackdom.[5]

2. Democratic: The short period between the revolution of February 1917 and the Bolshevik seizure of power in October 1917 has enormous significance for Russians who strive to be fully consistent democrats. These individuals often are driven to reject unequivocally both the Tsarist and the Soviet heritage. The historical memory of this period plays an important role in contemporary Russian politics, as demonstrated most powerfully in the movement to reconvene the Constituent Assembly that the Bolsheviks dispersed by force at the beginning of 1918. As conceived by its proponents, the Assembly had the task of making a clean break with the Soviet period by establishing a new Constitution providing for a division of executive, legislative, and judicial powers along Western lines.[6]

3. Soviet: Despite the dramatic changes currently underway, the Soviet period retains enormous weight in the Russian consciousness. It is, after all, the most recent of the four periods, and the one in which all living generations (except for a tiny minority of very elderly individuals) have grown to maturity. Moreover, in contrast to other peoples of the former USSR, most Russians considered the Soviet Union as a whole, rather than the Russian Federation (RSFSR), to be their homeland.[7] The loss of their "big homeland" has consequently had a deeply disturbing impact on many Russians' psyches. (Furthermore, in the institutional sphere there is still significant continuity with the Soviet period. Although the Communist Party has been ousted and the Su-

preme Soviet abolished, at the provincial and local levels many traditional Soviet elites retain power.)

In defining the various patterns of historical self-identification for post-
Soviet Russians, we can distinguish four ideal types, corresponding to the
most significant combinations of acceptance or rejection of each of these two
periods. Thus, the first category of self-identification (neo-Soviet) consists of
those who accept the Soviet and reject the Tsarist heritage; the second category
(archaic) consists of those who accept the Tsarist and reject the Soviet heritage; the third (statist) includes those who accept the heritage of both the
Tsarist and the Soviet periods; and the last (liberal) category comprises those
who reject the heritage of both the Tsarist and the Soviet periods, many of
whom draw inspiration from the democratic interlude in 1917.

The neo-Soviet type refers to Russians whose sense of historical self-identification derives mainly from the Soviet period. By no means does this include only or even primarily the communists who aim to restore the Soviet
system in roughly its previous shape. This category of self-identification also
includes the numerous ordinary people who simply take for granted the institutions and way of life inherited from Soviet times, and who are willing to accept change only on the condition that it is carried out gradually. It is such
people who constitute the mass base of powerful "centrist" forces like Arkadii
Volskii's Civic Union and Iurii Skokov's "Concord for the Fatherland." Aspects of this orientation include socialistic values of extensive welfare statism;
a multi-ethnic, pan-Russian approach to statehood; and a geopolitical focus on
the former Soviet area (perhaps but not necessarily including the larger Soviet
empire). One can even argue that, by dint of habit, the Soviet period exerts a
powerful influence upon the consciousness of all those who do not make a special effort to orient themselves toward some other frame of reference.[8]

According to the archaic self-identification, Tsarist Russia is the sole au-
thentic historical embodiment of the Russian state, and Bolshevism is excori-
ated as an alien intrusion into Russia's body politic. This orientation includes
highly fragmented features gleaned from various periods of Russian history, as
well as a set of rather nebulous qualities attributed to the Russian people, such
as *narodnost* (folk nationalism), *dukhovnost* (spirituality), *vsechelovechnost*
(universal humanism), and *sobornost* (organic, spiritual congregationalism).[9]

Table 1.1   Ideal Types of Historical Self-Identification.

	Heritage of Soviet Union	Heritage of Tsarist Russia
Neo-Soviet	Accept	Reject
Archaic	Reject	Accept
Statist	Accept	Accept
Liberal	Reject	Reject

The meaning of the "statist" ideal type requires further explication. It is logically impossible to fully accept both the Tsarist and the Soviet heritage, although some people would like to do so. The statist orientation aims to effect a compromise between the two heritages by combining elements of both, since taking either one to its logical conclusion would mean having to reject the other. For instance, statists may favor increasing the role of the Orthodox Church in state and society (this role was significant even during parts of the Soviet period), and may pay homage to the Cossack revival movement, but will not go so far as to advocate a restoration of the monarchy. The statist view recognizes both the Tsarist empire and the Soviet Union as successive forms of a historically continuous Russian state.[10] In this view, Russia has undergone occasional dramatic metamorphoses, but remains essentially the same.[11]

The unsatisfying eclecticism of the statist position makes it unattractive to intellectuals, although there are some prominent social theorists who advocate it.[12] However, it has great appeal to pragmatic officials, for whom it offers the broadest scope for political maneuver, conciliation of different social interests, and evasion of potentially destabilizing choices.[13] Indeed, statism is now the most influential form of historical self-identification in Russia.

Table 1.2 Main Characteristics of Ideal Types in Post-Soviet Russia

	Statist	Archaic	Neo-Soviet	Liberal
Soviet heritage	Accept	Reject	Accept	Reject
Tsarist heritage	Accept	Accept	Reject	Reject
Territory	Flexible	Slavic lands[a]	USSR	Flexible
Ethnic identity	Mixed[b]	Russian [*russkii*]	Pluralist	Pluralist
Religious identity	Pluralist	Orthodox	Secular	Secular
State structure	Flexible	Theo-autocracy	Federation of Soviet Republics	Federal Republic[c]
Perceived role	Eurasian	Special	Eurasian	European or Western

[a] Russia (possibly minus northern Caucasus and Tuva), Ukraine, Dnestr region, Belarus, northern and eastern Kazakhstan, northeastern Estonia.
[b] Often viewed as based upon a Slavic-Turkic combination.
[c] Usually on the American or German model.

The "liberal" ideal type in fact fuses two significantly different sub-types of Russian historical consciousness. It includes the awareness of those who look back to the abortive democratic republic of 1917 as well as the nineteenth-century liberal democratic tradition that prepared the way for it. At the same time, it includes a kind of "anti-historical" consciousness of people who do not believe that Russia actually possesses a serious liberal tradition; who consider the whole Russian historical heritage a benighted one; and who look for inspiration exclusively to foreign (Western) experience.[14] These are the "Russophobes" against whom the self-proclaimed Russian patriots rail.

The ways in which the four ideal types of Russian self-identification tend to be associated with specific conceptions of the territorial, ethnic, religious, constitutional, and historical identity of the state are set out below.

Territorial and Constitutional Structure

Those embracing a neo-Soviet self-identification naturally strive to restore a new union that will bear as close a resemblance as possible, in territorial extent as well as internal structure, to the USSR. In practice, this usually means a much strengthened Commonwealth of Independent States (CIS) within which the constituent republics retain considerable autonomy. Most people of neo-Soviet orientation realize that reimposition of a fully centralized state is neither a realistic nor a desirable goal. That is, they aim to create the reformed federation of Soviet republics that Mikhail Gorbachev strove for but never achieved, rather than a new version of the USSR that actually existed. Within this broader context, the exact borders of the Russian Federation are a less vital matter.

An archaic self-identification entails the use of the borders of the Tsarist empire as criteria for Russia's appropriate borders today. Some flexibility is provided by the choice of date: all accept the Tsarist empire as the frame of reference, but which period of the empire? The loss of relatively recent and poorly assimilated nineteenth-century acquisitions—Central Asia, Transcaucasia, perhaps the Northern Caucasus—is tolerable or perhaps even welcome. What cannot be given up are the "historic Russian lands," meaning Ukraine and Belarus (in the archaic mind set the existence of separate Ukrainian and Belarussian nations is not admitted); most of the present-day Russian Federation; and parts of neighboring republics long settled by Russians (northern Kazakhstan, northeastern Estonia, the Dnestr region, etc.). The constitutional goal of the most consistent archaists is restoration of a realm based on the fusion of the Orthodox Church and the autocracy. There is also an important moderate variant of archaism that advocates a religious orientation for state policy while maintaining a separation between church and state.[15]

Territory is not as important an issue for either the statist or the liberal orientations, since they are not so closely tied to specific historical precedents. Consequently, each possesses much greater scope for flexibility. Liberals generally seek to emulate federal republics like the United States or Germany; statists are not committed to any particular constitutional model, but rely upon a generalized historical legacy "averaged" over a long period of the past.

Ethnic and Religious Identity of the State

The archaic orientation typically seeks to establish a Russia that will be both ethnically Russian and confessionally Orthodox. Indeed, archaists generally equate the two: only an Orthodox believer can be a true Russian, although there is a reluctance to grant that a non-Russian who converts to Orthodoxy can also be considered a Russian.[16] In fact, this is a distortion of the historical record, as the Tsarist empire was not Russian in an ethnic sense, but rather incorporated the rulers of the peoples it conquered into its own nobility. Nevertheless, as is typically the case when ethnic and religious concerns predominate, the historical record is perused with a selective eye.

The statist orientation takes an instrumental approach to matters of ethnic and religious identity. At least as an ideal type, statism is committed neither to liberal, secular ideals, nor to any specific ethnic or religious cause. Instead, the state itself is the ultimate value. For this reason, statists tend to argue that Russia can be stable only on the basis of ethnic and religious pluralism.[17] Thus, the state as a whole should not be defined as ethnically Russian or Christian, so that non-Russians and non-Christians can be loyal to it. On the other hand, it may be considered useful to permit religion and ethnicity a role in state government at the local level. From this perspective Russia is conceived of as a mixed inter-ethnic (e.g., Slavic and Turkic) or inter-religious (e.g., Christian and Moslem) state rather than as a non-ethnic secular state of the Western type.

Interestingly, there appears to be some convergence on the questions of ethnicity and religion between the neo-Soviet and the liberal orientations. The liberal is loyal to the tradition of the non-ethnic secular state, in which individual citizens participate directly in the polity irrespective of their ethnicity or religion, which are relegated to the private sphere. The neo-Soviet inherits the tradition of the largely ethnically based sub-units of the USSR (union and autonomous republics, autonomous provinces etc.), but tends now to be critical of this aspect of the old Soviet structure, seeing in it the seeds of the current disintegration of the union. Therefore the neo-Soviet tends to agree with the liberal that federalism ought to be organized on a territorial rather than on an ethnic basis.[18] The neo-Soviet outlook also endorses a secular, if no longer anti-religious, state.

Historical Identity

There is a vast ongoing debate about the place of Russia in world civilization, influenced by both pre-revolutionary and emigre thought.[19] Three main
points of view are detectable. First there is the view, typical of the liberals, that
Russia is simply part of European (or, by extension, Western) civilization; it
has its own national peculiarities, but only in the sense that any European
country (say, France or Italy) also has its own national peculiarities. Second,
there is the Eurasianist school of thought, which sees Russia simultaneously as
part of both European and Asian civilization, an amalgam of the two or a
bridge between them. Neo-Soviets and statists find this philosophy convenient
for their purposes. Finally, the archaists see Russia as a special world in itself;
they share with the neo-Soviets reservations toward Europe and the West, but
they do not embrace the Asiatic/Turkic aspect of Russia's heritage, preferring
an emphasis on Slavdom.

Consolidation or Disintegration?

Having outlined the chief characteristics of the leading ideal types of historical self-identification, it remains to consider their potential impact on the
prospects for consolidation or disintegration of post-Soviet Russia.

First, the neo-Soviet orientation appears to be gradually losing its initially
strong consolidating potential, as the Soviet period recedes into the past and
loses its grip on the popular mind. On the other hand, it would be a mistake to
discount its potential for the foreseeable future, since the weight of the Soviet
past is felt not so much in specific institutions and practices as in a more diffuse set of attitudes, such as an orientation toward the post-Soviet geographical area and an attachment to a basically Soviet conception of the "social contract" between the individual and the state. These habitual elements are not
likely to disappear soon.

The archaic orientation seems likely to play a significant role in shaping
the public debate, even if it remains relegated to the sidelines of day-to-day
policy formation in most parts of Russia. Its influence probably will be detrimental to the integrity of the Russian state, since archaism is incapable of
playing a broadly consolidating role. There are very large sections of Russian
society that simply cannot accept restoration of Tsarist or other traditional
forms of social and political organization.

Perhaps the best example of why archaism cannot function as a consolidating force is the Orthodox Church. The obvious problem posed by the central role of Orthodoxy is the existence of other religions, especially given their
link with ethnicity—i.e., traditionally Moslem (on the Volga and in the north
Caucasus), Buddhist (in southeastern Siberia), Judaic, and pagan ethnic

groups (e.g., Mari or shamanist Siberian peoples). Seemingly reasonable arguments have been made that this does not matter a great deal; since the non-Christian ethnic groups are not a very large minority of the population and are geographically fairly compact, they can be allowed autonomy within a state that is elsewhere officially Orthodox Christian (as at certain times under Tsarism). However, the likely reaction of non-Christian religious communities is not the only problem facing those who would try to consolidate the Russian state on the basis of Orthodoxy. First of all, Christianity in Russia is not the same thing as Orthodoxy. Catholicism is acquiring an increasingly significant presence, and there are numerous Baptist, Lutheran, and other Protestant churches. Here again, there is some link with ethnicity, as with the Protestant affiliation of most ethnic Germans. Second, a very substantial part of society certainly will remain agnostic or atheist for a long time to come.[20] The observable tendency gradually to elevate Orthodoxy to the status of *de facto* state religion is just as much an affront to many non-believers as it is to the adherents of non-Christian religions and non-Orthodox Christian confessions.[21]

In addition, a factor that is not sufficiently appreciated is that Orthodoxy itself is very seriously and bitterly divided. The main divisions are between the established hierarchy inherited from the Soviet period; archaic branches dedicated to restoration of Holy Tsardom (e.g. the Orthodox Church Abroad, which is gaining an increasing number of adherents inside Russia); and modernist intellectual currents drawing their inspiration from such religious philosophers of the late pre-revolutionary period as Vladimir Solovev and Nikolai Berdiaev.[22] These modernist currents are especially strong among the religiously inclined elements of the intelligentsia. Such individuals tend to be adamantly secularist, arguing against the fusion of church and state.[23] It is perhaps this last factor—the existence of internal divisions—that is likely to be decisive in preventing Orthodoxy, and archaism generally, from playing a consolidating role.

The liberal orientation also faces significant difficulties in acquiring the necessary degree of popular support. This is the case not only for well-known reasons, such as the severe costs of liberal reform for the less adaptable and weaker parts of the population, but also because the "anti-historical" liberal sub-type so deeply offends the feelings of patriotism that are still entrenched in large sections of the population, especially in the provinces.[24] Despite Yeltsin's relative success in the 1993 April referendum, and regardless of the immediate outcome of the December elections, it is premature to claim that there exists anything approaching a popular consensus in favor of the liberal orientation.

Finally, the statist orientation is widely regarded within the Russian political establishment as the form of historical self-identification with the greatest consolidating potential. This judgment is undoubtedly correct, since a statist approach can satisfy, or at least avoid completely alienating, almost everybody.

The problem is that "statism" lacks inner coherence, so it is difficult to give it a stable intellectual form. On the one hand, this may not matter greatly, insofar as much of the population is unconcerned about conceptual coherence and may be willing to tolerate a considerable degree of ambiguity or dissonance as long as important emotional needs are met, or as long as political and economic stability can be provided. On the other hand, there appear to be limits to the practicality of this eclectic approach, since attempting to pursue traditional Tsarist and Soviet practices simultaneously may lead to institutional conflicts. An interesting early example of this may be the friction arising between Cossacks and local legislatures in southern Russia, where disparate elements of the statist mix reveal their incompatibility.[25]

Thus, in weighing the impact of the different types of self-identification, it is hard to avoid the conclusion that the disintegration of Russia is a likely prospect. Obviously, this will depend critically on other factors, including local ethnic unrest, spillover problems from the near abroad, and the ability of the government to stabilize the economy. Given reasonably favorable developments in these areas, we should not be too hasty in dismissing the possibility of stabilization on the basis of either a statist compromise, or an alliance between statists and archaists. Yet the underlying orientations around which political actors might coalesce, construct legitimate platforms, and mobilize social support, do not seem promising for the continued unity of the Russian state.

Notes

1. For useful discussions of the problems of historical self-identification faced by Germans and Japanese looking back on their pre-1945 states, see Chap. 3 in Gordon A. Craig, *The Germans* (Bungay, Suffolk: Penguin Books, 1984); and the Introduction to Haruko Taya Cook and Theodore F. Cook, *Japan at War: An Oral History* (New York: The New Press, 1992).

2. See the related argument by Mikhail Sivertsev, "Rossiiskaia politicheskaia kultura i perspektivy mnogopartiinosti," *SShA*, no. 1, January 1993, pp. 49-60.

3. For example, see A.A. Tarasov and V.L. Tsymburskii, "Rossiia: na puti k doktrine natsionalnoi bezopasnosti," *SShA*, December 1992, pp. 23-31.

4. There is currently in Siberia a revival of the philosophy of *oblastnichestvo* (provincialism), dating to the book of the nineteenth-century writer N.M. Iadrintsev, *Siberia as a Colony* (St. Petersburg, 1882). The provincialists consider the unification of Siberia and Muscovy a great tragedy for the people of Siberia. See Vera Tolz, "Regionalism in Russia: The Case of Siberia," *RFE/RL Research Report* 2, no. 9, February 26, 1993.

5. See N. Riasanovsky, *Nicholas I and Official Nationality in Russia, 1825-1855* (Berkeley and Los Angeles: University of California Press, 1959).

6. Marina Sale, a people's deputy affiliated with the Free Democratic Party of Russia, espouses such views in "Luchshe pozdno, chem nikogda," *Nezavisimaia gazeta*, November 25, 1992, p. 5.

7. For sociological data confirming this, see Leokadia Drobizheva, "Perestroika and the Ethnic Consciousness of Russians," in *From Union to Commonwealth: Nationalism and Separatism in the Soviet Republics,* Gail W. Lapidus and Victor Zaslavsky (Cambridge: Cambridge University Press, 1992), pp. 98-113.

8. This is borne out by numerous interviews and focus groups conducted by the author and his colleagues, Richard Smoke and Mark Kramer, in Russia during 1992 and 1993, in the context of the Security for Europe Project of the Watson Institute's Center for Foreign Policy Development. A common view was expressed by one woman participating in a focus group in May 1993 in response to a question: "What do you consider to be your country?" "My country," she replied, "I consider to be that state in which I grew up." None of the other participants dissented.

9. A relatively mild expression of archaism can be found in the quarterly journal *Vozrozhdenie,* founded in 1992 and edited by O.E. Kirillov, subtitled, "a free journal of Russian unification and statehood." For a more extreme form, see L. Okhotin, "Katastrofa i vozrozhdenie," *Sovetskaia Rossiia,* January 28, 1993, p. 4.

10. According to Otto Latsis, "The country that was called the Russian Empire and then the Soviet Union is a really existing unity. Not only a single economic and military-political space (that is subject to change), but a human unity." "Pochemu SSSR ne dozhil do svoego 70-letiia," *Izvestiia,* December 29, 1992, p. 3.

11. See the proclamation by the emigre writer Eduard Limonov in "Manifest Rossiiskogo natsionalizma," *Sovetskaia Rossiia,* June 12, 1992.

12. E.g., Aleksandr Tsipko, "'Demokraticheskaia Rossiia' kak bolshevistskaia i odnovremenno pochvennicheskaia partiia," *Nezavisimaia gazeta,* September 4, 1992, p. 5.

13. For an accessible statement of the statist perspective, see Sergei Stankevich, "Russia in Search of Itself," *National Interest,* no. 28, Summer 1992, pp. 47-51.

14. See also Viacheslav Petsukh, "Otkrytie Rossii," *Literaturnaia gazeta,* no. 4, January 27, 1993, p. 3.

15. Interview with Aleksandr Ogorodnikov, chairman of the Christian Democratic Union, in *Nezavisimaia gazeta,* October 29, 1992, p. 2.

16. See the writings of Ioann, Metropolitan of St. Petersburg and Ladoga, "Derzhavnoe stroitelstvo," *Sovetskaia Rossiia,* November 14, 1992, p. 1; and "Iz sily v silu," *Sovetskaia Rossiia,* December 31, 1992, p. 1.

17. Aleksandr Vladislavlev and Sergei Karaganov, "Tiazhkii krest Rossii," *Nezavisimaia gazeta,* November 17, 1992, p. 5.

18. For one of many articles calling for a de-ethnicization of the Soviet state structure, see Gasan Guseinov, Denis Dragunskii, Viktor Sergeev and Vadim Tsymburskii, "Ethnos and Political Power," *XX Century and Peace,* September 1989, pp. 13-18.

19. For a fairly recent overview, see Vera Tolz, "Russia: Westerners Continue to Challenge National Patriots," *RFE/RL Research Report,* no. 49, December 11, 1992. For a critical review of the earlier Russian debate between Europeanists and Eurasianists, see Mark Bassin, "Russia between Europe and Asia: The Ideological Construction of Geographical Space," *Slavic Review* 50, no. 1, Spring 1991, pp. 1-17. The current reworking of Russian historiography for pedagogical purposes addresses many of these same issues. For an insightful discussion, see Elizabeth K. Valkenier,

"Teaching History in Post-Communist Russia," *The Harriman Institute Forum* 6, no. 8, April 1993.

20. In an opinion poll of citizens of Russia conducted in 1992, 36 percent declared themselves believers and 31 percent non-believers or atheists, while 33 percent were unsure. See *Sotsialnaia i sotsialno-politicheskaia situatsiia v Rossii: sostoianie i prognoz* (Moscow: Institute of Socio-Political Research, 1993).

21. See the two letters written by atheists complaining about this tendency, in *Nezavisimaia gazeta*, January 28, 1993, p. 5. A survey conducted by "Vox Populi" in February and March 1993 showed Russian opinion evenly divided in its attitudes concerning the social role of Orthodoxy. Twenty-three percent thought that the revival of Orthodoxy might play a positive role in the fate of Russia; 22 percent thought it might play a negative role, while the majority were undecided. *Mir mnenii i mneniia o mire,* May 1993.

22. For the official condemnation of modernism, see Mikhail Ardov, "Ne renessans, no rassvet," *Nezavisimaia gazeta*, March 24, 1993, p. 8. For an example of the traditionalist approach and its criticism of the established hierarchy, see the interview with Metropolitan Vitalii, Patriarch of the Russian Orthodox Church Abroad, in *Nezavisimaia gazeta*, November 5, 1992, p. 5.

23. Konstantin Kedrov, "Istoricheskii vybor Rossii v trudakh Vladimira Soloveva," *Izvestiia*, January 28, 1993, p. 6. Writing on the 140th anniversary of Solovev's birth, Kedrov reiterated the poet-philosopher's question: "O Russia! . . . What kind of East do you want to be? The East of Xerxes or of Christ?" Kedrov then observed, "The question was posed in 1890, and we must answer it today." See also Zoia Krakhmalnikova, "Shturm Khristianstva," *Nezavisimaia gazeta*, December 4, 1992, p. 5.

24. For attempts to overcome this gulf between liberalism and Russian nationalism, see Aleksandr Rubtsov, "Byt russkimi! no -- segodnia: v preddverii 'liberalno-patrioticheskogo sinteza'," *Nezavisimaia gazeta*, December 29, 1992, p. 5; and Viktor Malukhin, "Nash vybor," *Literaturnaia gazeta*, no. 51, December 16, 1992, p. 4.

25. "Kubanskie kazaki idut 'na vy'," *Nezavisimaia gazeta*, March 27, 1993, p. 3. See also Igor Gamaiunov, "Kazaki -- razboiniki," *Literaturnaia gazeta*, no. 4, January 27, 1993, p. 12. Gamaiunov asserts that a group of bandits near Sochi who call themselves Cossacks (but are in fact unrelated) are planning to conduct ethnic cleansing of Caucasians. Thus, Cossackdom may be a strong force for disintegration rather than for consolidation.

2

Political Party Development in Russia: Integration and Disintegration

Eric Rudenshiold and N. Catherine Barnes

To Western observers, perhaps the most incomprehensible aspect of this emerging multiparty system is its amorphous nature. Russia's many-tiered democracy seems to be forever changing, with parties appearing, splitting, dissolving, and merging in a continual ebb and flow of political chiaroscuro. Although the players often remain the same, a factional fog that shrouds this evolutionary process also tends to obscure the nuances among party platforms. As such, efforts directed at image-building by nascent political organizations in Russia are simultaneously undermined by the identity crises that accompany this process. Even for informed spectators, if not the participants themselves, differences between and changes within some groups can seem ambiguous.

Failing to find the stability characteristic of Western multiparty systems, analysts question the viability of Russia's nascent multiparty system as well as its approach to democracy, which can rapidly turn today's front-running political organization into tomorrow's flotsam. However, many preconceptions regarding the weakness of Russian democracy stem from viewing it from a strictly Western perspective. With its Soviet roots, Russia's party system is a cogent example of a flexible alternative to the former communist monolith.

The Informal Roots of Party Democracy

One of the great strengths of Russia's evolving party system is its record of survival and its crucial, albeit brief, experience during the last days of Soviet history. Only a few years ago, many Western analysts assumed that the Russian polity was a brain-dead organism lobotomized by Soviet indoctrination and incapable of paying more than lip service to independent thought.

17

Yet Gorbachev's *glasnost* spawned hundreds of social and political movements that enthusiastically met his challenge of taking initiative and responsibility. Ranging from cultural preservation societies to environmental rehabilitation groups, from workers' organizations to youth movements, these associations and groups began to regenerate civil society in Russia.[1]

A singular aspect of these groups was that, although they appeared to mirror many existing, state-sponsored organizations, the "informal group" movement was a radical departure from officially sanctioned social activity. Unlike their shepherded counterparts, the broad spectrum of groups representing the new civic order eagerly criticized the bureaucracy and government programs. Analysis in the West all but ignored the potential impact of informal groups (save for certain militants, like the anti-Semitic Pamiat) and tended to focus instead on top-down models of reform and Kremlinological views of leadership and power consolidation. But organized pressure for change increasingly was being applied from the grass roots by civic initiative groups at all levels of the Soviet system. As these groups encountered bureaucratic inertia, they became increasingly politicized in order to achieve their goals.

Reinforced by the creation of, and interaction with, similar organizations throughout the fourteen other republics of the Soviet Union, Russia's "informal group" movement registered hundreds, in some cases thousands, of members. Curiosity, special interests, and a burgeoning belief that change was possible under *perestroika* were among the key motives that spurred membership and broader social support. For a great number of registrants, these non-state-affiliated groups captured the imagination of society and represented something fundamentally new, which was the hope that individuals and continued reform could have a positive influence on Soviet surroundings. Ties among informal groups from different republics developed further and extended the boundaries of Gorbachev's *novoe myshlenie* (new thinking).

In order to combat the bureaucracy, individual groups were often forced to coalesce and merge their memberships. By fighting the static forces of the *apparat*, larger movements and groups sought to enhance the process of reform by uniting under the banner of "democracy." An unwritten, anti-center *entente cordiale* developed between many such groups across the former union. Their spirit of unity was, in turn, reinforced by the bureaucracy's fear of such unprecedented activities. The resulting sense of solidarity that developed between informal groups spawned mass participation at rallies and protests against perceived inequities, in favor of extending reforms, and many other increasingly political issues. Although Gorbachev initiated the call for civic participation, he and other governmental leaders found it difficult to direct the process or to put the genie back into the bottle once fear of reprisal abated and mass participation became established.[2] The concentrated efforts of democratic informal groups and proto-parties played a part in precipitating the backlash attempt by conservatives to usurp authority in August 1991.

When Democracy Flew the Coup

The August 1991 cabal resulted in more than the downfall of the Soviet empire. It also dramatically altered the process of democratization in Russia. Before the events of August 1991, significant integration of democratic forces existed at three levels: between republics and at the all-union level; at the Russian national (Moscow) level; and at the regional and local levels. After August, the evolutionary process within Russia's neophyte "multiparty system" changed fundamentally.

The motives for cooperation between organizations in opposition to the Communist Party of the Soviet Union (CPSU) and other anti-reform elements disappeared after the coup. Until then, many democracy groups and organizations, though pursuing different goals, had shared an anti-Moscow perspective that enabled them to coalesce and cooperate on mutually advantageous issues. Hence, an independence-minded Ukrainian group like the Social Democrats was able to find common ground with the Russian Christian Democratic Movement and the National Front of Georgia in opposing the lack of accountability in the Soviet system of government. The breakup of the Soviet Union and the disbanding of the CPSU resulted in a concomitant devaluation of commonly held notions for many political groups and organizations. A vacuum of power existed in Moscow's post-coup political environment, forcing an intensive regrouping of political forces in Russia and throughout the former Soviet Union.

At the all-union level, centrifugal forces prevailed as many formerly allied political organizations separated in order to begin the process of nation-building and to fill the political void in their own back yards. Thus, whereas the Democratic Russia Movement once had shared experiences and discussed strategies with the Latvian Popular Front, the Baltic groups began to regard things Russian, including former political compatriots, as potential antagonists once independence from the Soviet monolith was achieved. Similarly, the process of nation-building combined with lingering imperialist traditions in Russia complicated relations with activists in the newly independent republics. The great tragedy of this turning inward was that newly emerging parties from different republics that were faced with similar social, political, and economic challenges no longer had the time, resources, or inclination to share ideas.

At the newly defined "national level" of Russian politics in Moscow, post-coup developments included the annulment of many marriages of political convenience. Coalitions that had formed for the purpose of fighting the communist center began to break apart rapidly as political leaders grappled with the notion of party discipline in non-communist organizations. In essence, larger organized groups began to splinter or, in an effort to maintain the broader organization at any cost, became semi-paralyzed by factionalism.

This process is continuing today and is exacerbated by the Soviet experience that has resulted in what political activists call a Russian "allergy" to the concept—as they understand it—of "party," which conjures up unpleasant associations with the CPSU. In an attempt to overcome this hurdle, many groups still refer to themselves as "movements," "unions," or "associations."

Because of this fear of being compared to the communists, many parties eschew rules for their membership. Consequently, individuals who belong to one organization might also belong to other political groups, or might even hold ideas diametrically opposed to the party's platform. For example, it is not uncommon for two people to be members of the same political coalition, the same group within the coalition, and even the same faction within the group, but to argue from opposing views on major political issues. Since many coalitions have allowed both individual and group memberships, instances abound of persons who may simultaneously be members of one political coalition and of a political party that has opted against group membership in the same coalition. Such internal confusion, combined with the frequent reticence of members to take strong positions, makes it difficult for any political party to present a united and cohesive front.

Another layer of confusion was added when elected officials who had been ushered into office under the auspices of the CPSU or its officially sanctioned organizations switched their party affiliation during the final months of the communist regime or after its collapse. In some cases, the political leeway provided by the disintegration of the CPSU allowed for the public announcement of more genuine political affiliations. In a larger number of cases, the move was motivated by political expediency, if not outright political opportunism.

The nominal change has proven to be considerably easier for elected officials than has the necessary metamorphosis in ideology and policy. For many such officials, finding a new political home symbolizes greater freedom coupled with the continued security of a political organization, rather than commitment to the party's platform or loyalty to its agenda. In the recent past, such officials often pursued an independent course of action in the public forum of the Congress of People's Deputies (CPD) or the Supreme Soviet (SS), often in direct contradiction to the party line. The chasm between nascent grass roots political parties and their official representation in parliamentary bodies also precluded the development of a clear, consistent, and unique identity that could be communicated easily to the Russian electorate.

Challenges at the National Level

Broad political coalitions in Moscow, like the Democratic Russia Movement (*DemRossii*), which provided an umbrella for dozens of political parties and civic organizations after its inception in October 1990, have had a difficult time moderating the political process and creating stability in Russia's body politic. This can be explained by many challenges arising from both internal and external factors. The response of groups like *DemRossii* to these problems may determine the success or failure of the democratic experiment in Russia.

Externally, there is a lack of common cause for uniting political parties in the absence of the CPSU and its central authority to act as a lightning rod for the opposition. Although many large issues pose common obstacles for Russian political parties, none provides as compelling a source that could unite a confederation as did the CPSU. And although the communists still exist, they often have gone underground and are no longer as easy to pinpoint. Hence, frictions arise within existing democratic coalitions, as individuals and groups seek to build names for themselves at the expense of broader, more difficult coalition objectives. The resulting turf wars threaten what measure of stability existed within the larger democratic movement.

Until very recently, the virtual absence of democratic electoral activity at the national and local levels, along with lagging political reforms and continued bureaucratic resistance to the development of a multiparty system, also have provided an external challenge for Russia's political movements seeking to maintain their momentum. The "democratic era" is popularly regarded as a phenomenon of economic decline, rising crime, and social chaos, a notion reinforced by conservatives and communist recidivists. Democratic parties and coalitions also are challenged at the national level by having to defend a record of failed initiatives, despite the fact that failures were often the result of bureaucratic intransigence and communist sabotage. The tolerance of the Russian populace has been sorely tried by economic hardship. Conservatives are widely regarded as offering a viable alternative to radical reform.

Along with the existence of communist groups, the growth of extreme nationalist groups and parties also poses an external threat to democratic parties and their coalitions. As Blum shows in Chapter 8, by appealing to patriotism and Russian nationalism, these groups call on Russia to disengage from Western "expansionism" and to avoid dependency on Western aid. Instead, they call for Russia to pursue a foreign policy based on Eastern or more "Eurasian" models, in order to return Russia to its "former glory." Although the specific claims are vague, the theme plays on popular concerns and fears that Russia's democratic leadership is dribbling away the country's wealth into the pockets of foreign businessmen and governments.

However, the primary reason for instability within Russia's political parties and movements is a significant degree of infighting among new political elites. Within the Democratic Russia Movement, for instance, the collective leadership initially collaborated to achieve common goals, but soon became frustrated in its efforts by internal division. The reasons for the fissures were both personal and political. At the Democratic Russia Congress in November

1991, the movement faced its first test of the post-coup era. At issue was the position to be taken by the movement in view of President Yeltsin's announcement that Russia's border with Kazakhstan should be redrawn to incorporate Russian communities in northern Kazakhstan. The ensuing debate revolved around whether or not Russia could legitimately make claims on territory beyond the Russian Federation; whether force should be used to further expansionist goals (or, as some would have it, defend the rights of Russian minorities living in the newly independent republics); and whether such aims were consistent with the principles upon which the movement was founded. In the end, disagreements over the permissibility of force separated the moderate from extreme nationalists. The Coordinating Council voted against endorsing Yeltsin's position, registering open criticism of his policy. Three parties chose to vote with their feet, and withdrew their membership from the movement. These parties, which formed their own alliance known as the People's Accord Bloc, included Nikolai Travkin's Democratic Party of Russia (DPR), the Christian Democratic Movement (RCDM), and the Constitutional Democrats (CDP).

While this important policy issue served as the catalyst for the split, additional issues—of both a technical and a personal nature—further convoluted the circumstances surrounding the event. Political parties, not only those aligned under the People's Accord Bloc, feared that they were losing potential members to *DemRossii*'s growing individual membership and demanded that the *DemRossii* charter be amended to exclude individual memberships. At issue was whether or not individual members, who held a majority of the seats on the Coordinating Council, were using *DemRossii* structures to create a "super party," thereby maneuvering to gain a competitive edge over other parties in the coalition. Not surprisingly, positions taken by prominent activists within the movement on both the technicality of membership and the issue of policy toward former republics tended to correspond to personal power bases established by the same individuals.

Even after the dust settled, the breach between the three parties and the movement was not resolved. In the case of the DPR and the RCDM, the parties' national leadership lacked the support of the rank and file, and their efforts to consolidate power exacerbated fissures within each organization. Some local chapters, angered by the unilateral move of their leaders and supporting the decision reached by the Coordinating Council of *DemRossii*, defied their national organizations and maintained their memberships in the movement. This option was made possible by *DemRossii*'s practice of offering group memberships to national parties both through their headquarters and through local party chapters. Moderate-to-conservative chapters of the DPR defected at Travkin's signal, while radical reformers stayed with the movement. Ironically, some chapters, perhaps unable to discern any inconsistency, supported both organizations. In Khabarovsk, for example, the local Democratic Russia chapter claims to support Travkin and the Democratic Russia Movement, which in Moscow is considered to be a contradictory position.

At the national level, prominent activists and even members of the parties' executive boards left to form new parties or became defunct leaders of AWOL chapters within their respective organizations. For instance, Father Gleb Iakunin and Valerii Borshov, both members of the Coordinating Council of Democratic Russia and the executive board of the RCDM, established a new Christian Democratic Party based on the RCDM's chapters within the movement. Several members of the DPR leadership in St. Petersburg came to symbolize widespread opposition within the party, but eventually left the party altogether. Only the Constitutional Democrats appeared to survive the breach with their organization intact. As for the alliance between the DPR, RCDM, and the CDP (People's Accord Bloc), it proved short-lived, as each group explored its own political aspirations. The DPR became a founding member of another coalition, the Civic Union, and the CDP established the "Russian Rebirth" bloc.[3] It is no surprise that the political vacuum created by the departure of such powerful figures as Travkin resulted in political maneuvering and power struggles within *DemRossii*, which led to some members of the Coordinating Council suspending their membership in January 1992.[4]

Given the already considerable overlap among the various political groups and platforms, the propensity for cleavage in party identity is not particularly useful when attempting to distinguish one political organization from another. Moreover, Russia's penchant for "cult of personality" politics makes party growth and consolidation based on shared principles virtually impossible. The fissures in the Democratic Party of Russia can be viewed in this context. According to one DPR activist in Voronezh, "those who joined the party based on its platform can no longer condone Travkin's activities. Those who followed because of the man continue to support his self-serving agenda." The impact of personality politics is not limited to the DPR. Virtually all of the major political parties, and even the smaller ones (there are over 800 "parties" in Russia) are led by prominent, strong-willed, charismatic leaders to whom supporters flock and around whom party identities form.[5] The lack of emphasis on party platforms and rules and broader political goals often has led to irresponsible leadership, and promoted organizations based on short-term interests rather than long-term institutional viability.

Of course, not all parties suffer from the same strain of the disease. While Travkin dominates DPR politics, parties like the Republican Party of Russia (RPR) were formed by several "co-chairmen." In the context of Russian politics, this arrangement also begs the question of party factions. The general lack of internal agreement as well as the primacy of personal ambition also extends to interparty development. When the left wing of the RPR expressed the desire to merge with the Social Democrats (SDP) to create a larger, more competitive organization, they were opposed by the right-wing faction of the party.

Eventually, the merger failed because neither the RPR nor the SDP could agree on how to combine each group's leadership. Other organizations, such as Civic Union, likewise have been unable to overcome the ramifications of competing personal agendas within a collegial leadership structure.[6]

Regional and Local Party Structure

At the regional and local levels, democratization and party development have proceeded at a slower and more tentative rate, albeit for completely different reasons. Away from Moscow's political infighting, there is still a clearly defined enemy for democratic forces to unite against. Thus, despite Moscow's own problems and regardless of its claims to the contrary, there is, by necessity, much more cooperation and coordination between political parties at the local level. These local groups do not have the luxury of being able to engage in political infighting and obfuscation. Communism may have been outlawed and the CPSU disbanded, but the bureaucratic machine it created, the army of *apparatchiks* it left behind, and the corrupt local officials who assumed considerable power under Communist Party tutelage remain hostile to reform and to the norms of a democratic society. The entrenchment of conservative forces in the Russian countryside has kept local reformist party organizations very much on the defensive.

Local party leaders are quite outspoken in their contempt for the lack of unity in Moscow and the relative lack of interest displayed by national party leaders for the needs and concerns of local activists. Vertical communication and coordination are not well-developed in nascent political organizations. As an example of the political and cultural leftovers discussed by Shenfield in Chapter 1, the communist method of management—i.e. dictation from above—still predominates. Input from the grass roots, when it exists, is taken lightly by Soviet-style party bosses in Moscow. In some cases local party members fall readily into the mold, awaiting direction from the top. To them, local initiative remains a foreign and empty concept. For the large majority, however, local political groups, ignored by their leaders and overshadowed by their competitors, have the single option of uniting. "Cooperation and coalition is the only way to defeat the communists," says one rural party leader from Novosibirsk. "They have had years to perfect their techniques and have inherited the spoils of the Soviet regime. Our time is limited."

Russia's rural parties and regional branches of national groups are also facing a new challenge posed by economic hardship. The hyperinflation and economic disenfranchisement resulting from marketization have produced a currency that is rapidly losing its value, rising unemployment, and a working public that regularly rides a roller coaster of emotions between anxiety and hopelessness. With most of the military-industrial complex standing idle and many rural dwellers facing an uncertain future, local parties have been left to bear the brunt of the blame for economic reform and anti-Yeltsin sentiment. The current situation is described by one retired college professor as *bezvykhodnost*, or exitlessness. "This is what democracy has brought us," he complains, "where once we were a proud world power, now we are reduced to beggary." In Cheliabinsk, where 90 percent of industrial output went to fulfilling military orders in the days of the communist regime, the local economy has virtually collapsed. Current requests from the military account for less than 10 percent of production, with nothing to make up the difference. Likewise, agricultural regions still pay salaries that lag significantly behind inflation. The result is an understandably hostile electorate. With virtually no access to or influence in local governments, regional parties often feel they are being hung for the crimes of their democratic colleagues in Moscow. Frustrated with the seeming inability of those in Moscow to "fix the system," Russian voters in the provinces wish for a strong hand. "You have to understand," explained one party activist in Barnaul, "people in my district would vote for Stalin if they could, because he could get things done!"

As in Moscow and other major cities, local pro-democracy organizations also are widely held accountable for stalemate in government. The coexistence of appointed officials (in the case of Yeltsin's presidential representatives) as well as elected executives and local legislatures with diametrically opposed agendas has paralyzed regional and city soviets. In the Autonomous Republic of Mordovia, for example, a Democratic Russia candidate, Gusliannikov, won the December 1991 presidential election. Coupled with a democratically controlled local government, the Mordovian president was repeatedly stalemated by a communist regional legislature, which also determined his cabinet. Stagnation prevented the implementation of any policy, due to the communist-dominated middle government structure. The consequence of this paralysis was that the democratic president was blamed for ineffective leadership, even by many of his former supporters. Seizing upon this discontent and following Moscow's lead, the chairman of the regional legislature—who not ironically is a close friend of Speaker of the Russian Parliament Ruslan Khasbulatov—led a move to oust Gusliannikov. On April 8, 1993, the national parliament voted to eliminate his position, and this act was upheld by the Russian Constitutional Court.

In the Siberian city of Barnaul, the regional soviet was controlled by communists, while the local administration was led by a Yeltsin appointee. As with other Yeltsin presidential representatives throughout the Russian heartland, the appointee began to see his role as power broker in the regional government rather than advocate of Yeltsin-Gaidar reform policies, and consequently he lost the support of pro-Yeltsin organizations, including *DemRossii*. In Khabarovsk, a Yeltsin appointee who was the self-styled "governor" of the city, but was also rumored to have links to the local mafia, was regularly accused of representing his own interests in the governing process. With parliaments controlled by holdover communists and, in some cases, self-interested or corrupt Yeltsin appointees, most local parties had no avenues for support in the regional political administration.

This circumstance is not, however, universal. In the city of Voronezh, the presidential representative has actively supported political groups through regular communication, coordination, and provision of his own office space and equipment. While the Voronezh City Soviet yielded a nominally communist-controlled parliament, democrats maintained enough seats to deny communists the majority needed to adopt legislation. The democratic bloc in the parliament offered its cooperation to the majority in return for the vice chairmanship of the body. To the north, in the city of Arkhangelsk, the democratically oriented chairman of the parliament and the mayor overcame stalemate by establishing a flexible and interactive working relationship. Both began to cooperate with opposing parties in the region.

Internally, the most challenging threat to political entities at the local level is the lack of resources and access to mechanisms of power. Rural parties and branches of larger national parties, particularly those without deep historical roots in local CPSU structures, have virtually no financial or technical resources. Operating out of apartments instead of offices, often with only a handful of dedicated activists, a pocketful of rubles, and perhaps a telephone, paper, and pens, local party organizations cannot realistically compete with their well-provisioned opponents. The communist network remains largely intact. Through its connections with printing house managers, newspaper editors, or newsprint suppliers it is able to effectively deny democratic activists access to these resources. Lacking the buildings, cars, equipment, publications, and established business relationships of the former communists, the key asset of nascent political groups is personnel. Yet the current generation of pro-democracy activists, while eager and dedicated, is relatively unskilled, having been barred from significant participation in Communist Party organizations and Soviet structures of government. Volunteer recruitment, necessary to ensure the continued growth of political parties in the countryside, is increasingly difficult in an environment of economic depression. Placed on the defensive by ample and well-entrenched communist forces and a disgruntled populace, local and regional democratic parties are faced with an increasingly uphill climb.

The Future of Russia's Democratic Pastiche

Apart from its fluidity, one of the most frustrating characteristics of Russia's democracy has been its lack of momentum among political groups. Having stumbled for a long period with no elections to prepare for, parties had little impetus to consolidate. Instead, national-level coalitions tended to engage in lateral maneuvering, leaving little room for vertical development or maturation. Hence, structural growth within parties and movements correspondingly was inhibited. Local parties were forced to concentrate their scant resources fighting rear-guard actions against the charges of former communists and entrenched conservatives. A hostile and almost nihilistic polity further confounded party plans to build, grow, and recruit new members. Even today, Russian citizens often confess to simply being tired of the political process; more talk on the streets is equated with less food on their dinner plates.

In general, Russia's inchoate political party system has been caught in a vicious cycle relating to its growth and development. Factionalization and the splintering of larger, powerful coalitions has weakened the national-level organizations' abilities to fight entrenched bureaucracies and maintain support for reform. Infighting among political elites and their indifference to grass roots structures have alienated and left many regional party branches demoralized. While the new elections may provide a catalyst for developing stronger party infrastructures, there is dwindling support for many "democratic" reforms at the rural level due to inflation and economic disenfranchisement. Thus, existing political party structures, which have little bottom-up input and little top-down influence, have serious gaps between their national and regional branches.

In the past, democratic forces and political movements could claim few elected officials across Russia. Yet, the country's economic malaise has been widely blamed on "democratic policies." Although the average citizen generally appreciates the increase in civic liberties in Russia, many political parties fear this emancipation will be traded away by voters who look to their pocketbooks. When party activists in Voronezh were asked what they needed most to prepare for upcoming elections, "sausage" was the not-so-lighthearted reply. Fissures within democratic organizations, heightened by party stagnation and inactivity, have been symptomatic of a much larger problem—the slow progress of reform in Russia to date.

Real privatization in Russia is still in its early stages. Property and power have shifted from central to regional levels, and from regional to local levels, but they generally remain in the hands of the government, which in many areas has remained in the hands of former communists. The resources and properties that have been pried away from the state have flowed mainly to party *apparatchiks* and regional "mafias" (as organized crime is called), rather than to budding entrepreneurs.

Enforced by guns and well-paid and well-positioned personnel, and in the absence of rule of law, mafias have sprung up in urban and rural territories with comparative ease. They have, in fact, tended to compound the problems faced by political parties, whose supposed policies of openness and reform have given rise to violence and corruption at all levels of government. Caught between entrenched former communists and burgeoning mafias (which are in no way mutually exclusive), local democrats feel they have little room to maneuver. Thus, ironically, the democratization process has empowered mafias to a greater degree than it has empowered political parties and community-based civic organizations.

"We are peasants," says one activist in Barnaul. "We don't know about politics." He wonders whether peasants should be involved in politics at all. Such notions are dying hard in Russia, further reinforcing the authority and power of conservative forces. Again, to echo Shenfield's theme from Chapter 1, when Russian voters question the "experiment in democracy," they betray a Soviet legacy of skepticism and passive participation. They are reluctant to commit themselves to democratic groups whose policies, however incompletely implemented, have yielded little but misery.

Those who understand democracy only in terms of events or personalities, rather than process and institutional consolidation, may be sorely disappointed by short-term developments in Russia. Western analysis has tended to concentrate on the fray at the top, and the pitched battle between Russia's political forces promises to be a protracted affair. And yet, there is still some reason for optimism when regarding the nascent democratic community. Although the concept of democracy has become tarnished in the eyes of the electorate, Russia's democratic political groups are quite active, and have new opportunities for exerting influence on the political process. Communists and other conservative forces in Russia have failed to come up with viable alternative programs. If global efforts to assist Russia's transition are tied to democratization and tangible reforms, such as privatization, the old ties to power will finally be severed. This, perhaps, could be the needed foothold that Russia's political parties have been lacking so far.

Russian political analyst Nina Beliaeva has frequently used the phrase "crisis as progress" to explain Russian democracy.[7] Taken in such a context, the confrontation between progressive and reactionary forces which culminated in the siege at the White House can be seen as a breakthrough for democratic institutions and processes. The elections of a new parliament—if they are accompanied by impartial and efficient administration, genuine competition between political parties based on a leveling of the playing field, and active and informed engagement by the electorate—may further the progress of democracy in Russia.

The utilization of proportional representation (based on party lists) to elect half of the seats to the State Duma (lower house) of the Federal Assembly in December 1993 should provide the necessary catalyst for the development and consolidation of viable political parties in Russia.[8] At the same time, the incredibly short campaign period raises cause for concern. There is a need for adequate preparation for new balloting procedures, a need for party planning and internal party organization, and a need to inform the voting public.

Furthermore, even if conditions are ideal and time is sufficient, there is no guarantee that democratic forces will triumph in upcoming elections. Reactionary forces of the extreme right and left wings have continued to dominate many government and bureaucratic structures at the local levels. The membership and support bases of communist and national-patriotic parties remain intact and could easily be consolidated into new political organizations or coalitions. Together with regional and local power structures, reactionary forces still command substantial resources compared to democratic parties and movements at the grass roots. Moreover, there has been considerable disillusionment and even disgust about the "fruits" of democratization and economic reform, which have been mostly bitter in rural regions and in respect to Russia's industrial dinosaurs. This may make conservative campaign themes, of both nationalist and communist hues, particularly appealing among certain segments of the voting population.

In addition, future success for reformers will require a degree of cohesion between democratic organizations at all levels, which has been lacking. In short, the lines will have to be clearly drawn. The April 1993 referendum process, in which some local party chapters (including the Democratic Party, the Social Democratic Party, the People's Party of Free Russia, and the Movement of Democratic Reforms) took positions contrary to those of the national headquarters, would amount to political suicide within the context of competitive parliamentary elections. Communication and coordination, as well as a campaign plan which is both flexible (to allow for certain local circumstances) and binding (to ensure that local actions do not undermine overall party or coalition objectives), will be necessary to devise a winning strategy. This is also essential to guarantee that reform-oriented organizations do not split the pro-democracy vote, thereby giving reactionary forces a winning majority.

In the final analysis, future elections in Russia undoubtedly will be more democratic and more chaotic than before. Western observers should be cautious in their predictions and expectations. As Smyth argues in the next chapter, a more democratically elected parliament does not necessarily mean a more democratic parliament, nor one less inclined to gridlock and inaction. At the same time, an accelerated election cycle, including presidential and local elections, does provide a vital opportunity for parties to take their rightful place in political life. Beyond organizing forces for the campaign, they may now be able to serve as an institutionalized mechanism for representing the interests of various segments of the Russian electorate, whether a majority or minority, in the difficult debates that lie ahead.

Notes

Eric Rudenshiold is a program officer with the International Republican Institute (IRI). Formerly with the IRI, N. Catherine Barnes is currently a program officer with

the International Foundation for Electoral Systems (IFES). Both authors have conducted research, training, and assessment work for the International Republican Institute with political parties in the former Soviet Union. The research for this piece was
drawn from interviews and discussions as part of the authors' regional program work
in Russia. Special thanks to democratic activists in Moscow, St. Petersburg,
Arkhangelsk, Barnaul, Chelyabinsk, Khabarovsk, Novgorod, Novosibirsk, Saransk,
and Voronezh for their invaluable contribution to this article.

1. For an overview of the roots of informal group development during glasnost
and perestroika, see Gail Lapidus, "State and Society: Toward the Emergence of Civil
Society in the Soviet Union," in *The Soviet System in Crisis*, edited by Alexander
Dallin and Gail Lapidus (Boulder: Westview Press, 1991), pp. 130-147; and Victoria
Bonnell, "Voluntary Associations in Gorbachev's Reform Program," also in *The Soviet
System in Crisis*, pp. 151-160. See also Nadia Diuk and Adrian Karatnychy's explana-
tion of the national, cultural and historical roots of informal group development, *The
Hidden Nations* (New York: William Morrow and Company, Inc., 1990).

2. For a discussion of the evolution of the informal group movement into a proto-
party system see *After Perestroika: Democracy in the Soviet Union*, edited by Brad
Roberts and Nina Belyaeva, CSIS Significant Issues Series 13, no. 5, (Washington,
DC: CSIS and Interlegal, 1991); Aleksandr Meerovich's "The Emergence of Russian
Multiparty Politics," in *The Soviet System in Crisis*, edited by Alexander Dallin and
Gail Lapidus (Boulder: Westview Press, 1991), pp. 161-171; and Vera Tolz's *The
USSR's Emerging Multiparty System*, CSIS Washington Paper 148, (New York:
Praeger, 1990).

3. Interestingly enough, Travkin considers the "bane" of Russia's party politics to
be their penchant for splits. See Gerald Nadar, "Fickle Russians Prefer 'Raskols' to
Party Politics," *The Washington Times*, March 27, 1993.

4. For a detailed and well presented history of the development of the Democratic Russia Movement, see Yitzhak Brudny, "The Dynamics of Democratic Russia,
1990-1993," *Post Soviet Affairs* 9, no. 2, April-June 1993, pp. 141-170. Another perspective is presented in Julia Wishnevsky, "The Rise and Fall of Democratic Russia,"
RFE/RL Report 1, no. 22, May 29, 1992, pp. 23-27.

5. An introduction to the larger parties and significant political coalitions can be
found in Vera Tolz, Sandy Slater, and Alexander Rahr, "Profiles of the Main Political
Blocs," *RFE/RL Report* 2, no. 29, May 14, 1993, pp. 16-24; and Vladimir
Pribylovskii, *Dictionary of Political Parties and Organizations in Russia* (Washington, DC: CSIS and PostFactum/Interlegal, 1992).

6. By the summer of 1993, the increasing radicalization of certain Civic Union
leaders, in particular Aleksandr Rutskoi's confrontation with Boris Yeltsin, resulted in
the emergence of fissures within the coalition. Nikolai Travkin removed the national
organization of the DPR from Civic Union, giving local chapters the option to retain
their membership. With the exception of Moscow and several other chapters, this was
a moot point since many local organizations had never left the Democratic Russia
Movement.

7. N. Beliaeva, "Russian Democracy: Crisis as Progress," *The Washington Quarterly*, Spring 1993, pp. 5-17.

8. V. Tolz, "More on Preparation for Elections," *RFE/RL Daily Report*, October
14, 1993, p. 1.

3

The Russian Parliament and Political Consolidation

Regina A. Smyth

Democracy legitimizes political conflict and invites opposition. As a result, a viable democratic system demands procedural certainty to assure individual commitment to the system. Political actors must have confidence that the process of conflict resolution is regularized; that all actors have access to the same information about how the system operates; and that they can work through the system to obtain political objectives. Actors must also have some sense of "mutual security" that assures them they will still have a place in the system even if they lose a battle over policy.[1]

In established democracies, parliamentary institutions are crucial mechanisms of conflict resolution. The legislature provides the means for direct representation of popular demands in government and the reconciliation of these demands when they come into conflict. Equally important, the legislature provides a forum to incorporate local interests into national policy solutions. In Russia, the legislature became the focus of conflicting demands from both society and political elites as the processes of democratization and marketization continued. Before its dissolution in the fall of 1993, the Congress of People's Deputies had the power to enact a new constitution, control spending, and formulate policy. Thus, it was responsible for redistributing political and economic property rights in accordance with democratic and market relationships. In essence, the success or failure of reform hinged on the ability of the legislature to establish a system of governmental institutions that were able to force compliance with the new property rights at elite and lower social levels within the bounds of the Constitution.[2] This, in turn, required a majority consensus on principles within the parliament that would provide a basis for bargaining over critical details.

The dissolution of parliament and subsequent violence demonstrated that parliamentary structure alone cannot guarantee the emergence of democracy in Russia. The paradox of representative institutions is that they may either promote or prevent the consolidation of power, depending on the range of preferences held by individual deputies. The Russian parliament was unable to form a stable majority that could provide a basis for consolidation. Rather, the constant struggle for control of the institution, and of subsequent policy outcomes, led to the stalemate that paralyzed both the government and the parliament, and accelerated the disintegration of Russia.

Many of the same structural problems continue to plague the Russian polity today. This must be understood from a somewhat broader theoretical perspective. In a representative democracy that lacks supporting institutions such as strong leadership, legislative factions, parties, and electoral goals, individual legislators have little incentive to search for and commit themselves to a consistent set of policies. This inability to commit can be described in terms of a collective action problem.[3] Benefits to the public—in this case, policy that supports the goals of democratization and marketization—are costly, and these costs must be borne by a majority of deputies in order to make them politically possible. However, what seems a sensible action for the group to take might not be sensible for its individual members. Each individual has the option of shirking by voting against legislation that is costly to either his district or to himself, thus ensuring that collective progress will not be achieved. In the Russian legislature, the result has been a shifting set of coalitions that has prevented adherence to any consistent policy path.

Moreover, the legislature operated within a parliamentary system in which the executive was independently elected and could not be recalled through parliamentary action. At the same time, the legislature had the power to recall cabinet posts and negate executive decisions. This created two bases of institutional power that moved opposition politics from conflict within the legislature to conflict between the legislature and the government. There were no formal institutions to regulate this conflict, so it became a struggle to co-opt the parliamentary structure in order to assure passage of competing political programs.

This chapter explores the problems observed in the Congress of People's Deputies from 1990 to 1993 with an eye toward the future role of legislative politics in the process of democratic consolidation. The first section examines the problems faced by the legislature as it attempted to develop internal institutions, and speculates about how the proposed change in the electoral law and legislative structure will affect institutional formation. A survey of the role of legislative institutions such as parties, committees, and leadership illuminates efforts to make the legislature an autonomous source of effective policy and a viable actor in the new political system. It also demonstrates the enormous complexity of the problem the legislature faces in trying to build consensus around a set of political and economic institutions that will define state-society relations in the new regime.

The second section explores the ability of the legislature to maintain its independent power base when confronted by predatory action from other actors in the political landscape. Much of this capacity will be determined by the election law, which will influence the distribution of political preferences in the new parliament, and by the new structure of the parliament. In a system of divided government the legislature must compete with other actors such as the president, the executive bureaucracy, and court systems to perpetuate its influence over policy. In addition, in a participatory democracy, the legislature must compete with strong organized interests that seek to dominate policy outcomes. The power and effectiveness of legislative institutions can be evaluated only in the context of this larger political environment. In large part, the ability of the legislature to maintain its position in the future will depend on the strategies that newly elected representatives pursue, as well as the strategies followed by external actors in pursuit of their own political and institutional goals.

The Evolution of the Russian Legislature

The Russian Federation's Congress of People's Deputies was chosen in three rounds of elections beginning in March 1990. The electoral law, nominating procedures, campaign regulations, and district lines were drafted under the communist regime. Many have argued that this introduced a conservative bias into the deputy corps.[4] In earlier work, I contended that despite these efforts to control electoral outcomes, the deputy corps was not obviously skewed from its constituent base.[5] Early voting data revealed a strong conservative trend in rural areas, a pattern consistent with societies moving away from traditional peasant farming.[6] In contrast, urban representatives tended to be more liberal. The latter observation presents an important problem for urban representatives who wish to be reelected. Urban deputies advocating marketization are essentially introducing the possibility of massive unemployment among their constituents, most of whom are skilled workers.[7]

Clearly, the distribution of preferences in the deputy corps will be profoundly affected by the new electoral law. According to the law, one-half of the deputies will be elected directly, as voters choose one of several candidates to represent a given district. The other half will be elected indirectly, through balloting for party slates. In this case, individual deputies are drawn from party lists depending on the percentage of votes each party receives. The inclusion of the list system is designed to reduce the advantage that local notables have in rural regions by offering a set of candidates with a distinct party platform and national profiles.

Further, changes in the structure of the legislature will also influence the distribution of deputies' preferences. According to the presidential decree of October 21, 1993, the new legislature will be bicameral.[8] The lower house, the State Duma, will consist of 400 deputies elected to four-year terms. The Upper House, the Council of the Federation, will include two representatives from each of the eighty-eight constituent regions of the Russian Federation, who will also be elected to four-year terms.[9] Much of the effect of bicameralism will depend on the institutional structure and distribution of responsibility between the two bodies. The State Duma will have the bulk of legislative responsibility, although the Council of the Federation will have the power to object to proposals within three months after they are passed by the Duma. In addition, the Duma will control much of the financial policy for the federation in conjunction with the government. It also appears that the institutions will be elected from different constituencies, and therefore will reflect very different interests. If this is the case, there is potential for the bicameral system to slow down legislation and impede consolidation.

Building Internal Institutions

Deputies in the Russian parliament face two tasks if they are to foster democratic rule. The first is to dismantle the command economic system that politicized all economic transactions and that remains a source of power for old political elites. This process demands difficult policy choices that mandate enormous redistribution of wealth within the population. The second is to promote the viability of the legislative institution in a competitive and uncertain political environment. The tasks are often incompatible, and individual deputies find it difficult to cooperate in pursuit of either goal. In many cases, cleavages cut across these issues, creating a multi-dimensional conflict rather than a clear schism between conservatives and radicals, or between urban and rural deputies. As a result, it is easier to develop an opposition strategy that prevents changes in the status quo than it is to find a strategy that fosters consolidation around a coherent alternative.

In order to be an effective source of policy within a political system, the legislature must build a stable majority around a vision of how the government and economy should operate.[10] In the past this proved to be extraordinarily difficult, given the composition of the deputy corps. In the first session, groups divided the Congress into thirds: a "conservative" group that voted consistently against all reform measures regardless of their policy implications; a "radical" group that supported reform measures in both the economic and political realms; and an independent group that seemed to vote according to individual policies, not according to an overarching political or economic world view. Subsequent roll call voting analysis showed that the strength of both the conservative and radical groups diminished over time, but the overriding difficulty remained the same. No group of deputies had enough support to form a majority that was able to control the outcomes of votes on policy or procedure. This persistent division has profound implications for the strength of the legislature in the future and its role in establishing democratic rule.

Bargaining to construct consensus on an issue-by-issue basis entails a great deal of negotiation and transfer of political influence through a process of vote trading. Faced with external pressure from the president and strong, independent interests, the process can paralyze the legislature and render it ineffective in the larger political system. To counter this threat, the legislature must solve the collective action problem (building a stable majority) by establishing mechanisms that enforce individual commitment to a set of policies and a coherent view of the Russian future.

The process of building consensus is complicated by the realization that no issue confronting the legislature has a single dimension. The merits of policies can be debated in their own right, or evaluated as part of a broader program for reaching larger goals. For example, a central debate in the reform of the Constitution has been the appropriate federal structure for the new republic. Within this framework, each proposed piece of legislation can be considered from at least two angles. Privatization of agriculture may be thought of as a reallocation of economic or political power, or as an effective or ineffective policy. Key procedural questions exist over who should control the redistribution of land, the federal, provincial, or local governments; over who should receive tax revenues and in what form; and over who should determine land use. Such questions are important in determining the relative balance of power among levels of government.

Potential members assess the cost of joining a group against expected benefits of membership. Individual deputies accrue benefits in two ways. As citizens, they benefit directly from government action. This is significant in a period of massive redistribution and may be even more significant for those deputies such as industrial managers or *kolkhoz* chairman who controlled economic resources under the old system. They also benefit indirectly if their constituents reward them with support and, ultimately, reelection for providing effective legislation. Costs are incurred in two ways. First, there is the cost of providing the good. These—for example, the cost of organizing—may be borne entirely by group members. There may also be direct costs in terms of popular support to individual legislators for supporting bills that are unpopular among their constituencies.

The obvious political benefits for individual deputies who agree to establish a majority coalition create an incentive for leaders and groups to solve the collective action problem by organizing internal institutions.[11] Parties, committees, and leadership structures are an example of internal institutions that can aid in the formation of a stable majority coalition.

Several mechanisms can be employed to initiate collective action to foster political consolidation. Entrepreneurial behavior by legislative leaders, including committee chairmen and faction leaders, can be crucial for group formation.[12] The entrepreneur accepts the initial cost of identifying and allocating incentives that will entice reluctant individuals to support his cause. He may see group organization as an instrument to further his policy interests; he may also link his own career to the prestige and power of the group or institution.[13] Regardless of motivation, however, such entrepreneurs play an important role in group activity. They identify group organizational strategy, target potential members, and establish property rights over parliamentary resources. They struggle to capture leadership positions in the Congress.

Throughout the first year of the Congress, Yeltsin was able to use his strong team of advisers and high level of popular support to enact much of his own program, although he was never able to determine parliamentary outcomes. Later, opposition to Yeltsin and his team mounted sharply as the struggle over a new constitutional framework intensified. Since government ministries were largely loyal to Yeltsin and were not responsible to the legislature and its constituent parties (as they are in normal parliamentary systems), the legislature tried to develop its own mechanisms for information collection and dissemination. Yet such opposition efforts were always hampered by the lack of infrastructure available to deputies, as they formulated strategy for building a majority coalition to insulate them from Yeltsin's attempt to gain control over the parliament.

This point may be illustrated with the example of taxation. Before deciding on a tax scheme, deputies need to understand its implications for themselves, their districts, and the national budget. Yet these are complicated relationships even in the best of times, and in current conditions it is extremely difficult to anticipate policy outcomes, particularly since implementation mechanisms are not in place. The element of uncertainty underscores the importance of control and dissemination of information to individual deputies. A major source of information collection and dissemination in parliament is the committee system. According to the guidelines established by the preparatory committee before the first session, committees and commissions of the Supreme Soviet and Congress were established to address particular areas. However, committees were very poorly equipped to carry out their functions. They were not allocated sufficient office space, and even office supplies and equipment were hard to obtain. In addition, all draft legislation had to pass through the "editorial commission" to ensure compliance with the Constitution and other laws. This commission, which was controlled by the executive, acted as a gatekeeper, screening proposals and amending them in favor of the president's platform. This kept the committee system at a disadvantage.[14]

In addition, committees were not well staffed, and they relied heavily on the executive branch or "volunteer" specialists for expertise and accurate information. This practice led to disproportionate representation of certain interest groups. For example, in a study of banking reform, the committee writing the new banking laws drew largely on the advice and expertise of private commercial bankers, disregarding the Central Bank and Ministry of Finance.[15] The demands for information provided a strong incentive for committee chairmen to turn to such "expert" representatives of economic and political interest groups. In turn, the committee system provided an opening through which these interest groups could press their policy concerns. For these reasons, the Russian parliament was unable to establish its own, fully independent sources of outside information.

However, organized factions within the legislature play an important role in informing deputies. They also play an important role in solving the legislative collective action problem.[16] Factions can provide a strong base from which political entrepreneurs can foster group coordination. They reduce the costs of negotiating bargains by decreasing the number of actors involved in the decision-making process; by linking individual proposals as packages of legislation; and by routinizing decision-making. Most important, parliamentary factions transfer the costs of bargaining from the floor of the legislature to the party caucus rooms, thus limiting the range of possible outcomes. In practice, factions in the Russian parliament have focused on the tasks of drafting alternative legislation and providing information about policy alternatives or procedural issues to individual members.

In addition to providing information, internal institutions such as parties, committees, and factions provide incentives for individual deputies to commit to consistent platforms. Such institutions also create career opportunities that ambitious deputies can follow to increase their influence within the legislature, and subsequently within their districts. The prospect of climbing through the ranks from committee member to a leadership position gives junior members an incentive to strengthen the institution. Members trade votes on controversial policies in return for committee assignments and support from the party during elections. This is particularly true in proportional representation systems. Failure to establish a strong committee system or an electoral connection further inhibited the process of consolidation within the former parliament.

Two very active umbrella organizations were founded at the first Congress: Democratic Russia (DR), which organized the reform elements of the Congress, and Communists of Russia (CR), which organized the conservative elements. These groups provided leadership for the deputies and exerted a great deal of influence through media attention, but had little ability to enforce voting discipline. Indeed, despite the subsequent development of other blocs, preliminary analysis of individual voting scores showed a wide range of opinion among members in each bloc.[17] For example, economic issues remained in the background for a long time because democratic coalitions could not agree over the appropriate pace, process, and extent of economic reform.[18] Party platforms remained vague in order to maintain membership support in the face of controversial issues and cross-cutting cleavages. More important, there was little effort on the part of nascent parties to reach out to the electorate to build popular support that might bolster their position for the next elections. And, as Rudenshiold and Barnes show in Chapter 2, there was (and remains) little cohesion between central and regional party organizations. It is not surprising, then, that as many as several hundred deputies remained unaffiliated at the time that parliament was dissolved.

The imposition of the list system will require that candidates adhere to a party platform during elections and vote accordingly once they are elected. The end result will be stronger party coherence by the next election period, particularly if elections are held every four years, as proposed. However, one half of the deputies still will be elected in single-member districts, which diminishes the likelihood that a single party will be able to dominate elections. Over time, these deputies will have an incentive to ally with the parties represented in the legislature in order to enhance their individual influence. As potentially decisive swing votes, they are likely to be pivotal players in future legislative development. If they do ally quickly with existing parties, these deputies will provide the basis for a stable majority coalition that will strengthen the legislature. What is more likely, however, is that these deputies will refuse to enter into stable coalitions and will become an impediment to the consolidation of legislative power.

For these reasons, individual deputies will remain the crucial unit of analysis for factions, committees, and leadership organizations. So it is difficult to make definitive statements about the legislative structure without knowing something about the personal motives of individual deputies.[19] Determining the goals of Russian parliamentarians is a complex puzzle. Indeed, deputies who do not run on party platforms are likely to have very diverse policy positions, which will further complicate efforts at consensus building.

For example, during the early sessions of the Congress of People's Deputies, members of Democratic Russia were willing to support parliamentary autonomy as long as they controlled the Congress and won the battle on most important votes. Once this control was in doubt, however, they were willing to sacrifice the structural question of parliamentary autonomy in order to save the reform effort. DR shifted its support from the legislature to the executive once the former was captured by moderate and conservative forces.

Viewing the process of institutional selection from this perspective introduces two important elements into the picture of legislative development. The first is the role of the larger political environment, which is often unstable. Nascent institutions (such as factions) can be profoundly affected by unintended consequences of policy, or by the introduction or disappearance of political actors, or by a sudden redistribution of political resources. All of these events have occurred in recent Russian history. The unexpected coup of 1991, the resignation of Mikhail Gorbachev, and the break-up of the Soviet Union are examples of events that fundamentally affected internal legislative politics. In addition, events may be interpreted by opposition groups as undermining or enhancing the position of embryonic political organizations. For example, efforts by nationalist groups to blame the Yeltsin government for the break-up of the Soviet Union opened the way for a nationalist-communist opposition coalition. The significance of such factors is considered in the next section.

External Challenges

The former Russian parliament existed in a tumultuous political environment. It was a competitor in an increasingly complex governmental system, with all actors fighting for control of political resources. The parliament was also an enormous resource to be captured. Although it proved strong enough to resist presidential domination, it did not present effective policy solutions and therefore was unable to insulate itself from political predators. As a result, the legislature was transformed from an institution that channeled political conflict to one in open conflict with other branches of the government. The vestiges of the Soviet system, which remained intact even in 1993, undermined the operation of the legislature. These included the perpetuation of state ownership in all spheres, the power of local officials over the daily lives of citizens, and an ingrained mentality of clientelism and support for sweeping social guarantees. In a real sense, the Russian legislature struggled against Soviet domination as well as presidential domination.

In an environment of competing institutions, it is difficult to protect the autonomy of the legislature. Unclear institutional boundaries provide the opportunity and incentive for forces outside the legislature to compete for control of the legislative majority. In this circumstance, legislative leaders and leaders of outside forces, such as the executive or organized lobbies, fight to form and control the majority coalition. Leaders may pursue either of two strategies. They may try to attack the legislature, or they may use it as a forum in which to express legitimate political opposition. The first strategy weakens the integrity of the legislature *vis-a-vis* other actors in the system. The second strategy weakens the institution if competing interests cannot reach a compromise. Failure to compromise results in stalemate or an attempt to enlist the support of groups external to the legislature to resolve the conflict.

The first strategy, undermining the legislature, may take the form of limiting the policy prerogatives of the legislative branch. For example, nationalist leaders have questioned the parliament's legal right to make decisions that violate the boundaries of the former Soviet Union, or to ratify treaties with the successor states. This strategy was also used by Yeltsin in his bid to increase the power of the presidency.[20] Most dramatically, in the wake of the April 1993 referendum, Yeltsin attempted to undercut the parliament by creating a new Constitution to extend his prerogatives.[21]

The second strategy, use of the parliament as a forum for articulating opposition, was pursued after the seventh session of the Congress of People's Deputies. The Civic Union and other independent groups sought to capture a majority that would ratify their programs for the future.[22] This was a workable strategy, since the prospect of creating ties to political groups and social movements was attractive to deputies who wished to seek reelection. Many deputies agreed to vote for certain legislation in return for endorsements and political help during their own campaigns. This process in itself may not necessarily be a bad thing. As long as it does not lead to domination by external interest groups, or to a stalemate that cannot be resolved, it may have the useful effect of encouraging disciplined voting.

This second strategy may also be pursued by the executive. In fact, in Russia the parliament was designed precisely to prevent arbitrary executive rule. The law gave the Congress of People's Deputies the power to finance the president's programs; to repeal presidential decrees; and to impeach him if he violated either the Constitution or Russian or Soviet laws. The president was also forbidden to join any political party or public organization, or to hold any other office. While the law allowed considerable discretion to the executive, it was firmly dedicated to the supremacy of the legislature as the chief ruling body in the Russian Federation. Yet when various attempts to forge a centrist coalition aimed at future elections failed, and the parliament continued to resist the president's attempts to circumvent its power to create a new Constitution, Yeltsin broke the stalemate by dissolving parliament.[23]

A final challenge to parliament may come from the constitutional court. Although the court did not impinge directly on the parliament's autonomy, it took an activist stand in defending the constitution by attempting to broker a deal between the legislature and executive. The former chairman of the court, Valerii Zorkin, argued during the seventh Congress against holding a referendum that Yeltsin desired, and later identified himself as a supporter of conservative political forces in parliament.[24] The chief justice promoted an overtly political agenda during the constitutional assembly and parliamentary crisis. The constitutional court had the power to review presidential decrees, and used it to declare unconstitutional Yeltsin's decree dissolving the parliament. After the crisis Yeltsin abolished the court, and a new court was to be established following ratification of the new Constitution and election of the parliament. The future disposition of the court is uncertain. But as long as it retains institutional autonomy it potentially retains the political ability to challenge parliament over a given issue.

It is impossible to overlook the potential for popular opinion to influence the parliament through mass protests, strikes, or through organized interests.

In extraordinary times protests have proven to be very influential. The combination of the March 1991 referendum and the massive political protests in support of Yeltsin seem to have been important factors in shaping the office of the president.[25] Protestors also influenced government actions in the abortive coup attempt of 1991 and the parliamentary standoff of 1993. The opposing interpretations of public opinion after the April 1993 referendum also illustrated its importance in legitimating government institutions. In the future, the direct expression of public opinion through elections—even if limited by the ban on parties, control of media, and the election law itself—will provide additional incentives for policymakers to act in response to their perceptions of public opinion.

Conclusion

The effort to institutionalize democratic rule in Russia and to reallocate political and economic property rights has proven to be extremely difficult. In part, this failure has reflected the lack of consensus within the Russian polity about whether democracy and the market are desirable goals, and disagreement over the definition of these terms. In part, too, it has reflected the absence of strong parliamentary institutions.

Parliamentary institutions alone are not sufficient for forging stable coalitions necessary for majority decision-making. For this, it is necessary to have robust and cohesive parties, strong leaders, and well-institutionalized and coherent rules.

Yet while a parliamentary system cannot ensure stable democratic rule, it may well be an essential element of a Russian democracy. The development of a stable legislature within a system of checks and balances on the other branches of government could be a strong force in the consolidation of democracy by channeling conflict and fostering compromise. In order to foster consolidation, such compromises must be meaningful and direct, not ambiguous and general. In the recent past, the legislature has served as both an arena in which political battles could be played out and as an actor in those battles. In the future, these two roles must be balanced in order for the situation to stabilize.

It also remains to be seen whether external actors will dominate legislative policy processes and diminish legislative autonomy. In order to do so, such forces must provide sufficient incentives to attract the allegiance of individual deputies or parties and overcome the collective action problem. It is conceivable that either the new president or a nascent party could provide long-term political opportunities for ambitious deputies, thus assuring their support on crucial issues. This hold might grow stronger as the electoral mechanism is regularized and candidates for parliamentary seats seek resources to run their campaigns.[26] While this sort of strategy might lead to consolidation of power, it may not necessarily lead to democracy. Much will be determined by the parameters of institutional power outlined by the new Constitution. In addition, much will depend on the individuals elected and the preferences they hold on major issues such as democratization and marketization. We have already seen that institutional structure alone does not guarantee a political outcome. However, structure does help shape outcomes in important and predictable ways. The past has shown that the legislature is vulnerable to external pressure, but it has also shown that, short of extra-constitutional action, the legislature can be very resilient.

In sum, the legislature must find a way to organize itself internally, to provide mutual security for the multitude of opinions that exists among the deputy corps. At the same time, it must stabilize its position in the larger environment. This requires formation of a majority coalition that can sustain support for legislative initiatives designed to solve the problems of building new institutions. In order to build such a coalition, individual deputies must commit to support the program over time despite the costs associated with that support.

If the primary commitment mechanism is based on electoral incentives, the key question will be the response of the Russian people to the new institutions, and to the policy solutions that emerge from them. Recent events have shown that Russian elites in both the parliament and government are concerned with the willingness and capacity of the population to participate in the political process in a productive manner. It remains unclear how vast numbers of Russians outside major industrial centers feel about recent political changes, or whether the population will accept democratic consolidation through reform from above. In order to function as a consolidating force, the legislature must be prepared to address the powerful interests in society that so far have remained unformed or unspoken.

However, in order to retain its influence relative to these interests, the legislature must be able to establish its own political property rights over a segment of the policy process. If it is unable to do so, the body stands a strong chance of being captured by another institutional actor or by a dominant organized interest in society.

The implications of this outcome for the question of consolidation versus disintegration are unclear. The long-standing conflict between the legislature and executive paralyzed the policy process, and was an enormous impediment to consolidation of either Yeltsin's power or democratic governance.[27] It is likely that the relative power of these institutions will not be resolved with the ratification of a new Constitution, but will be settled through an evolutionary process carried out over a number of years. The key to resolution will be a set of stable institutions that yield implementable, effective policy outcomes that are broadly acceptable to participants.

The legislature's unique ability to give voice to local concerns, including those of the autonomous regions within Russia, also affords it a potentially important position in the multi-ethnic state. Although Yeltsin was able at first to build a network of support among the new republican leaders through his local representatives, as Khrushchev shows in Chapter 6 this support has deteriorated in the face of negotiation over resource allocation. On the one hand, it seems likely that some sort of mutually acceptable compromise between center and periphery will have to be found, including a legitimate mechanism for accommodating the demands of diverse ethnic and particularist groups, in order for democracy to take root in Russia. On the other hand, bargaining between regional interests and the center is extraordinarily difficult, particularly in a democratic context. Still, it may be that stable negotiations can take place only within a legislative setting, in order to foster compromise over difficult redistributive issues through universal legislation or political deals. Thus, parliament's ability to maintain coherent internal institutions, and to prevent capture by narrow interest groups, will be a key factor in determining the prospects for consolidation at the central and regional levels.

Notes

1. For illuminating discussions of the problems inherent in building democratic and market institutions see Adam Przeworski, *Democracy and the Market. Political and Economic Reforms in Eastern Europe and Latin America* (Cambridge: Cambridge University Press, 1991); and Guiseppe DiPalma, *To Craft Democracies: An Essay on Democratic Transitions* (Berkeley: University of California Press, 1990). Both scholars reach similar conclusions about the relationship between uncertainty and individual commitment in nascent democratic systems.

2. Blondel argues that legislative institutions are not well-suited to the promotion of democracy because they are indecisive and require strong leadership. Jean Blondel, *Comparative Legislatures* (Englewood Cliffs: Prentice Hall, 1973). In a similar vein, Huntington argues that "The primary problem of politics is the lag in the development of political institutions behind social and economic change." Samuel Huntington, *Political Order in Changing Societies* (New Haven: Yale University Press, 1968), p. 5.

3. For the initial theoretical statement of the role of the collective action problem in political life see Mancur Olson, *The Logic of Collective Action: Public Goods and the Theory of Groups* (Cambridge: Harvard University Press, 1965); and see also Russell Hardin, *Collective Action* (Baltimore: Johns Hopkins University Press, 1982). Both authors seek to explain why individuals with common interests may not take action to further that interest without added incentives to do so.

4. Thomas Remington, "Elections in the RSFSR," edited by Darrell Slider, *Elections and Political Change in the Soviet Republics* (forthcoming); Michael Urban, *More Power to the Soviets: The Democratic Revolution in the USSR* (Brookfield: Edward Elgar, 1990).

5. Regina Smyth, "Ideological vs. Regional Cleavages: Do the Radicals Control the RSFSR Parliament?" *Journal of Soviet Nationalities* 1, no. 3 (1990), pp. 112-157. This study was based on roll-call votes, which provide information on how individual deputies voted on various issues. In areas that appeared to be strongly conservative (based on content analysis of regional newspapers), deputies' voting patterns were also quite conservative; similarly, in more liberal regions, the deputies voted a more liberal line. For an alternative analysis based on modernization theory, which stresses demographic variables, see Gregory J. Embree, "RSFSR Election Results: Election Results and Roll Call Votes," *Soviet Studies* 43, no. 6, 1991, pp. 1065-1084.

6. Stephen Wegren, "Private Farming and Agrarian Reform in Russia," *Problems of Communism*, no. 3, May-June 1992, pp. 107-121. Fear of losing private plots and input subsidies if collective farms are disbanded is an important factor in shaping rural opinions about reform.

7. This presents a puzzle for scholars looking for an "electoral connection." Despite this paradox, the preliminary results of the referendum held in April 1993 indicate that urban voters continued to support Yeltsin and his reform program. See "Nation Divided by Money, Power, and Sentiment," *Financial Times*, April 26, 1993, p. 2.

8. The law on the election of deputies to the State Duma and on the Federal Organs of Power in the Transition Period were published in *Rossiiskie vesti*, September 28, 1993, pp. 1-5.

9. Steven Erlanger, "Yeltsin Decrees Russians to Elect Both Houses of a New Parliament," *The New York Times*, October 13, 1993, p. 5A.

10. John Aldrich argues that coalitions in American political parties historically formed around a single dimension, or "great principle," that defined the structure of American government. The principle at stake became the overriding concern of individual legislatures, rather than multi-dimensional, cross-cutting issues. John Aldrich, *Why Parties?* (forthcoming).

11. Robert Bates, "Contra Contractarianism: Some Reflections on the New Institutionalism," *Politics and Society* 16, nos. 2-3 (1988), pp. 387-401; Barry R. Weingast and William J. Marshall, "The Industrial Organization of Congress: Why Legislatures, Like Firms, Are Not Organized as Markets," *Journal of Political Economy* 96, no. 11, 1988, pp. 132-152.

12. Political entrepreneurs are individuals who invest personal resources to coordinate pursuit of a collective good. See Angelo Panebianco, *Political Parties* (Cambridge: Cambridge University Press, 1988).

13. On the theory of political entrepreneurs, see Norman Frohlich and Joe A. Oppenheimer, *Modern Political Economy* (Englewood Cliffs: Prentice Hall, 1978); an opposing view is Russell Hardin, *Collective Action* (Baltimore: Johns Hopkins University Press, 1982). For an application of the concept to interest group formation, see Terry Moe, *The Organization of Interests: Incentives and the Internal Dynamics of Political Interest Groups* (Chicago: University of Chicago Press, 1980).

14. Personal interview with parliamentary consultant Georgii V. Barabashev, in April 1991. Barabashev participated in the drafting of the law on local self-governance.

15. Joel Hellman, *Breaking the Bank: The Political Economy of Banking Reform in the Former Soviet Union*. Unpublished Ph.D. dissertation, Columbia University, 1993.

16. Yeltsin initially eschewed parties as divisive forces, but by the second session of the fifth Congress was arguing for the formation of a party that could control parliamentary activity. Interfax, October 27, 1991, in FBIS-SOV-91-208, October 28, 1991.

17. Smyth, "Ideological vs. Regional Cleavages." Early analysis showed that the voting indices of individual members ranged from 0 to 100 with a standard deviation of 30. I am grateful to the East-West Center at Duke University for providing the roll call voting data used in the analysis for this paper.

18. Personal interview with Viktor L. Sheinis, a People's Deputy from the 47th territorial district in Moscow.

19. Joseph Schlesinger, "On the Theory of Party Organization," *Journal of Politics* 46, no. 2 (1984), pp. 369-400.

20. See Evgenii Krasnikov, in *Nezavisimaia gazeta*, May 1993, p. 1; FBIS-SOV-93-102, May 28, 1993, p. 16.

21. The provisions for the operation of the Constitutional Assembly were detailed by Sergei Filatov in his speech at its opening on June 5, 1993. See *Rossiskie vesti*, June 8, 1993, p. 3.

22. *Kommersant*, April 10, 1993, p. 2, in FBIS-SOV-93-068, April 12, 1993, p. 22.

23. This was an act of dubious legality, since the parliament rejected the executive's authority to issue decrees, and moved to impeach Yeltsin. The resulting "war of laws" served to deepen popular cynicism about the political process, and eroded what little legitimacy these institutions had managed to attain.

24. Other members of the constitutional court publicly endorsed Zorkin's proposal as well. ITAR-TASS, February 9, 1993, in FBIS-SOV-93-026, February 10, 1993, pp. 20-21.

25. Urban, *More Power to the Soviets*.

26. In the wake of the referendum, the ninth Congress passed a resolution calling for early presidential and parliamentary elections to be held on October 10, 1993; Interfax, March 26, 1993; FBIS-SOV-93-058, March 29, 1993, p. 21.

27. For example, see "Ukaz prezidenta Rossii 'o deiatelnosti ispolnitelnykh organov do preodoleniia krizisa vlasti'," *Izvestiia*, March 25, 1993, p. 1.

4

The Disintegration of the Russian Economy

Michael Spagat

Introduction

Russia is experiencing an extraordinarily severe drop in economic activity. In a recent report, the World Bank estimated that Russian Gross Domestic Product (GDP) fell by 9 percent in 1991, and projected that it would fall by 15 to 20 percent in 1992.[1] Former Russian economic minister Andrei Nechaev stated that the drop in output for 1992 was 20 percent, and the figure has been confirmed by Western calculations.[2] An additional decline of 5 to 10 percent was predicted for 1993. In 1993, the level of Russian imports and exports should be less than half of what they were in 1990.[3] These figures indicate a drop in output comparable to that experienced by the American economy during the Great Depression.

The World Bank attributes the collapse to two factors: the unraveling of supply links between enterprises, and the reduction in foreign trade.[4] These ideas are not necessarily wrong, but they do not explain very much. The question remains: why should inter-enterprise links and foreign trade disintegrate so dramatically in such a short time?

To understand the sudden collapse of the Russian economy on a deeper level, it is necessary to take a historical perspective. The Soviet economy was built up over six decades according to rules that suddenly are no longer in effect. The economy was never created to function as a market system. When even a weak attempt was made to enforce financial discipline on this anomalous creation, a general economic disintegration was inevitable. This argument is developed in detail in the following pages. Next, I review the likely impact of current Russian government policies that attempt to reverse the collapse. Finally, I discuss the long-term future of the Russian economy.

First, a definition of "economic disintegration" is needed. This term should be understood to mean a severe drop in economic activity. This chapter is concerned mainly with the reasons for this collapse and the prospects for its reversal. Note, however, that "disintegration" is used occasionally to refer to the fragmentation of the Russian economy into isolated regional economies.

The Creation of the Russian Capital Stock

It is useful to think of the capital stock as being divided into two components: physical capital and human capital. Physical capital includes buildings, equipment, machines, seeds, livestock, and infrastructure such as railroads, roads, bridges, airports, and storage facilities. Human capital is comprised of the skills, knowledge, and training of the work force.

Capital is gradually built up over many years through investment. In the developed West, possible investment projects are subject to sophisticated scrutiny before they are approved. Commercial banks, investment banks, and brokerage firms spend billions of dollars on the evaluation and finance of investments. They employ many of the brightest people available in these societies to carry out the analysis. Although the many scandals of the 1980s made clear that corruption and incompetence are pervasive in the financial sector, finance actually has performed rather well historically.

The roots of the current Russian economic collapse lie in the highly distorted nature of that country's capital stock. The Soviet investment process was uniquely unsuited to the task of developing capital that could survive a market test. In other words, capital created under Soviet conditions is very unlikely to be profitable in an economy that operates according to market prices, for a variety of reasons that are considered below.

First, the former Soviet Union maintained a structure of prices that by any reasonable standard was highly distorted.[5] As a crude first approximation, one could say that the millions of prices in the economy were selected at random. Any investment decisions based on such prices would be entirely arbitrary from the viewpoint of market prices. Only through sheer luck would a project undertaken as profitable at randomly chosen prices also turn out to be profitable at market prices.

Of course it is an exaggeration to think of Soviet pricing as purely random. It is possible to identify certain systematic tendencies in pricing practices, along with their impact on investment decisions. Raw materials prices were held down to negligible levels. Heavy machinery was valued very highly. Consumer necessities such as food and housing had very low prices. Material objects such as steel were valued very highly compared to nonmaterial services such as transportation. All of these pricing tendencies ran counter to the structure of world market prices. They also were out of line with the price structure that would have prevailed internally under market conditions without international trade. The point is that even if investment decisions had been based on sound economic methods, the results would have been grotesquely warped. The prevailing prices encouraged the adoption of projects that were profligate in their use of artificially cheap items such as raw materials. At the same time these prices overemphasized the production of artificially expensive items such as heavy machinery. The Soviet development process followed this pattern to a pronounced degree.

A second reason for the many poor investment decisions stems from the official investment methods that were used.[6] First, because of the Soviet interpretation of the Marxian labor theory of value, firms paid little or nothing for the use of physical capital. Consequently, managers tended to demand as much capital as they could possibly get, making it extremely difficult for investment planners to gauge where additional capital would be most useful. Second, Soviet methodology generally rejected the principle that time should play a crucial role in investment decisions. This led to the adoption of many projects that took years or even decades to complete. This practice contributed significantly to the current obsolete nature of much of the Russian capital stock. Finally, an even greater contributor to capital obsolescence is the near complete refusal to retire old capital. Official ideology held that one of the most wasteful practices of capitalism was to abandon machines that were still physically capable of continued operation. The Soviets entirely missed the point that in many cases it is possible to save resources by replacing an old machine with a new and more efficient machine, rather than continuing to repair and operate dilapidated equipment.

A third major distortion in investment policy came about because in many cases, perhaps even in the typical case, economic criteria played little or no role in the decision-making process. Investment funds were allocated to politically powerful individuals or institutions. For example, a well-connected manager of an old-fashioned steel firm would get funding to build another plant using the outdated open-hearth method despite the economic folly of such an endeavor. Regional Communist Party power brokers could pull investment funds into their regions, even if far better economic opportunities were going unfunded elsewhere.

An important legacy from the past is the way that human capital was developed in the Soviet Union. The regime invested heavily in training people as scientists, engineers, and technicians of various sorts. Moreover, despite its many shortcomings, the general education system was rather effective at teaching basic skills to a fairly wide group of students. Of course, just as many items of physical capital are totally inappropriate for a market environment, many human skills of Russian citizens will not be useful under market conditions. Nevertheless, people tend to be much more adaptable than machines, so the high level of education in Russia is an important resource to be tapped in the future. The potential significance of the Russian human capital stock is much greater than that of the physical capital stock.

Sustaining Inefficient Industry and Agriculture
Through Raw Materials Subsidies

The value of the raw materials that were extracted by the Russian economy in 1993 was about $100 billion, which works out to about $670 per capita. A dollar value of the Russian per capita annual GDP is difficult to estimate. However, no reasonable measure places it much above $5,000, and it is arguably less than $2,000. This indicates that raw materials account for a substantial fraction of the wealth created in Russia in any given year.[7]

As mentioned above, internal prices of raw materials in relation to other goods' prices are maintained at levels far below world market prices. For example, the price of oil is less than one-third of the world market price, while zinc and copper sell for less than 80 percent of their world prices. On the other hand, computers are at least 37 percent more expensive in Russia than in the West.[8] These very low prices encourage domestic users to waste raw materials on a colossal scale.[9] The Soviet government always made raw materials available to domestic industry at a negligible cost, acting as if their natural-resource base had virtually no limits.

These heavy raw materials subsidies have made it possible for many inefficient firms to survive. This was possible in the Soviet Union since the raw materials came from the country's awesome natural resource endowment. The state also provided a variety of other subsidies, but they were probably less significant overall than raw materials subsidies.

Soviet officials often argued, incorrectly, that since the Soviet Union had raw materials in abundance it would not make sense to treat domestic users the same way as Western users by charging each group the same price. But any raw materials not used domestically can always be sold on world markets for badly needed hard currency. So, even though the Soviet Union always had plenty of raw materials, the cost of using them wastefully on domestic industry was always high. Wasteful domestic usage threw away the opportunity to earn and then spend substantial amounts of hard currency on world markets.

In many cases, energy was used to produce poor-quality domestic goods that sold for less on world markets than sale of the energy used to produce them would have earned. Such activity was clearly not in the interest of Soviet citizens, who could have benefited much more from the effective distribution of foreign-trade earnings. Moreover, now that the most easily accessible deposits of natural resources have been tapped, the cost of providing Russian industry and agriculture with extremely cheap natural resources is escalating rapidly.

On the basis of these arguments international organizations like the International Monetary Fund and the World Bank have pushed hard to convince Russia to raise raw material prices to world market levels, and to force domestic firms either to make profits while paying these prices, or to go bankrupt.

Such a policy would force domestic industry to use raw materials more efficiently. The most hopeless raw materials wasters would go out of business and the surviving firms would strive to improve their efficiency. To get a grasp on the possible benefits of such a policy, it is necessary to examine the extent of inefficiency in the Russian economy.

The Physical Capital Stock: Degrees of Inefficiency

Arkadii Volskii of the Russian Union of Industrialists and Entrepreneurs has claimed that at world market prices 16 percent of Russian industrial capacity would definitely survive; 28 percent would almost surely go bankrupt; and 56 percent would be in a precarious situation.[10] Although the basis of these figures is unclear, they represent a widespread fear that a huge part of Russian industry would collapse in the face of world market prices.[11] Several recent Western studies that have tried to measure the amount of value created in the Russian economy have concluded that much of Russian industry is actually destroying value rather than creating it.[12] An industry is value-destroying when the value of its final product on the world market is less than the value of the raw materials that it uses up in the production process.

The diamond industry provides a simple example. The crudely cut and polished diamonds that this industry produces actually sell for less on the world market than the rough unprocessed diamonds the industry starts with. A value-destroying industry cannot be profitable even if workers work for free. When people actually receive positive wages, they are being paid to do economic damage. Such an industry can be shut down while paying unemployment compensation to all laid-off workers equal to their previous wages, and there still will be money left over equal to the economic destruction no longer being committed.

Senik-Leygonie and Hughes estimate that almost 8 percent of the output of Russian industry in tradeable sectors is produced in such a value-destroying fashion.[13] Thornton finds that five of eighteen sectors in the Russian Far East are value-destroying, although she does not calculate the percent of Far Eastern industrial output produced by these sectors.[14] This would be bad enough, but an examination of the methods used in these studies indicates that they probably understate the magnitude of the problem by tending to make difficult choices in favor of helping Russian industry look better.[15] For example, hypothetical world market prices are assigned to output from various sectors based on the actual world market prices of the portion of that sector's output that is sold on the world market. So a sector like machine-building and metalworking receives a world market valuation based on the few high quality products that are exported, even though most of the output of that sector is of such a low quality that it could not be sold on world markets at any profitable price. Given the extremely uneconomic nature of value-destroying economic activity, these studies point to a very serious problem.

A second category of inefficiency includes firms whose products can be sold only at world market prices that are lower than the value of the raw materials plus the labor they use. These firms would lose money if their current resource flows were evaluated at world market prices. However, a firm with negative cash flow that is not a value-destroyer could have positive cash flow if it could pay a low enough wage and still find enough people to work at this wage. Workers in these industries are receiving more in wages than the wealth that they are creating for society. So if one of these firms were closed down, money would be saved but the savings would not be enough to pay full unemployment compensation. Therefore, closing firms of this type would probably cause social problems, because the government would be forced to cut the compensation paid to the released workers, unless it was prepared to raise more funds from other sources. Of course, the option of keeping these firms in operation at much lower wages would also be very unpopular with workers.

Senik-Leygonie and Hughes estimate that almost 2 percent of the output of Russian industry in tradeable sectors results in negative cash flow, but not negative value added.[16] Thornton found that one sector out of the eighteen she studied in the Far East produced negative cash flow, but not negative value added.[17] These estimates can probably be taken as a lower boundary of the true magnitude of the problem.

In a third category of inefficiency are firms with positive cash flow, but with profits that are too small to justify their setup costs. These firms never should have been built, but since they exist it would be a mistake to close them down. Senik-Leygonie and Hughes estimate that almost 26 percent of the output of Russian industry is insufficiently profitable but has positive cash flow.[18] Finally, there are firms that should have been built, but that should be using less labor and materials to produce their products. Probably the remaining two-thirds of Russian output falls into this category.

All types of firms can improve their efficiency to some degree if they can mobilize sufficient funds to finance a restructuring. Even some value-destroyers could become viable at a reasonable price, so that it would not necessarily be efficient to close them all down. This issue will be considered in detail below.

The Attempted "Big Bang"

On January 2, 1992 Russia followed in the footsteps of Poland and launched what was supposed to be a "Big Bang" reform.[19] The idea was to free prices while simultaneously forcing firms to sink or swim, depending on whether or not they could generate profits, without subsidies, at these liberalized prices. The government was to get its budget deficit down to below 5 percent of GDP while reducing inflation to single digits per month. At the same time, trade was to be liberalized while the ruble was to be stabilized in preparation to become a convertible currency.

The program has deviated significantly from these basic principles. First, many prices remained fixed at levels well below market values. The most important examples have been many raw materials, particularly energy, and consumer staple items. Second, varying limits on price markups have been applied at both the national and local levels. Third, many enterprises that were struggling soon started receiving large direct subsidies, in complete contradiction to the spirit and letter of the reform. The budget deficit is currently about 20 percent of GDP; inflation is above 20 percent per month; and the ruble has fallen to over 1,000 to the dollar.[20]

Despite these contradictions, I believe that the deepest cause of the Russian economic depression is the shock therapy that was implemented in the first half of 1992. Many firms saw their subsidies cut dramatically and suddenly were threatened with bankruptcy. Many unprofitable firms were put under tremendous financial pressure by the attempted "Big Bang."

Unable to get the quick and automatic reimbursement for their losses to which they had been accustomed for decades, many firms were forced to cut losses by producing less. To stay in business, Russian firms were expected to be profitable at market prices, even though none of them had been created with this capability in the first place. They could hardly respond to the challenge overnight, so the result of the shock therapy is entirely unsurprising

The industrial sectors that contracted the most in the first half of 1992 tended to be the least profitable, while those that contracted the least tended to be the most profitable. In Table 4.1, the left column lists six internationally traded sectors in ascending order of short-term profitability at world market prices. Food processing yielded large losses, while wood products, engineering, textiles, and footwear yielded small losses. Chemicals, oil and gas, and metallurgy are separated because they earned much higher short-term profits than the other four sectors.[21]

The right column in Table 4.1 shows basically the same industries. This table starts with light industry, whose total share in industrial output decreased by the largest percentage, to metallurgy, whose total industrial share increased by the largest percentage amount.[22] The last two entries are the only listed industries that increased their total share, and both showed large increases. Although the categories do not overlap perfectly, it seems clear that high calculated profitability was closely related to an increased share in industrial production, and vice versa.[23]

Table 4.1 Profitability and Share of Industrial Output

Short-Term Profitability (Lowest to Highest)	% Change in Share of Industrial Output (January-July, 1992)	
Food processing	Light industry	-38%
Wood products	Food industry	-17%
Engineering	Machine building & metal processing	-12%
Textiles, footwear	Timber & wood processing industry	-6.8%
Chemicals, oil, and gas production	Chemical, oil, and fuel industry	+35%
Metallurgy	Metallurgy	+71%

Sources: Claudia Senik-Leygonie and Gordon Hughes, "Industrial Profitability and Trade Among the Former Soviet Republics," *Economic Policy* (October, 1992), pp. 363; and *The Uncertain State of the Russian Economy* (New York and Moscow: Institute of East-West Studies and Institute of Economic Policy, 1992), p. 94.

As shown by Table 4.1, profitability at world market prices is directly related to the percentage change in an industry's share in industrial output in the first half of 1992. Research on Soviet foreign trade also supports this explanation of the Russian economic disintegration. Marrese and Vanous show that Soviet trade with Eastern Europe consisted largely of the exchange of Soviet raw materials, primarily energy, for heavily overpriced East European goods, mainly low-quality machinery.[24]

They argue convincingly that these subsidies were given in exchange for political obedience. This implies that Russia was borrowing against the future by giving away its natural resources at extraordinarily low prices. So when the Soviet empire collapsed, trade with Eastern Europe disintegrated because Russia no longer had an interest in mortgaging its own future. Economically this was good for Russia and bad for Eastern Europe. But this view implies that most of the supply links with Eastern Europe were severed because they did not make economic sense in the context of a market economy.

This analysis gives a new perspective to the World Bank's explanation of the Russian economic disintegration: the collapse of foreign trade and the severing of supply links. The World Bank report at times almost creates the impression that these causes were exogenous occurrences, and indeed in a few cases supply links were destroyed by capricious factors such as war or nationalism.

However, the report emphasizes the dismantling of the central planning apparatus as the primary factor in the disintegration of both domestic and foreign economic links. Obviously, firms have not simply lost connections with their suppliers. The economic depression cannot be reversed by opening up the Gosplan records to discover and then reconstitute the old economic links.

In most cases, supply links, both domestic and foreign, were broken because they were not mutually beneficial. A major part of Soviet economic activity was economically irrational; it was sustained by the coercive force of central planning and it relied on government subsidies. The planning apparatus was able to force firms to engage in unprofitable activities while it imposed the losses on the natural resource base, health care, the environment, safety, and many other areas. When central planning was dismantled and subsidies were removed many supply links simply became untenable.[25]

Note that this explanation of the economic disintegration implies that the degree of collapse has been exaggerated by the official statistics. The fall in the output of industrial products is very real, but at least the nation is not using resources as inefficiently as in the past, and this drop-off in the waste of resources may not show up adequately in official statistics. And yet, although there has been substantial progress in reducing waste, natural resources are still significantly undervalued, so that the benefits of conservation continue to be underestimated.

The claim that the "Big Bang" caused the current economic disintegration is not, by itself, a criticism of this economic policy. If shock therapy is applied scrupulously, the most inefficient economic activities are hurt the most. Subsidizing these activities soaks up funds that could be used to help in a variety of crises that Russia faces. Since many opponents of shock therapy sidestep this point, it is worth considering in some detail some of the alternative uses for the resources that are now subsidizing loss-making operations.

The health system is in utter disarray. Doctors' salaries are well below average wages and there are perilous shortages of even the most basic medicines and equipment.[26] The education system is falling apart mainly because teacher salaries are falling much faster than other wages are. Dozens of environmental crises must be addressed. Retired people are experiencing traumatic hardship as the value of their pensions has eroded under severe budgetary pressure. Shock therapy can allow these problems to be addressed by mobilizing the funds that are supporting loss-making enterprises.

Perhaps more important, subsidies to the state sector severely inhibit the growth of the private sector, for a number of reasons. First, large subsidized enterprises are able to pay relatively high wages. Any new private firm will have to pay wages that can compete with these state sector wages.

Second, fledgling private firms will have to compete in the marketplace with large state firms that can absorb huge financial losses with help from the subsidies they receive from the state. Third, private firms must compete with the state firms for bank loans that are needed to make investments.[27] Since the future of the Russian economy ultimately lies primarily with the private sector, the continued subsidization of old capital has a very large cost.

Watering Down Shock Therapy

Industrialists responded to shock therapy by quickly organizing to lobby the government for a significant softening of its subsidy policy. Indeed, many managers had never believed in the government's resolve, and they acted on the assumption that the policy eventually would be reversed. These managers continued producing their products as before, accepting in return promises of payment that the managers knew could never be fulfilled. They simply assumed that the government would step in at some point and make good on these debts. This type of behavior was fundamentally harmful to the economy, because it introduced complicated networks of debt that are now a nightmare to unravel.[28]

By the middle of 1992 the balance of power had shifted decisively in favor of the "Industrial Lobby," which was able to invade the government with several representatives. Most prominent was Viktor Gerashchenko, chairman of the Russian Central Bank, who started in July. The bank immediately began the process of resolving the inter-enterprise debt problem by paying off the bad debts.[29] This retrenchment from the "Big Bang" is particularly counterproductive, because it rewards precisely those firms that have been obstructing government policy the most.

The power of the Industrial Lobby rose to a new high with the appointment of Viktor Chernomyrdin as prime minister in December of 1992. He made it clear that his top priority would be to revive economic output by increasing industrial subsidies. In fact, his first major act as prime minister was to reward his old colleagues in the energy sector with a major program of fresh subsidies. He planned to gradually phase out subsidies only after output stabilized. He claimed to believe that firms should be forced eventually to sink or swim on their own, but he wanted to give them time to adapt slowly rather than to force immediate adjustments.

The Central Bank responded vigorously to the encouragement of the new government by flooding the economy with new money. By January of 1993 Russia may have crossed over briefly into the realm of hyperinflation, where prices more than double every six weeks. By early February the value of the ruble had plunged to 572 to the dollar, and by early June it crossed the threshold of 1,000 to the dollar. Apparently, the Chernomyrdin government was so disturbed by these obvious consequences of its behavior that it reversed its own priorities, announcing that inflation stabilization would now supersede output stabilization as its first goal. While this change of heart was probably sincere, the credibility of the government was now so low that the conditions for a new stabilization program were extremely unfavorable. Any time a government announces a plan to introduce painful measures it faces an uphill struggle, since many people simply will not believe that the government will have the nerve to carry out a policy that will bring so much pain. In the Russian case many managers never believed that Yeltsin and Gaidar would really implement shock therapy. Of course the doubters were proven correct. Certainly the Chernomyrdin reversal only deepened the cynicism with which all reform efforts are greeted.[30] It would be very surprising if the man who personified the abortion of the "Big Bang" turned out to be the first Russian prime minister to finally phase out subsidies.

Nevertheless, in the spring economic transformation was revived. Yeltsin's major victory in the April referendum created momentum that allowed the government to achieve an agreement with the Central Bank aimed at reducing inflation to less than 10 percent per month by the end of the year through simultaneous limitations on government spending and credit creation.[31] Legal support was provided by a bankruptcy law that had gone into effect in April. This law has the potential to help rein in industrial subsidies and control government spending.[32] The ruble stabilized at around 1,000 to the dollar as the budgetary situation began to look hopeful. The Western world rewarded this behavior in July by promising $44 billion in foreign aid.[33]

Unfortunately, these hopeful developments were seriously marred when, beginning in July, the parliament and the Central Bank began an all-out assault on Yeltsin's economic program. First, the parliament passed a budget that was so out of balance that, if enforced, it would undoubtedly push the economy into hyperinflation. Second, the parliament attempted to undermine the government's privatization program by diminishing the value of people's privatization vouchers. But the most important sabotage came from the Central Bank when, on July 24, it declared invalid all ruble notes printed before 1993 while giving citizens only one week to exchange a small amount (35,000 rubles) of old currency.[34] While the government did manage to water down this measure, it had no means to prevent another shattering blow to both domestic and world confidence in the ruble.

The situation was once again reversed when Yeltsin's dramatic crushing of the Russian parliament completely changed the balance of economic decision-making authority. First, the Central Bank was declared to fall under the jurisdiction of the executive branch of authority. As of mid-October 1993 the bank remains feisty, but it appears likely that it will soon be brought under control.[35] This would bring considerable credibility to the government's efforts to reduce subsidies and fight inflation. Indeed, these goals have now been declared to be a top priority of the government.[36] Second, the new parliament is likely to be significantly more receptive to Yeltsin's economic transformation program than the previous parliament was. It seems unlikely that it will attempt to spend irresponsibly and to stall privatization in the manner of its predecessor. Finally, Egor Gaidar has been brought back into the government as a first deputy prime minister and apparently will have considerable control over economic policy.

Since a prolonged period of inflation, if not hyperinflation, still seems likely in Russia, it is worth considering the probable consequences. First, high inflation is generally correlated with high variability in the inflation rate, which makes any kind of economic planning extremely difficult. Solid investment decisions become particularly hard to achieve since these decisions require reasonably accurate forecasting of economic conditions over several years, and good forecasting is impossible under unstable conditions. This means that badly needed foreign and domestic investment simply will not be forthcoming unless Russia can bring its inflation rate down to a reasonable level. In fact, avoidance of inflation is now causing a high level of disinvestment, in the form of capital flight. Second, high inflation encourages the newly independent countries of the former Soviet Union, as well as republics within Russia, to introduce their own currencies in order to achieve financial security. Since it will be difficult to make these new currencies convertible into one another, trade within the region will become very difficult. This process will accelerate the transformation of trading relations into a barter basis and damage the economic integration of the region. In other words, the Russian hyperinflation is a force for economic disintegration, and consequently for the general political dismemberment of Russia and the former Soviet Union. Third, certain powerless groups will be put into a very precarious position, since they will have great difficulty achieving salary growth in line with inflation. Affected groups are likely to include pensioners, teachers, and doctors, i.e., those who depend on the government for support.

Adaptability of Enterprises and the
Medium-Run Future of the Russian Economy

The Russian economy is so inefficient that any rationalization of the economy will eliminate a huge amount of current economic activity.[37] Bankrupting a large part of Russian industry and agriculture by removing subsidies will inevitably throw millions of people out of work and cause wages to plummet. Almost all of this unemployment will be temporary, because the private sector will absorb unemployed people as it grows. But no one knows exactly how flexibly the private sector will respond to the withdrawal of state sector subsidies. The Russian government will be very hard-pressed financially to provide an acceptable standard of living for the unemployed if there are too many of them at one point.[38] Moreover, unemployment is a serious political problem if too many people are out of work at the same time. This suggests that the government is likely to phase out subsidies gradually to spread out unemployment over time.[39]

The Gaidar government gave another justification for eliminating subsidies in stages over several years. The government argued that Russian industry needs time to adjust to financial discipline. The government claimed that too big a shock would break industry rather than force it to adjust to harsh new realities. Russia would then become "Kuwaitized" as a mere raw materials appendage of the West. It was argued that with a gradual approach a significant fraction of Russian industry would have the opportunity to restructure itself so that Russia could remain a major industrial economy. The Chernomyrdin government increased the emphasis on temporary industrial subsidies for this reason.

A variety of viewpoints have been expressed on the probable consequences of this policy of the Russian government. *The Economist* magazine regularly argues that the Russian economy is tremendously inefficient, and is sustained largely by cheap raw materials. According to this view, a large fraction of existing resource flows cannot be justified on efficiency grounds. Therefore, the magazine advocates the Kuwaitization of Russia, and considers subsidies in support of restructuring a costly and futile exercise.[40] Lipton and Sachs argue, in effect, that Russia would not become Kuwaitized if raw materials and other subsidies were suddenly removed.[41] These analysts have emphasized a supposed underlying flexibility of post-communist economies that would allow them to adapt remarkably quickly to new conditions. But they do not believe that subsidies are necessary for enterprises to carry out their restructuring plans, so they also view the government's policy as a vast waste of resources. On the other hand, Murrell argues that virtually none of the existing industrial structures in post-communist economies is capable of restructuring itself to be viable in a market economy.[42] A new industrial structure must, in his view, be built up essentially from scratch. Murrell is so pessimistic that he, like the Russian government, advocates a gradual approach to removing subsidies. This is not to give existing industry a chance to adapt, but rather to close it down in an orderly fashion, reducing the social consequences of the transition process.

Unfortunately, the degree of adaptability of Russian industry is unknown, so it is difficult to assess the likelihood that current government policy can successfully turn it around. It is perhaps useful to conceptualize the issue in terms of energy efficiency. In many cases, factories, homes, and machines that were not built to be energy efficient in the first place cannot be sufficiently transformed through after-the-fact alterations; there is only so much that can be done with Band-Aids and rubber bands. Alternatively, one can imagine that there are, in many cases, significant and inexpensive opportunities for major improvements such as installing insulation in a very leaky building. Since energy was practically free under the previous regime, managers never bothered to implement even the simplest measures to save energy. But with energy subsidies taken away, managers will move decisively to make simple improvements. Which of these two outcomes prevails is crucial to determining the real value of the existing physical capital stock.

Suppose for the moment that much of Russian physical capital is fairly adaptable. Even then, most economists would expect that government subsidies for restructuring would be wasteful and unnecessary. Specifically, suppose that a firm is temporarily unprofitable, but could become profitable after a suitable restructuring at a reasonable price. In a standard Western economy it would be possible to borrow money to carry out its restructuring plan. But conventional Western credit markets do not exist in Russia and will not exist for a long period of time, for the following reasons.[43] First, considerable expertise is needed to evaluate loans in any country, and that expertise is not present in Russia after seven decades of communism. In the Soviet Union, firms received credit from banks, but the banks were hardly concerned about whether or not the firms paid back these loans; the Central Bank would always be willing to cover the debts. Therefore, it was not necessary to train prudent loan officers. Second, in an economy that is undergoing massive structural change it is much more difficult to evaluate the quality of various investment projects than in a more stable environment. In the Russian economy the uncertainty now is tremendous, so even experienced Western loan officers would not be able to make good decisions about which projects were worth supporting in Russia. They would be forced to rely on crude rules of thumb, such as supporting projects in the underdeveloped service sector and not funding the restructuring of factories whose technology is beyond a certain age.

This analysis sets up the following dilemma. Given the absence of credit markets, removing subsidies too rapidly runs the risk of forcing the shutdown of many firms that could be capable of adapting to market conditions. Thus, the Chernomyrdin subsidized readjustment program could be viewed as a crude substitute for the missing Russian credit market. It is crude because the subsidies would not or could not be targeted effectively on the most promising investment projects. Choosing the best projects would have been the role of a well-functioning credit market if such a market existed in Russia. On the other hand, this policy runs the risk of throwing a huge amount of good money after bad by supporting many firms that would never be able to survive under market conditions. The present government has decided, rightly or wrongly, that cutting off all these hopeless industries from their subsidies would have the costlier side effect of forcing out of business too many firms that have the potential to adapt to the market.

A further factor driving government behavior is the concern that even firms that can survive without subsidies may be prevented from carrying out reasonable restructuring plans to raise their efficiency in the absence of well-functioning credit markets. Without credit they will have to generate their restructuring funds internally, and this may not be possible. Therefore, subsidies are given even to profitable firms, even though many do not have a good chance to improve their efficiency.

Although the Chernomyrdin policy may have a logically coherent (although an empirically incorrect) basis, it has one more major drawback.

There is a real possibility that managers would simply pocket the subsidy money even when their firms were worth restructuring. This problem is especially acute under the current murky regime of property rights. Managers do not know who their future bosses will be. Consequently, managers' reward structure is unclear. This creates an incentive for short-term benefit maximization. This probably implies that simply taking subsidy money would be preferred by managers to carrying out complicated restructuring plans. This problem presents a serious challenge to the privatization process that is just beginning.

Human Capital and the Long-Run Prospects of the Russian Economy

A key feature that distinguishes Russia from a typical developing country is the fact that Russia has a large stock of human capital.[44] Of course, all of the arguments developed earlier to explain the distorted nature of the Russian capital stock apply to the human capital stock. Therefore, many of the particular skills that exist are not appropriate or useful for the economy of the future. Nevertheless, the high numeracy and literacy of the work force is a very valuable asset for the economy, and one that cannot be matched by many developing countries. Moreover, Russia possesses a large stock of highly trained individuals such as scientists, engineers, doctors, and technicians of various sorts. Many of these people are at or near world levels of competence, and even those who are below world levels often have a useful knowledge base to draw on. For example, many Russian engineers would be designated as technicians in the West. But every economy needs good technicians, so the knowledge these people have is potentially of great commercial use under the right conditions.

In any society knowledge is built up cumulatively over many generations in such a way that younger generations find it easier and more natural to acquire human capital when older generations are themselves highly educated and skilled. A highly educated older generation will have a large pool of potential teachers who can serve all levels of the educational system. It is easier for children to learn at home when their parents are educated, and in this case the parents are likely to encourage their children to learn. The general climate in a highly educated society will be conducive to learning. Thus Russia is a country where the relatively high general level of education and skills makes it relatively easy for younger generations to become educated and skilled. This is a rare example of a positive legacy from the Soviet past.

Unfortunately, the strong Russian human capital base must contend with a very weak physical capital base. This implies that many people with potentially useful skills are not very productive, because they do not have the right machines or equipment to work with. The low labor productivity in turn implies that Russian wages are very low. Conversely, the strong human capital base makes good physical capital very productive. Plenty of educated and skilled labor is available to work with physical capital at very low wages. Thus, Russia has a major potential niche in the world economy: high human capital at low wages.

This state of affairs would, under normal circumstances, work as a magnet for both foreign and domestic investment. The Russian economy is an untapped reservoir of inexpensive human talent waiting to be matched with the right physical capital. Indeed, some American companies like Sun Microsystems and Corning have moved to take advantage of these opportunities. However, under present circumstances foreign investment will be very slow in coming. The uncertainty that will plague the Russian economy for some time to come will make it a prohibitively risky market for most investors. Private domestic investment also will be a slow process, not only because of the risks but also because of the continued subsidizing of old capital and the underdevelopment of domestic financial institutions. Therefore, the deficit of good physical capital is likely to persist for a long time.

This prolonged shortage of good physical capital causes two serious problems for the future. First, the wages for educated labor will be held down to levels that will not encourage the younger generations to acquire human capital. Most young people will be better served financially by simply taking unskilled jobs or by developing schemes to capitalize on the murky legal system, rather than spending the time and money necessary to become educated and skilled. Many students are not concentrating on their studies, because they have to make money to get by, or they are attracted by opportunities to make quick money.

Second, older generations will abandon their professions in Russia, allowing their own skills and education to erode while not transmitting them to younger generations. The research institutes are under heavy pressure because most of them cannot generate much revenue on their own. Many of the most qualified people have already left the country. General education is suffering severely under serious budget cuts as many teachers are leaving their profession to work in unskilled jobs.

Of course, these choices are reasonable for individuals to make, and in most cases they also provide strong benefits for society. Most people who are making money are doing so by providing the kinds of goods and services that the Soviet economy never provided adequately. However, once the general educational level of the population falls substantially, it will become very difficult and costly for future generations to educate themselves. Thus, the general disintegration of Russia threatens to precipitate a collapse of the Russian human capital stock. This would ensure that by the time that the investment climate has become reasonably stable, Russia will have lost its special niche in the world economy as a country with high human capital at low wages. It would be forced to begin its development process from a position akin to that of a typical developing country. To summarize, this analysis suggests that the short-term benefits of small-scale, unskilled business activity must be weighed against the long-term cost due to the erosion of the Russian human capital stock.

Although it goes beyond the scope of this chapter, I believe that there are policy measures worth taking that could maintain the Russian human capital stock relatively intact. For example, wages for skilled labor should be subsidized to encourage people to acquire expertise and education. In addition, the education sector should be supported by raising teacher salaries and providing students with financial incentives to stay in school.[45] If this were done and if the general economic environment could be stabilized—a very difficult task— it is quite likely that Russia would experience rapid growth in the future. Foreign capital could start pouring into Russia to take advantage of its inexpensive and well-educated work force. At the same time, as internal financial institutions developed they could enable a spurt in domestic investment. In fact, in the long run it is possible for the Russian economy to do very well indeed on the basis of its strong underlying human capital base.

Conclusions

It is very difficult to find any grounds for optimism about the short-run prospects for the Russian economy. Indeed, in this chapter I have argued that a severe drop in output is an inevitable consequence of the transition process to a market economy. Government decision-making and the Central Bank have been strongly influenced by the philosophy of the Industrial Lobby. Total subsidies for 1993 will be in the trillions of rubles. This subsidization may prop up output to some degree, but the practice of coddling highly inefficient state enterprises inevitably hinders the growth of a market environment. Existing firms will not be forced to adapt to reality, and private firms will be at a disadvantage. Moreover, needy areas like health, education, the environment, and pensions will continue to suffer from lack of funding.

Nevertheless, there are substantial reasons for optimism on the medium-term future of the Russian economy. First, the return of Gaidar as economics minister signals a renewed governmental commitment to economic reform. Second, the political turnaround of October 1993 provides an impetus for stabilization. Finance Minister Boris Fedorov has already taken advantage of the moment by pushing a new initiative to cut the budget deficit. There is mounting pressure on the Central Bank to implement a more rational monetary policy. Third, it is important to note that for an entire year privatization has been proceeding apace.[46]

On the negative side, the political upheaval of the fall of 1993 may encourage various regions to assert their sovereignty more strongly. As Khrushchev discusses in Chapter 6, the central government has faced considerable difficulty in collecting taxes from recalcitrant localities. Moreover, economic development has been seriously inhibited by confusion over property rights. A renewed struggle between local and central government for control of various economic entities would further constrain growth. These problems may actually be exacerbated by Yeltsin's heavy-handed tactics in asserting his power.

However, if the investment climate can be stabilized and the human capital stock can be maintained relatively intact, Russia's long-term economic prospects are quite good. Unfortunately, these prerequisites will be very difficult to satisfy. However, with the right combination of domestic leadership, foreign support, and good fortune, it is not out of the question that today's young people can have a prosperous future to look forward to.

Notes

1. See *Russian Economic Reform: Crossing the Threshold of Structural Change* (Washington, D.C.: World Bank, 1992).

2. *Radio Free Europe/Radio Liberty* (hereafter *RFE/RL*) *Daily Report*, no. 29, February 12, 1993, and "Russian Economic Monitor," *PlanEcon Report* 9, nos. 5-6, March 10, 1993.

3. See World Bank, *Russian Economic Reform: Crossing the Threshold*, p. 39; for 1992, see "Russian Economic Monitor," *PlanEcon Report* 9, nos. 5-6, March 10, 1993. For trade figures, see "The Bread Battle," *The Economist*, October 9, 1993.

4. Ibid., p. 15.

5. For a recent, sophisticated, and detailed treatment of Soviet prices, see Morris Bornstein, "Soviet Price Policies," *Soviet Economy* 3, no. 2, 1987, pp. 96-134.

6. For a survey of Soviet investment methodology, see Janice Giffen, "The Allocation of Investment in the Soviet Union: Criteria for the Efficiency of Investment," in *The Soviet Economy on the Brink of Reform*, edited by Peter Wiles (Boston: Unwin Hyman, 1988.)

7. For more detail on these magnitudes, see "How Big Are the Soviet and East European Economies," *PlanEcon Report* 6, no. 52, 1990.

8. The oil figure is based on *The Wall Street Journal*, November 12, 1992, p. C12, and personal communication with Paul Hunt of PlanEcon in Washington. The other figures are from *Finansovye Izvestiia*, October 27, 1993, p. 7.

9. Among many references the reader can consult IMF, World Bank, OECD, and EBRD, *A Study of the Soviet Economy* 3, Chap. V.6, Washington D.C., 1991.

10. See Arkadii Volskii, "Zashchitit natsionalnuiu promyshlennost," *Ekonomicheskaia gazeta*, no. 47, November, 1992. Leonid Paidiev, an official from the economics ministry, believes that 70 percent of Russian firms are on the verge of bankruptcy. See V. Golovachev and L. Paidiev, "Two Steps from Bankruptcy," *Trud*, no. 190, December 4, 1992.

11. Clearly the government holds this view. See, for example, the first part of the "Official Program of Deepening Economic Reforms," *Ekonomicheskaia gazeta*, no. 30, July, 1992.

12. See Claudia Senik-Leygonie and Gordon Hughes, "Industrial Profitability and Trade Among the Former Soviet Republics." *Economic Policy*, October, 1992, pp. 354-386, for an analysis of all republics of the former Soviet Union. Also, Judith Thornton, "Structural Change and Integration of the Soviet Far East into the World Market: The Case of Negative Value Added," unpublished manuscript, University of Washington, 1991 does a similar study of the Russian Far East. See Ronald McKinnon, Chap. 12 in *The Order of Economic Liberalization: Financial Control in the Transition to A Market Economy* (Baltimore: Johns Hopkins University Press, 1991) for a theoretical argument why negative value-added should be a major problem in formerly centrally planned economies.

13. Senik-Leygonie and Hughes, "Industrial Profitability and Trade Among the Former Soviet Republics."

14. Thornton, "Structural Change and Integration of the Soviet Far East."

15. This is probably the right approach for initial studies that are attempting to document with a high degree of certainty that a substantial problem indeed exists.

16. Senik-Leygonie and Hughes, "Industrial Profitability and Trade Among the Former Soviet Republics."

17. Thornton, "Structural Change and Integration of the Soviet Far East."

18. Senik-Leygonie and Hughes, "Industrial Profitability and Trade Among the Former Soviet Republics."

19. I use the terms "Big Bang" and "shock therapy" interchangeably. For a detailed description of the government's economic program, see World Bank, *Russian Economic Reform: Crossing the Threshold*.

20. See "The Bread Battle," *The Economist*, October 9, 1993.

21. I have dropped industries listed in Senik-Leygonie and Hughes, "Industrial Profitability and Trade," that do not have corresponding listings in *Uncertain State of the Russian Economy*. Although chemicals is separated from oil and gas in Senik-Leygonie and Hughes, "Industrial Profitability and Trade," I have joined the two in Table 4.1 to facilitate comparison with Table 2 of *Uncertain State of the Russian Economy*. Note that by itself chemicals is a bit less profitable than textiles, footwear.

22. Again I have dropped industries that do not have corresponding listings in Senik-Leygonie and Hughes, "Industrial Profitability and Trade." To facilitate comparisons I have joined ferrous and nonferrous metallurgy, and the chemical and oil industry with the fuel industry.

23. I believe that there is substantial overlap between engineering and machine building and metal processing.

24. See Michael Marrese and Jan Vanous, *Soviet Subsidization of Trade with Eastern Europe: A Soviet Perspective* (Berkeley: University of California, Institute of International Studies, 1983.)

25. A common explanation of the Russian economic collapse is that it resulted from freeing big monopoly firms from government controls. However, monopolized and highly concentrated industries have not cut their output levels any more on average than other industries. See John Parker, "Russia: The Sixth Wave," *The Economist*, December 5-11, 1992, p. 13.

26. To get a sense of the gravity of the situation note that in 1988 15 percent of the hospitals in the Soviet Union had no water supply system and 49 percent had no hot water. See Murray Feshbach and Alfred Friendly, Jr., *Ecocide in the USSR* (New York: Basic Books, 1992). This book provides an exhaustive catalogue of health and environmental horrors in the USSR.

27. For further discussion of the role of subsidies in stifling the private sector, consult "The Russian Economy During the First Half of 1992: 'We Pretend to Reform Our Economy and the West Pretends to Lend Us Money'," *PlanEcon Report* 8, nos. 33-34, 1992.

28. For a thorough analysis of the problem, see Barry Ickes and Randi Ryterman, "Inter-Enterprise Arrears and Financial Underdevelopment in Russia," unpublished manuscript, Pennsylvania State University, 1992.

29. This was possible without the approval of Boris Yeltsin and the acting prime minister, Egor Gaidar, because the Central Bank was subordinate to the parliament, the power base of the Industrial Lobby. For a general discussion, see Michael Ellman, "The Economic Program of the Civic Union," *RFE/RL Research Report* 2, no. 11, March 12, 1993, pp. 34-45.

30. Remember that financial discipline has been a theme of Soviet economic reform dating back at least until 1965.

31. See "The Agreement of the Central Bank and the Government Will Hasten the Path of Economic Reform," *Finansovye Izvestiia*, no. 29, May 15-21, 1993, p. 1.

32. This law began to show results in September. See "Bankruptcy Law Claims First Victim," *Financial Times*, September 17, 1993.

33. See "While the Rich World Talks," *The Economist*, July 10, 1993, pp. 11-12.

34. See "The Rouble Used as a Bomb," *The Economist*, July 31, 1993, pp. 41-42, which covers the general clash between the parliament and the government and "The People Do Not Need a Government that Lies to It," *Finansovye Izvestiia*, no. 139, July 27, 1993, p. 1. Note that the currency confiscation was apparently carried out with the approval of Chernomyrdin.

35. The bank has refused to place its currency reserves at the disposal of the executive branch, as ordered, and it has declared against the government's wishes that beginning on January 1 all transactions in foreign currencies will be banned. See RFE/RL, *Daily Report*. no. 193, October 7, 1993.

36. See Steven Erlanger, "Now that Parliament's Gone, Can Yeltsin Really Reform Russia's Economy," *The New York Times*, October 6, 1993.

37. On a paradoxical bright note, there are many cases of value-destroying operations that can be closed down in a manner that leaves everyone better off. But in general, unemployment will impose a severe hardship on anyone who experiences it.

38. Of course when the government is committed to paying unemployment benefits, the costs of these payments should be included in the cost of shutting down a firm, i.e., these potential government expenditures should be added to the firm's profits.

39. Note that unemployment in Russia is still negligible by Western standards, so that up until now social considerations would not be a valid ground for slowing down the withdrawal of subsidies. However, unemployment has the potential to grow very rapidly if stringent financial discipline were suddenly enforced.

40. See for example *The Economist*, October 24, 1992.

41. See David Lipton and Jeffrey Sachs, "Creating a Market Economy in Eastern Europe: The Case of Poland," *Brookings Papers on Economic Activity*, no. 1, 1990, pp. 75-147, and David Lipton and Jeffrey Sachs, "Prospects for Russia's Economic Reforms," *Brookings Papers on Economic Activity*, no. 2, 1992, pp. 213-283.

42. See Peter Murrell, "Evolution in Economics and in the Economic Reform of the Centrally Planned Economies," Chap. 3 in *The Emergence of Market Economies in Eastern Europe*, edited by Christopher Clague and Gordon C. Rausser (Cambridge, Mass.: Blackwell, 1992).

43. These arguments are taken from Barry Ickes, "What To Do Before the Capital Markets Arrive: The Transition Problem in Reforming Socialist Economies," unpublished manuscript, Pennsylvania State University, 1991, and Ickes and Ryterman, "Inter-Enterprise Arrears and Financial Underdevelopment in Russia," where they are developed in detail.

44. See *Human Development Report* (New York: Oxford University Press, 1992), p. 190.

45. Note that such measures would undoubtedly be expensive and the continued subsidization of loss-making firms is absorbing many of the needed financial resources. See C. Simon Fan and Michael Spagat, "Human Capital and Long-Run Growth in Transition Economies: Gradualism versus Shock Therapy," unpublished manuscript, Brown University, for detail on the above argument.

46. See "Russia's Struggle," *The Economist*, October 2, 1993, p. 22.

5

Russia's Labor Relations: Consolidation or Disintegration?

Linda J. Cook

Introduction

From the outset, labor relations in the independent Russian state faced a dilemma: how to maintain labor peace while implementing market reforms. Russia emerged from the Gorbachev period with a mobilized and activist, if somewhat fragmented, labor movement. Protracted and often politicized strikes had done much to destabilize Mikhail Gorbachev's government, and President Boris Yeltsin sought to avoid further unrest by establishing a "social partnership" with labor unions.

At the same time, Yeltsin's government committed itself to a reform program of fiscal discipline and market transition that threatened to impose great costs and hardships on workers, including declines in real wages, decreases in social spending, layoffs and unemployment. For much of 1992, unions and workers struggled to protect themselves from these costs by trying to weaken or delay various provisions of Acting Prime Minister Egor Gaidar's 'economic shock therapy.' Labor and reform, in short, made contradictory policy demands.

I will argue below that the dilemma was resolved more often in favor of labor's short-term interests. Efforts to maintain labor peace—both the institutional arrangements Yeltsin made with the unions and the pattern of governmental and legislative concessions to workers' demands—helped undermine the economic reform program, and achieved only a temporary stabilization of labor relations.

The Structure of Russian Labor Relations

As the Soviet Union collapsed in the fall of 1991, Boris Yeltsin's government moved quickly to establish a cooperative relationship with Russia's labor
unions. In October Yeltsin promised to consult with republic trade union associations before adopting any major legislation on social and economic issues.
In a November edict "On Social Partnership and the Resolution of Labor Disputes," he proposed that a comprehensive annual socio-economic agreement
be negotiated between unions and government. In January 1992, Yeltsin proceeded to formalize his social partnership with labor by establishing the Tripartite Commission on the Regulation of Social and Labor Relations. The
commission, which was clearly influenced by European corporatist models of
labor relations, brought together representatives of organized labor, organized
management, and government in a three-sided negotiating structure. It was
empowered to review and set wage levels, monitor working conditions, and
mediate industrial disputes. Unions were to take a no-strike pledge in return
for their role in top-level decision-making. Yeltsin appealed for their cooperation in riding out the early stages of Russia's economic reform.[1]

The Tripartite Commission was comprised of fourteen representatives
from labor unions, fourteen from employers, and fourteen from government.
Of labor's seats, nine were allocated to the Federation of Independent Trade
Unions of Russia (known by its Russian acronym, FNPR); one each to the Independent Union of Miners and the Independent Union of Civil Aviation Pilots; and three to the Union of Social Trade Unions (Sotsprof). Management
was represented by several organizations, including the Russian Union of Industrialists and Entrepreneurs (RUIE), most of whose members were managers
of large state enterprises, and the Congress of Russian Business Circles, representing managers of commercial banks, insurance and stock companies.[2] The
government's share of seats was occupied by officials of state ministries.
Yeltsin's state secretary, Gennadi Burbulis, was assigned to coordinate the
commission, and his labor minister from that time, Aleksandr Shokhin, is
known as the architect and major proponent of the tripartite bargaining process.[3]

The FNPR was the successor to the Russian branch of the old official
Communist trade unions (the All-Union Central Council of Trade Unions—
AUCCTU), in which all Soviet workers were automatically registered. The
AUCCTU had adapted remarkably well to Gorbachev's political democratiza-
tion. It reorganized itself in 1990 as the General Confederation of Trade
Unions (with republic-level affiliates called Federations of Independent Trade
Unions). It also repudiated its past subordination to the Soviet state, and
adopted an activist stance in defense of workers' interests. After the August
1991 coup attempt the Russian federation, the FNPR, inherited the old union's
republic-wide apparatus, property (including offices, rest homes, and vacation

facilities), monopolistic role as distributor of social security benefits and membership roles. Although FNPR unions suffered from extremely weak rank-and-file loyalty because of their communist past and bureaucratic operating methods, workers continued to depend on these unions for distribution of social benefits, so most stayed on the membership rolls. So the FNPR was able to claim more than 50 million members (from a total employed labor force of approximately 73 million), and on this basis it promoted itself to Yeltsin's government as the exclusive bargaining agent for Russia's workers.[4] The FNPR also had established itself in 1990 and 1991 as a 'constructive opponent' of government in the reform process, presenting itself as a union that preferred negotiation to strikes and cooperation to confrontation. The FNPR fit well into Yeltsin's 'social partnership' scheme; even though it was denied the exclusive right to represent workers on the Tripartite Commission, it gained the dominant position.

By contrast, the independent miners' and pilots' unions, each given token representation (a single seat) on the Tripartite Commission, were authentically independent products of democratization. The Independent Miners' Union (known by its Russian acronym, NPG) emerged from the grass roots coal miners' strike movement of summer 1989 and played a major leadership role in the 1990 and 1991 strikes. The NPG's influence in the coal basins greatly exceeded its limited membership (approximately 5 percent of miners). It was from the outset a militant, strike-prone union, given to ultimatums over negotiation. The Pilot's Union, with some 30,000 members, also had established itself through strikes and strike threats.[5] Sotsprof, which gained three seats, was an independent trade union with approximately 250,000 members. It included affiliates in many regions and branches, mostly small unions that had broken away from the FNPR or developed as grass roots initiatives. Established in 1989 and split in 1990, Sotsprof was quite closely connected with the Labor Ministry under Shokhin and the Social Democratic Party. Sotsprof's representation on the Tripartite Commission, and its influence with the Labor Ministry, far outweighed its size, and prompted protests from the FNPR.[6] The independent unions were generally pro-reform, but their small memberships limited their influence.

The Yeltsin government intended the Tripartite Commission to be an institutional mechanism to manage, mediate, and diffuse workers' discontent during the initial stages of market reforms and the commission did contribute for a time to stabilizing labor relations. The commission held frequent meetings, and helped negotiate settlements to several strikes in the winter and spring. However, Yeltsin's early commitment to social partnership and comprehensive socio-economic agreements placed labor unions in a position to try to resist reform at the policy-making stage. And while its leaders claimed support for market transition, the FNPR used its influence mainly to press for social guarantees that would protect workers from the effects of reform policies, usually at the expense of fiscal discipline and other reformist goals.

The Tripartite Commission also connected the FNPR institutionally with a strong ally against economic shock therapy: Arkadii Volskii's Russian Union of Industrialists and Entrepreneurs. In liberal corporatist theory, the government's representatives are supposed to mediate conflicts between management and workers in the tripartite bargaining structure. In practice, because the Russian state still owned most enterprises and controlled financial and other resources, managers of state enterprises and the unions that represented their workers were less often adversaries than allies in claiming resources and resisting demands from the state. The RUIE continually pressed Yeltsin's government to maintain industrial subsidies; provide substantial new soft credits; and reduce taxes in order to keep their enterprises, which were in many cases obsolete, inefficient, and unprofitable, afloat in the reform period, thereby protecting workers' jobs and incomes. Unions and industrialists generally cooperated in efforts to maintain real wage levels, subsidies, and continued high employment levels.

As a mechanism for bargaining and seeking compromise over policy, the Tripartite Commission worked poorly. Its meetings were marked by dissension; government officials were often absent; and efforts at policy-making were conflictual and generally ineffective. Almost from the beginning, FNPR officials protested the government's failure to consult with them on critical issues or to keep its commitments, and FNPR Chairman Klochkov periodically threatened to withdraw his union from the tripartite process. Nevertheless, the union did gain some limited concessions. The first comprehensive General Agreement on socio-economic policy, which was signed in late March 1992, illustrates the policy directions in which tripartism pushed Yeltsin's government.[7] This agreement followed a price liberalization in January that had freed 90 percent of retail prices from administrative controls. This resulted in an overall rise of prices of 300 to 500 percent, forcing a precipitous drop in real wages.[8] The FNPR insisted that the state regulate prices for necessities, so the March General Agreement provided for state regulation of a limited range of consumer and energy prices. The government also promised to introduce (by the third quarter of the year) a mechanism for quarterly review of minimum wages, pensions, etc., and to take into consideration changes in the minimum subsistence level. In exchange, the FNPR promised to refrain from strikes on matters relating to the agreement, and management agreed not to lay off workers or close down factories. Price controls and wage and income increases flew in the face of reform goals, and the provision for quarterly wage reviews constituted the first step in the FNPR's campaign for wage and income indexing. While one can surely see the legitimacy of demands for wage increases in the face of such large price increases, in the end rising wages contributed to inflation and fed the ongoing wage-price spiral.

The FNPR also sought support for its positions in the Russian Supreme Soviet. The Supreme Soviet's committees and commissions regularly consulted with interested parties as part of the legislative process, and the FNPR was heavily involved in deliberations on social and economic issues. Beginning in the fall of 1991, the union prepared a program of legislative activity focused on increasing wages and benefits, restricting privatization, and protecting its status. The union's positions received a sympathetic hearing in the legislature's Commission on Social Policy, which sponsored large increases in minimum wages and pensions and the introduction of income indexing during 1992.[9] Whether because of effective lobbying or coincidence of views with anti-reform deputies, the FNPR's legislative initiatives had considerable success in the Supreme Soviet, where they contributed to growing conflict between legislative and executive branches over the reform program.

Labor Strikes: Grievances and Concessions

Compared to 1991, 1992 was a year of relative industrial peace in Russia. Strikes continued, but they focused on economic grievances and were settled quickly. With the exception of the Tyumen oil workers, no one demanded the government's resignation. The protracted, anti-government strikes of 1991 did not reappear, nor did the large-scale social and labor unrest of that spring. In the early months of 1992 the pattern of strikes shifted from the critical energy sector (i.e., coal and oil) to the service sector, which accounted for some 90 percent of strikes in the first quarter.[10] The spring and summer brought a strike wave across many sectors, but the unrest abated again in the fall. The Tripartite Commission played its most significant role in successfully settling many of these strikes; indeed, government spokesmen credited the tripartite mechanism with reducing strike activity. However, it seems likely that the wage concessions made by Yeltsin's government in the face of strikes and strike threats also played a major part in damping down unrest.[11] We will consider below the major causes of strikes in 1992, the sectors they affected, and the terms of their settlement.

Workers in the raw materials sector, by far the most disruptive under Gorbachev, continued to present a serious challenge to Yeltsin. In the aftermath of the January price liberalization, the Independent Coal Miners' Union threatened to strike unless its wages were raised to cover the price increases. In response, Yeltsin agreed to triple these wages, essentially "buying off" this most militant sector of the labor force.[12] The miners nevertheless remained restive, demanding that their wages and pensions be indexed to inflation. A second strike by Kuzbass miners in March was mediated by the Tripartite Commission, and wage concessions were made again. In May, oil and gas workers struck, demanding large wage increases as well as decontrol of oil and gas prices. Their wages also were tripled, and the government agreed to higher energy prices, but not to complete deregulation. The strikes led to sharp reductions in extraction of oil and gas, as well as an ongoing dispute over price levels.[13]

By far the largest number of strikes in the first months of 1992 took placed in the service sector, among workers who were paid directly from state and municipal budgets—teachers, medical personnel, municipal transport workers, pilots, and air traffic controllers. These workers in budget-financed organizations were suffering most from the January price liberalization and general inflation, because they had received much smaller wage increases than had industrial workers, whose wages were determined by factory managers. In late January, health care workers in seventy-three of Russia's seventy-seven administrative regions threatened a strike to protest their 'poverty' wages and inadequate allocations for medical services; the strike was preempted by a 45 percent across-the-board salary increase and other concessions.[14] In late April and early May medical workers and teachers struck in various regions. Schools and day care centers were closed, and medics withheld non-emergency services and threatened to stop all forms of medical assistance. Both demanded that their wages be increased several times to equal the average monthly pay of industrial workers.[15] Again the Tripartite Commission helped negotiate a settlement, and again substantial concessions were forthcoming. Although an 80 percent wage increase for all budget-financed employees was scheduled to go into effect shortly, teachers got a 160 percent pay increase, in a combination of wage rates and productivity-linked bonuses and supplements.[16]

As in the past, transport workers also were restive and strike-prone. Both civil aviation pilots and air traffic controllers had established independent unions, and in February both threatened strikes. They demanded indexing of their wages and pensions to inflation; special hardship status for their profession; and guarantees of property rights during privatization. The government preempted strikes by meeting most of their demands, but pilots' and controllers' unions continued to issue demands and strike threats.[17] Trolley, bus, and tram drivers also struck in various cities. In April they threatened an all-federation transport strike, demanding higher wages and the modernization of their vehicles. Elsewhere, dock workers, agro-industrial workers, meteorologists, and undertakers struck. Their demands varied but always included wage increases. In most cases settlements were accompanied by workers' threats to resume the strike if the government failed to deliver on its promises, a testament to low public confidence in that government's effectiveness and integrity.

In late spring and summer a new wave of strikes, over non-payment of wages, spread across Russia. Raging inflation (averaging 20 to 25 percent per month) and large wage increases, combined with the Gaidar government's efforts to combat inflation by limiting new currency emissions, had produced a serious cash shortage. This created disruptions of wage payments in many regions. Protests and warning strikes broke out again among Kuzbass miners, who claimed that the government owed them seven billion rubles in back wages. Nuclear industry workers in Krasnoiarsk, who had not been paid in three months, claimed the right to appeal through foreign news media to the world public for financial aid if their demands were not met promptly. Workers in Novosibirsk, in Kamchatka, and in the Far East struck for back wages, typically claiming two to three months' arrears. Many strikers added demands, including cancellation of enterprise debts, extension of additional credits, and indexing of wages and working capital to inflation.[18] The strikes were settled, but disruptions in wage payments continued in the summer.

Delegations from the Tripartite Commission played a role in settling the spring strikes, but the 'social partnership' began to break down in this period. In June FNPR Chairman Klochkov said that, "The inability of the Russian Tripartite Commission to regulate social and labor conflicts effectively forces us to look for other ways to tackle urgent problems." The FNPR threatened to call a nationwide strike unless the government provided the cash to pay overdue wages in all regions.[19] The union also demanded that the government protect the population from any further decline in its living standard, and that it guarantee the solvency of enterprises. The FNPR would seek conciliation with Yeltsin's government again, but it would also engage in separate negotiations with anti-reformist groups outside the government; would periodically threaten to violate its no-strike pledge; and, in the fall, would publicly demand the dismissal of Gaidar's government. There is some evidence that the FNPR in fact lacked the authority to call its membership out on strike. In any case it never actually tried to do so, and labor unrest tapered off in the fall of 1992.

Wages

The government's pattern of concessions in the face of strikes and strike threats contributed to increasing wage levels, but it was only one of several factors. While parliament legislated increased wages, raises were also often granted independently by factory managements. The cumulative effect was to produce rapid increases in nominal wages. These increases did not, however, improve or even maintain living standards, because consumer prices increased much more dramatically than wages did.

In order to partially compensate for the effects of the January price liberalization and inflation, the Russian government legislated a number of wage increases for specific categories of workers during 1992. In June the minimum monthly wage was increased by 50 percent, to 900 rubles from 600 rubles, and pensions and student grants were raised. In July, the government announced a planned increase of 80 percent in the wages of all those employed in budget-financed organizations. In November the Russian parliament approved a new minimum wage of R2,250 per month. The FNPR remained dissatisfied with these increases, and insisted in the fall wage negotiations that a still-higher minimum, of R3,375 to 4,000, was required to maintain minimal subsistence levels.[20]

The FNPR also pressed continually for full indexation of all incomes, meaning that increases in prices would be fully compensated by increases in various forms of income (including wages, pensions, stipends, and other transfer payments). Claiming that the January price increase had pushed 90 percent of the population below the poverty level, the union included demands for a wage indexation mechanism in all its negotiation packages.[21] The government ruled out full indexation on grounds that it would lead to hyperinflation, but began moving reluctantly toward partial indexation with the March General Agreement. The June resolution on the minimum wage promised to introduce a mechanism for raising the wage quarterly to preclude its lagging more than 30 percent behind future consumer price increases. In July the Labor Ministry confirmed its support for partial quarterly compensation for price increases as well as additional payments to the most vulnerable population groups. In June, Gaidar promised to index 80 percent of unpaid salaries. New wage regulations passed in the fall provided for quarterly upward adjustments of wages to partially offset inflation in 1993.[22]

The cumulative effect of these and other wage increases can be seen in Table 5.1, which shows growth in average monthly nominal (money) industrial wages in the first nine months of 1992. As shown in Table 5.1, the wage rate more than quadrupled over the nine-month period. While industrial wages are somewhat higher than wages for all workers and employees, the overall average showed the same trends, equalling R3,052 per month in April; R3,650 in May; and R4,400 in June.[23] But the trend in real wages was quite a different story. As Table 5.2 indicates, real wages dropped precipitously after the January price liberalization. Wage increases and other measures produced some real improvements over the following months, but double-digit inflation kept recovery modest despite the scale of nominal increases.

Table 5.1 Average Nominal Industrial Wage, 1992 (rubles per month)

Jan	Feb	Mar	Apr	May	June	Sept
1,801	2,567	3,464	3,769	4,296	5,948	8,140

Sources: *PlanEcon Report* 8, no. 37, Oct. 7, 1992, p. 14, for January through June figures; Elena Belyanova and Sergei Aukutsenek, "Russia's Economic Decline," *RL/RFE Research Report* 2, no. 4, Jan. 22, 1993, p. 43, for September figure.

Table 5.2 Real Industrial Wage, 1992 (month to month change in percent)

Jan	Feb	Mar	Apr	May	June
-53.2	14.9	11.5	-4.6	2.5	22.5

Source: *PlanEcon Report* 8, no. 37, Oct. 7, 1992, p. 14.

Overall, these wage statistics meant a dramatic fall in real wages early in 1992 followed by some recovery. By spring, monthly wage increases nearly compensated for (and in some cases exceeded) monthly price increases, but wages never made up for the initial price jump in January. Though the statistics are inconsistent and unreliable, analysts generally agree that overall consumer prices increased at least twice as much as wages in 1992. So most workers experienced a substantial drop in their real incomes and living standards. These effects were, of course, differentiated for various sectors of the labor force and population, with wages ranging, for example, in September 1992, from more than R10,000 in construction to R4,000 to R5,000 in health, education, and culture. Those dependent on state transfer payments (i.e., pensioners) and employees of budget-financed organizations suffered most.[24]

At the same time, aggregate economic output declined at an accelerating rate throughout 1992.[25] Rapid increases in money wages, when taken in the context of declining production, helped feed a wage-price spiral. In short, the government's wage concessions to striking workers and to the unions shored up workers' incomes to some extent, but at the expense of fiscal stabilization. Both inflation and the budget deficit worsened dramatically in the second half of the year, while workers' real incomes remained well below their 1991 levels. Continuing price increases led to demands for further wage increases and indexing of incomes against future inflation. Yeltsin's government could find no escape.

Employment

The Yeltsin government's policies of market transition should have produced substantial unemployment as old, inefficient enterprises collapsed, and others began to shed workers and use labor more efficiently, under market pressures.

Though the numbers varied, both Russian labor experts and informed outside observers such as the International Labour Organization anticipated several millions of unemployed by the end of 1992.[26] In fact, as we can see from Table 5.3, actual numbers of registered unemployed remained quite low, reaching only 518,000, or 0.7 percent of the labor force, by December.

Table 5.3 Registered Unemployed, 1992

Jan	Mar	June	Aug	Oct	Dec
69,600	118,401	202,900	300,000	367,500	518,000

Source: Figures for January through October are from *PlanEcon Report* 8, no. 37, Oct. 7, 1992, p. 14; figure for December is from *Trud*, Dec. 23, 1992, p. 2.

Even if we accept the common assumption that these figures seriously underestimate joblessness, they should still tell us something about its scale and rate of increase. While they do indicate that the system no longer provided virtually full employment as in the past, at the same time they clearly do not reflect what one prominent labor expert has called "the massive shake out of surplus labor that will accompany a real market reform."[27]

State sector employment nevertheless was declining significantly, but in forms that were not clearly reflected in the figures. First, large numbers of employees were being put on part-time work or sent on extended, unpaid leaves by enterprises that lacked the materials or money to keep them on full time. By the fall such practices had been adopted by one in four industrial enterprises and reportedly affected some two million industrial workers (or 9 percent of the industrial work force), with considerably higher numbers in some regions. Second, a substantial shift of labor from the state to the non-state sector (i.e., cooperatives, leased, joint stock, and privatized enterprises, joint ventures) continued. Overall state employment declined by some 6 million in 1992; only about one million of these workers actually were dismissed, and most of the others apparently moved into the private sector within or outside of their enterprises. Finally, unemployment was a problem in certain areas and for certain sections of the population, including women and first-time entrants into the labor force. Some 70 percent of all registered unemployed were women, and they were disproportionately well-educated, urban, and white-collar.[28]

The Russian government did take steps to create a 'safety net' for unemployed workers. A relatively liberal rate of unemployment compensation was available to laid-off workers who qualified, and the state set up programs for job referral and retraining. In May Prime Minister Gaidar signed a resolution on the provision of public work for laid-off workers who could not find new employment, and in June a law was passed mandating that 1 percent of the wage fund be channeled into unemployment insurance, with the legislation to become effective in 1993.[29] But these measures were universally considered inadequate to manage even the modest levels of joblessness that materialized. Job referral services were available in few locales and were technically primitive by the standards of Western market systems. They proved incapable of organizing retraining programs or providing information on jobs across regions (an especially critical function since regionally-concentrated unemployment, for example, in large Siberian cities dominated by defense plants, was anticipated). The 1 percent unemployment tax was considered too little even at the outset. The 'safety net' was, in short, weak and porous, while even a much stronger one could have accomplished little in the face of the mass layoffs that were anticipated.

That those layoffs did not take place partly explains the relative stability of labor relations. However, low unemployment was premised on continuing government subsidies (industrial managers negotiated an additional R200 billion in April); inaction on enterprise debt; a general softening of monetary and credit policy (with gross indebtedness of enterprises to banks and to one another growing rapidly); and the government's failure to enact and implement bankruptcy legislation. (Yeltsin pressed for this legislation, but the Supreme Soviet resisted.) Nearly full employment was maintained, moreover, in a context of a 20 percent drop in output for the year and, by summer, slightly improving real wages. This brought into full relief the paradox that high employment and real wage levels simultaneously contributed to and undercut social stability in the context of looming hyperinflation.

Nor were the system's structural problems with the use of labor addressed; full employment in the existing economy kept much labor occupied inefficiently. There was no mass release of workers to stimulate development of a labor market and rapid movement of labor into the private sector, as World Bank economists urged.[30] Continued subsidies relieved the pressure on the many insolvent and poorly-performing enterprises without providing either sufficient means or incentives for them to modernize and improve efficiency and output quality. The Yeltsin government effectively left in place the fundamental problem of Soviet industry that reform is intended to resolve—the thousands of inefficient, overstaffed, obsolete production facilities that tied up labor, investment funds, energy, and materials.

Labor, Democracy, and Reform

It should be interesting at this point to consider the relationships among labor, democracy, and reform. Gorbachev had clearly believed that democratization would provide popular support for economic reform; it was partly for this reason that he opened up the Soviet system to societal organization and participation in politics. Yeltsin could claim—much more clearly than Gorbachev—an electoral mandate for reform. When he was elected president of Russia in the spring of 1991, Yeltsin was well-established as a proponent of radical economic reform (specifically, the Shatalin or 500-Day Program, which Gorbachev had rejected as too extreme). Yeltsin, however, inherited a system in which labor was already mobilized politically, both in old official and in new unions, and somewhat experienced at pressuring and bargaining with the state. At the same time, the institutional mechanisms for managing and moderating labor's demands were weak; workers regularly ignored restrictions on their right to strike and legislation requiring that their grievances be submitted to arbitration. Moreover, since the state still owned and controlled most of the economy, workers generally held it responsible for their well-being and believed it to be financially capable of meeting their demands. Yeltsin's state lacked both the repressive controls of its authoritarian predecessor and the labor management mechanisms of established democracies. Nor could it appeal to the market and hard budget constraints to insulate itself from political responsibility for wage and employment issues. In sum, the new Russian state's capacity to manage labor's demands was weak.

Yeltsin needed to find a way to impose costly reforms on newly-empowered workers. His approach, understandably enough, was to try to incorporate the unions into a structured bargaining relationship with the state. However, the dominant union, the FNPR, though it mouthed qualified support for reform policies, used its privileged position to try to protect its massive membership from the inevitable effects of reform. In fact, Yeltsin inadvertently shored up the position of the FNPR, which was held in low esteem by the vast majority of its rank-and-file, by making it the state's designated representative and bargaining agent for labor. The FNPR's main resource was its near-monopoly over the distribution of social security benefits to workers. Its dominance in the Tripartite Commission placed the FNPR in an advantaged position to try to secure and distribute additional state benefits, while excluding potential new bargaining agents (or unions) for most workers. The FNPR had little incentive to support reform policies, and strong incentives to protect its rank-and-file against layoffs and falling incomes. Democratization had forced the old unions to become responsive to the interests of their own memberships, and the FNPR's conception of those interests was highly conservative and status quo-oriented. As Yeltsin's government began implementing the reform program, the FNPR became increasingly strident in its opposition.

Even if the Tripartite Commission was divided over reform policies, it might have constituted an institutionally stable mechanism for state-labor-management cooperation. In the event, both the FNPR and the RUIE were soon seeking alliances and means of access to the policy process outside the state, and threatening mass action. Volskii's RUIE allied with other centrist political parties to form the influential Civic Union, which sought successfully to strengthen its influence in the largely anti-reform Supreme Soviet and to articulate a distinct, more moderate reform agenda of "regulated transition to the market."

In summer 1992, the FNPR's leadership made a formal agreement on cooperation with the Civic Union, and in the fall the union joined an alliance of mainly anti-reform elites in a successful campaign to dismiss the Gaidar government. Frustrated with the uncompensated decline in workers' real incomes and critical of the government's privatization program, the FNPR condemned the Tripartite Commission as ineffective and sought other means of political influence.[31] In the end, neither government, managers, nor unions maintained their commitment to the 'social partnership,' so no stable mechanism for state-labor relations was established.

In contrast to the FNPR, the independent unions that occupied labor's other five seats on the Tripartite Commission were generally pro-reform, favoring transition to the market, price liberalization, and some version of privatization. Sotsprof and the NPG especially supported Yeltsin's economic policies and often cooperated with the government in the commission. However, such open support for Yeltsin has led many observers to regard the leaders of these unions as too politicized. This is an especially serious problem for Sotsprof, because in many cases its local affiliates do not support the national leadership's pro-reform stance.[32] In addition, the independents (with the exception of Sotsprof) have relied heavily on strikes and strike threats to press their members' demands, and have rejected legislative regulations on labor conflict and arbitration. Overall, their small memberships (fewer than half a million in total), internal divisions, and militancy contributed to limiting the independents' influence in the political process.

The Yeltsin government also proved very vulnerable to the strikes and strike threats of workers in the democratized polity. It placed priority on settling strikes quickly, usually by means of wage and other concessions, and often with the mediation of the Tripartite Commission. Workers and trade unions regarded the state's resources as highly elastic. More important, the managers and industrialists who would have driven a hard bargain with labor in a market system were generally on labor's side, often giving large wage increases to their workers independently of the state's concessions. Still, when we consider that most of the Russian labor force experienced a significant decline in its real income in 1992, strike movements were actually quite limited and mostly concentrated in a few sectors: social services, transport, and energy. The reasons for militancy in these sectors are specific to their workers' conditions and opportunities. Workers in health and education struck in 1992 over their extremely low wages. As employees in state budget-financed organizations, they had seen their wages stagnate while industrial workers gained large increases from their managers and prices skyrocketed. After the January price liberalization, health and education sector wages stood at a fraction of the cost of living, while modest promised raises remained months in the future. Even after strike concessions, workers in these sectors remained at the bottom of the wage scale. Transport workers are, by contrast, comparatively well-compensated. They strike because their collective threat to paralyze public transport has usually been effective in wresting concessions from municipal and other governments.

Coal miners, the most militant and organized sector of the Russian labor force, have a history of unrest that began with their national strike in the summer of 1989 and continued with protracted political strikes in 1990-1991 that helped bring about the downfall of Gorbachev's government. Miners, in the former Soviet Union as elsewhere, tend to militancy in part because they often live in concentrated settlements and perform hard, dirty, dangerous work; both conditions contribute to their sense of solidarity and shared grievance. It has also been argued that, in the Soviet case, the comparatively high wages of miners drew many educated men to the pits, and that this substantial group of worker-intelligentsia played a major leadership role in the strikes. Finally, miners share with other workers in energy sectors (oil and gas) a belief that their product, unlike much of the Soviet/Russian economy's output, has value on international hard currency markets. Despite wage levels that were many times the national average (many miners were earning R30,000 per month in the spring of 1992, for example), workers in all three sectors have struck repeatedly to demand a share in that value.[33]

There was growing pro-reform sentiment among some groups of workers and labor activists. The official metal workers' union split from the FNPR to support Gaidar's reform policies. Again, the structure of opportunity played a central role: many metal workers believed that the enterprises in their sector, which had been privileged for investment under state socialism, were potentially profitable and could benefit from reform.[34] Coal, oil, and gas workers also supported some aspects of the reform program, including the removal of state price controls from their product (a demand they shared with the IMF) and self-management rights. Still, their strikes brought costly concessions that were detrimental to other reform goals. Some workers took initiative in schemes to modernize their factories and improve efficiency. Most, however, behaved defensively in the face of Gaidar's program and looked to their managers to protect them from declining income and unemployment.

For the most part, then, workers' use of their democratic rights to lobby, bargain, and strike worked to the detriment of economic reform. In the industrial sector, the groups that were organized and mobilized in the system—both labor and management organizations—saw their interests mainly in avoiding austerity policies, plant closings and industrial restructuring, and used their influence to press against these policies. Yeltsin's efforts to co-opt these organizations did not produce any significant re-definition of their interests or moderation of their tactics. The FNPR and Civic Union talked about a more gradual, 'regulated transition' to the market, but spent most of their energies building alliances against reform.

Largely as a consequence of these pressures, Yeltsin's labor policy has been confined mainly to temporary, piecemeal responses to immediate problems. His policies have facilitated substantial development of the private sector and movement of labor into more entrepreneurial (and, one hopes, more efficient and profitable) endeavors, and this should surely be counted as progress toward the goals he set. However, his government has made little progress in creating the infrastructure for a functioning national labor market, or even for significant interregional labor mobility. It failed to address the fundamental structural problems of industry, or to halt a drastic decline in output. Nor did it manage to enforce wage and income constrains, or to control inflation.

Most important, the combination of policies that Yeltsin's government used to avoid labor unrest could not be sustained for long. These policies provided nearly full employment in the context of declining output and rapidly-rising nominal wages. The result would be (indeed, has been) an uncontrollable wage-price spiral. The private sector has compensated for the output shortage to some extent, but only at the very high prices that the still semi-monopolistic market will bear. The Yeltsin-Gaidar government sought to control this spiral by limiting cash emissions early in 1992, but, as we have seen, a combination of strikes, and union and parliamentary opposition defeated that effort. With the leadership unable to either reduce employment or sufficiently constrain wages, the result could only be continued inflation, leading to renewed demands for wage increases and general discontent and hardship.

In sum, then, the Yeltsin government in 1992 did achieve a temporary stabilization of labor relations, preventing further descent into the socio-economic and political chaos of 1991. But it was able to do so only at considerable expense to its reform agenda and its control over socio-economic policy-making. Further, it failed to establish either policies or institutional mechanisms for long-term stabilization. The tripartite mechanism facilitated the efforts of both organized labor and organized management to oppose Gaidar's reform program. At the same time, neither Yeltsin's government, the FNPR, nor the RUIE was fully committed to that process, or fully agreeable to its constraints. Limited progress was made in creating a 'safety net' that could ease transition to the market; most of the government's efforts and resources were needed to respond to current demands. Finally, the set of policy concessions that Yeltsin's government made to maintain labor peace were not viable in the long term, with or without transition to the market.

Labor Relations and Russia's Future

Is the future of labor relations, then, tending toward integration or disintegration? In addressing this question, we will first consider the situation with Russia's labor unions, then the relationship between labor and the state.

The FNPR is very likely losing its near-monopoly over representation of

Russian workers. During the political confrontation in the fall of 1993, the leadership of the FNPR condemned Yeltsin's actions as an illegal usurpation of power, and called on its members to respond with strikes and protests.[35] However, the actual course of events only revealed the FNPR's weakness: its calls to action produced no apparent public response, and some branch unions openly opposed the leadership. Meanwhile, most independent unions either supported Yeltsin or took a neutral position on the conflict between president and legislature.[36]

Under *de facto* presidential rule, Yeltsin's government passed a series of measures that will probably have great significance for the trade union's future. On September 24, First Vice Premier Shumeiko signed a directive that prohibited financial organs from collecting trade union dues, in effect undercutting the FNPR's financial base. Next, Russian Federation pension funds were placed under the control of the government and Finance Ministry. In the most significant move, Yeltsin signed a decree on September 28 transferring management of the social security fund to the government, thereby depriving unions (mainly the FNPR) of their most significant function.[37] Moreover, Yeltsin's government has long proposed nationalizing the federation's property and Sotsprof has asserted rights to a portion of it, proposing that administrative offices and other facilities be divided among all existing unions.[38] Yet regardless of the property issue, the government's decrees will likely lead to the collapse of the FNPR in most regions and sectors.

For the future, the key questions are whether the labor movement will be a powerful expression of mobilized social interests; and whether it will be consolidated in the form of stable institutions and negotiating mechanisms, or disintegrate into chaotic, weakly organized local protests. In both cases, one can offer only informed speculation.

To a great extent, the future of the Russian labor movement is inseparable from the larger problems of attaining social and political equilibrium. The government's ability to find effective policies to stabilize the economy and to overcome the crisis of authority will strongly affect the level of worker unrest. This, in turn, will be determined partly by the nature of political forces at the center.

Because the RUIE, the Civic Union, and others opposed to Gaidar's reforms spent most of 1992 trying to block the government's policies, it is unclear what kind of positive program they might attempt, if they indeed gained greater influence. Virtually no one wants a return to central planning, least of all industrial managers who have gained much autonomy and control over their enterprises in the reform process. At the same time, Volskii and the industrialists favor a large, ongoing state role in the economy. They could conceivably make the state a somewhat effective instrument of modernization in the defense and heavy industrial sectors, while allowing privatization to continue in other sectors. The state could target subsidies and bank credits to fund conversion programs, and ease out hopelessly obsolete factories. Workers would still suffer unemployment, but the impact would be moderate and probably manageable. Such conversion programs are rife with technical, resource, and management problems, and have not been very successful in the past; but the situation now is more desperate, and the managers arguably may gain the power to design and carry out a comprehensive policy. If they fail in this and the economic decline continues at its present rate, labor discontent is likely to escalate as living standards fall. And if economic shock therapy is seriously implemented, a significant level of labor discontent seems unavoidable.

Yet the relative level of labor discontent raises another question, that of the strength of the labor movement and its institutions. There are, of course, serious divisions within the labor movement over the economic reform program. Unions in energy and advanced manufacturing branches with export potential support reform because they expect to benefit from independence and privatization. Oil and gas workers (as noted above) favor Yeltsin's policies, and behaved independently without ever formally leaving the FNPR. The two million-strong Trade Union of the Mining and Metallurgical Industry, the first branch union to split from the FNPR, defected mainly to support reform. In short, the independents have tended to represent the more modern, competitive branches, and they have generally supported Yeltsin's policies.[39]

At the same time, as we have seen, strong independent unions have become established in only a few sectors. While grass roots organizing initiatives have appeared throughout the labor force, new unions face a daunting range of obstacles: emergent leaders have little organizing experience and few resources; levels of activism among workers are generally low; workers fear loss of benefits and other costs if they leave the FNPR. As a consequence, most remain small locals or poorly consolidated confederations, though a wave of activism could transform many into dynamic new unions which would replace the old in many sectors. The independents have also sought to change the "rules of the game" of wage and contract negotiations at the enterprise level (where the FNPR was firmly entrenched), lobbying for legislation which would guarantee the right of any trade union to negotiate a separate collective agreement with management.[40] It remains unclear, then, whether present trends in the labor movement will lead to its diversification and development, or weakening and disintegration.

There is another, larger question: whether Russia's central government will be able to govern effectively at all. As Khrushchev discusses in Chapter 6, centrifugal forces are rife throughout Russia, with non-Russian ethnic groups pressing for autonomy, regional governments controlling their own economic and financial policies, and resource-rich regions claiming ownership of their raw material deposits. If the central government continues to waste time and energy in internal bickering, its capacity to make and implement policy will erode further, while regionalization of power and policy-making will intensify.

The potential consequences of such a development for labor and labor policy are complex. First, the position of workers could become quite disparate in different regions. Workers in energy sectors (especially oil and natural gas) could find themselves in quite privileged positions, since their regional governments would be able to earn considerable hard currency as they deal and bargain on international markets. Other regional governments, particularly in developed urban areas, might make steady progress toward privatization and large concessions to attract foreign investment. Remote provincial cities built around large, obsolete factories that depend heavily on the central government for subsidies would suffer by comparison, and endure all the negative effects of radical reform with no Moscow-sponsored safety net. In short, some workers would gain while others would lose; disparities would likely widen; and patterns of discontent would become more diverse. Labor as a political force would become fragmented and weakened. Unions would likely become less capable of defending workers' interests in full employment and income maintenance, and, by the same token, less capable of blocking market reforms.

Yet even if extreme fragmentation is avoided, the future of the Russian labor movement is highly uncertain. Perhaps now independent unions, freed from the need to compete with the massive hold-over union, will flourish and articulate a more differentiated and sophisticated conception of their members' interests (though the state's control over pension and social security funds also deprives them of potential constituency-building resources and functions).[41] Or perhaps, instead, most workers will be left without national organizations to articulate and defend their interests, without institutional means to fight for limits on the costs they will bear in the name of economic liberalization.

Notes

* The research for this chapter was funded in part by a grant from the National Council for Soviet and East European Research, Contract No. 807-24.

1. Elizabeth Teague, "Russian Government Seeks 'Social Partnership'," *Radio Free Europe/Radio Liberty* (hereafter, *RFE/RL) Research Report* 1, no. 25, June 19, 1992, pp. 16-23; *Trud,* Jan. 15, 1992, p.1.

2. On the Russian Union of Industrialists and Entrepreneurs, see *Rabochaia tribuna,* Feb. 11, 1992, pp. 1, 2; *Ekonomika i zhizn,* no. 13, March 1992, p. 10.

3. Teague, "Russian Government." See also Peter Rutland, *Business Elites and Russian Economic Policy* (London: Royal Institute of International Affairs, Post-Soviet Business Forum, 1992), pp. 43; 63-64.

4. At some points the FNPR claimed as many as 65 million members; see *Izvestiia,* Apr. 4, 1992, p. 2; lower figures of 55 million to 60 million were also cited

at various points; for total employed labor force see *PlanEcon Report* 8, no. 37, Oct. 7, 1992, p. 14; for background on the FNPR and its predecessors, see Walter D. Connor, *The Accidental Proletariat: Workers, Politics, and Crisis in Gorbachev's Russia* (Princeton: Princeton University Press, 1991), pp. 290-302.

5. See Elizabeth Teague, "Trade Unions in Post-Communist Society: The USSR Learns from Eastern European Experience," *RFE/RL Research Reports* 3, no. 41, Oct. 11, 1991, pp. 21-22; Valentin Rupets, "Trade union movement in post-totalitarian Russia," *New Labor Movement,* no. 3-4, 1992, pp. 39-44. On strike treats by pilots and air traffic controllers, see Foreign Broadcast Information Service: Soviet Union (hereafter, FBIS: SU), May 14, 1991, p. 28, citing Radio Rossii, May 13, 1991; May 16, 1991, p. 38, citing TASS, May 16, 1991; May 20, 1991, pp. 26-27, citing *Komsomolskaia pravda,* May 17, 1991, p.1.

6. Vladimir Pribylovskii, *Dictionary of Political Parties and Organizations in Russia,* edited by Dauphine Sloan and Sarah Helmstadter (Washington: Center for Strategic and International Studies and Moscow: Postfactum, 1992), pp. 97-98.

7. For the terms of the General Agreement see *Izvestiia,* March 27, 1992, p. 1.

8. On the January price liberalization, see Keith Bush, "Russia: Gaidar's Guidelines," *REF/RL Research Report* 1, no. 15, Apr. 10, 1992, pp. 22-25; for its impact on real wages, see *PlanEcon Report* 8, no. 37, Oct. 7, 1992, p. 14.

9. Interviews with Russian Federation Supreme Soviet Deputies Vladimir I. Makhanov, member of the Supreme Soviet Commission on Social Policy, May 25, 1993; and Alexander K. Utkin, member of the Commission on Social Policy and chairman of the Sub-Commission on the Population Level and Living Indexation, May 26, 1993, Moscow.

10. On the 1991 strikes see Connor, *The Accidental Proletariat,* pp. 304-312; Linda J. Cook, Chap. 7 in *The Soviet Social Contract and Why It Failed: Welfare Policy and Workers' Politics from Brezhnev to Yeltsin* (Cambridge: Harvard University Press, forthcoming 1993); on distribution of strikes by sector in 1992, see *Trud,* April 25, 1992, p.2.

11. Teague, "Russian Government."

12. The government reportedly raised miners' wages to some R30,000 per month, twelve times the national average; *Rabochaia tribuna,* Feb. 25, 1992, pp. 1, 2.

13. See *Rossiiskaia gazeta,* June 3, 1992, p. 1. It might be added that the oil and gas workers shared with the radical reformers and the IMF a desire to deregulate Russian energy prices, a measure that would force down domestic consumption and increase marketing abroad.

14. See *Pravda,* Jan. 25, 1992, p. 2; "Economic and Business Notes," *RFE/RL Research Report* 1, no. 6, Feb. 7, 1992, p. 45; no. 7, Feb. 14, 1992, p. 59.

15. See *Nezavisimaia gazeta,* May 6, 1992, p. 2; "Economic and Business Notes,"*RL/RFE Research Report* 1, no. 19, May 8, 1992, p. 46; vol. 1, no. 21, May 22, 1992, pp. 37-38; vol. 1, no. 22, May 29, 1992, p. 53.

16. See *Izvestiia,* May 16, 1992, p. 2.

17. See "Economic and Business Notes," *RF/RLE Research Report* 1, no. 12, March 12, 1992, p. 45; FBIS:SU, Feb. 20, 1992, p. 59, citing TASS, Feb. 20, 1992; Feb. 21, 1992, p. 55, citing Radio Rossii, Feb. 21, 1992; Feb. 27, 1992, p. 50, citing Interfax, Feb. 26, 1992.

18. For reports on strikes over non-payment of wages see FBIS:SU, May 14,

1992, p. 43, citing ITAR-Tass, May 8, 1992; FBIS:SU, May 18, 1992, pp. 38-39, citing MosTel, May 13, 1992; FBIS:SU, June 10, 1992, p. 51, citing ITAR-Tass, June 9, 1992; FBIS:SU, June 16, 1992, p. 4, citing MosTel, June 11, 1992; "The Year 1992: 'Shake-up' for Russia's Reform," *New Labor Movement,* no. 3-4, 1992, pp. 27-38.

19. Quote is from *Rossiiskaia gazeta,* June 16, 1992, p. 1.

20. See *Rossiiskaia gazeta,* May 1, 1992, p, 2; *Izvestiia,* May 16, 1992, p. 2; "Economic and Business Notes," *RFE/RL Research Report* 1, no. 46, Nov. 20, 1992, p. 45; vol. 1, no. 47, Nov. 27, 1992, p. 48. The new minimum wage, effective Jan. 1, 1993, applied to state employees—approximately 70 percent of Russia's labor force.

21. See, for example, *Izvestiia,* Jan. 11, 1992, p. 2.

22. See *Rossiiskaia gazeta,* May 1, 1992, p. 2; *Izvestiia,* June 2, 1992, p. 2; FBIS:SU, July 30, 1992, p. 23, citing ITAR-TASS, July 29, 1992.

23. For average monthly wage figures see *Izvestiia,* June 27, 1992, p. 2.

24. For *Goskomstat* figures on wages and incomes see Sheila Marnie, "Economic Reform and Poverty in Russia," *RFE/RL Research Report* 2, no. 6, Feb. 5, 1993, p. 33; for *Goskomstat* statistics on wages in selected sectors, see Elena Belianova and Sergei Aukutsenek, "Russia's Economic Decline: State Manufacturers Suffer Less," *RFE/RL Research Report* 2, no. 4, Jan. 22, 1993, p. 43.

25. See *PlanEcon Report* 8, no. 37, Oct. 7, 1992, pp. 1, 2.

26. See, for example, the interview with the chairman of the Russian Ministry of Labor's Committee for Employment, who projected 3.5 million to 4 million unemployed by the end of 1992; FBIS:SU, May 5, 1992, p. 31, citing MosTel, Apr. 29, 1992; for ILO projections of 10 million to 11 million unemployed by year's end, see Philip Hanson, "The Russian Economy in Spring, 1992," *RFE/RL Research Report* 1, no. 21, May 22, 1992, pp. 27-29.

27. Quote is from Elizabeth Teague, "Tackling the Problem of Unemployment," *Report on the USSR* 3, no. 45, Nov. 8, 1991, p. 7.

28. See Sheila Marnie, "How Prepared is Russia for Mass Unemployment," *RFE/RL Research Report* 1, no. 48, Dec. 4, 1992, pp. 44-50; *Komsomolskaia pravda,* June 9, 1992, p. 2, reported this figure for women; Keith Bush, "Conversion and Unemployment in Russia," *RFE/RL Research Report* 2, no. 2, Jan. 8, 1993, p. 31.

29. *Izvestiia,* June 22, 1992, p. 3; FBIS:SU, May 19, 1992, p. 20, citing Interfax, May 18.

30. See, for example, *Russian Economic Reform: Crossing the Threshold of Structural Change* (Washington, D.C.: World Bank, 1992), pp. 141-159.

31. Elizabeth Teague, "Russia's Industrial Lobby Takes the Offensive," *RFE/RL Research Report* 1, no. 32, Aug. 14, 1992, pp. 1, 2. *Trud,* Sept. 20, 1991, p. 1; *Rabochaia tribuna,* March 7, 1992, p. 2; April 17, 1992, p. 1.

32. See, for example, *Nezavisimaia gazeta,* Feb. 29, 1992, p.2.

33. On causes of the miners' militancy see Peter Rutland, "Labor Unrest and Movements in 1989 and 1990," *Soviet Economy* 6, no. 3, 1990, pp. 345-384; Linda J. Cook, "Lessons of the Soviet Coal Miners' Strike of Summer, 1989," *Harriman Institute Forum* 4, no. 3, March, 1991, pp. 1-10.

34. Interview with Boris G. Misnik, president, Trade Union for Mining and Metallurgical Industry of the Russian Federation, June 1, 1993, Moscow.

35. For the text of the statement by the FNPR's Executive Committee, issued on

September 22, see FBIS:SU (Supplement), Sept. 24, 1993, pp. 38-39, citing *Rossiiskaia gazeta,* Sept. 23, 1993, p.4.

36. See FBIS:SU (Supplement), Sept, 24, 1993, p. 39, citing *Rossiiskie vesti,* Sept. 22, 1993, p. 1; FBIS:SU (Supplement), Sept. 27, 1993, pp. 50-51, citing *Nezavisimaia gazeta,* Sept. 25, 1993, p. 2; FBIS:SU (Supplement), Sept. 28, 1993, p. 31; citing Radio Rossiia, Sept. 27, 1993; FBIS:SU (Supplement), Sept. 30, 1993, p. 37, citing *Kommersant-Daily,* Sept. 29, 1993, p. 4; at this point Klochkov acknowledged, with reference to the all-Russia strike, that "workers on the ground were unprepared for this action."

37. On these measures, see FBIS:SU, Sept. 28, 1993, p. 24, citing *Kommersant-Daily,* Sept. 24, 1993, p.3; FBIS:SU, Sept. 28, 1993, p. 18-19, citing *Izvestiia,* Sept. 25, 1993, p. 2; FBIS:SU, Sept. 29, 1993, p. 16, citing ITAR-TASS, Sept. 28, 1993; the decree specified that the government would manage social insurance "with the participation of...trade unions."

38. *Nezavisimaia gazeta,* Feb. 29, 1992, p.2.

39. This division between old and new unions is suggested in Leonid Gordon and Eduard V. Klopov, "The Workers' Movement in Postsocialist Perspective," *Labor and Democracy in the Transition to a Market System* (Armonk: M.E. Sharpe, 1992), p. 35.

40. *Trud,* Feb. 25, 1992, pp. 1, 2.

41. Unions, including some that were not affiliated with the FNPR, protested the decree on the social insurance fund as strengthening the state's monopoly, violating the labor code, and "groundlessly imposing legal restrictions on the right of Russian trade unions to manage the...insurance fund." See FBIS:SU (Supplement), Sept. 30, 1993, p. 37. citing ITAR-TASS, Sept. 30, 1993.

6

The Political Economy of
Russia's Regional Fragmentation

Sergei Khrushchev

To assess the relative prospects of Russia's regional disintegration and the country's preservation, it is essential to understand the factors that once held the country together. These included economic connections; dictatorship of the Communist Party of the Soviet Union; ideological and moral factors; defense against the common enemy; and control by the KGB. It was arguably the centralized economy, more than any other factor, that kept the republics and regions together.

In the post-Soviet period, however, these factors dissipated. The continuing collapse of production; the disruption of economic relations; the refusal of the central authorities to maintain economic governance; the physical breakup of the Soviet Union—all these factors have forced regional leaders to ask themselves what kind of center they need, or whether they need any center at all.

Regionalism as a Means of Survival

The same questions regarding the continued existence of the center have arisen for the authorities in Moscow. Caught in an extreme budget deficit, in 1992 the Gaidar government essentially proposed that enterprises struggle for survival and create new economic relations without any help from the center. Deprived of the old economic linkages, managers were forced to choose between two means for adapting to the new conditions. The first, regional isolationism, has grown immeasurably since the breakup of the Soviet Union. Customs posts sprang up at the frontiers of the former republics, and interstate commerce required special licenses as well as payment of customs duties.

On the other hand, managers whose products were virtually indispensable and who depended on cooperation with outside suppliers often tried to preserve the old structures or to create new structures similar to the old ones. For example, Urals metallurgists had an interest in preserving ties with their Kazakh partners. Indeed, connections between economic managers from different republics often are more fruitful than connections at the intergovernmental level. In spite of their political squabbling, cooperation between Russian and Lithuanian enterprises in electronics and in the manufacture of computers, TV sets, and electrical meters has continued with practically no interruption. But traditional ties with former Soviet republics generally proved very difficult to maintain. For example, difficulties arose with Ukraine because of regular interference by the Russian government in mutual payments between Russian and Ukrainian enterprises. Even as it proclaimed market freedoms, the Russian government delayed payments, or imposed, and then canceled, new customs duties. Although the aim was to defend Russian national interests, measures like these resulted in further destabilization. While the new economic union within the CIS may rectify this situation in the future, there has already been a strong trend toward local self-sufficiency within the Russian Federation.

The cascading collapse of old, often irreplaceable relations seriously undermined production by Russian enterprises. In 1992 the total volume of output in Russia dropped 18.8 percent. The national income dropped by 20 percent, capital investments by 45 percent; transport of goods by 22 percent; and turnover of retail goods by 39 percent. Compared to December 1991, prices of consumer goods and services increased 26 times.[1]

Trade in goods and services among regions was disrupted as the regional authorities began introducing *vizitki* and *kupony* (special visiting cards and rationing coupons), and placed restrictions on the export of consumer goods. For example, the authorities in Tatarstan and in the Krasnodar and Stavropol provinces introduced quotas for the export of agricultural products. In Voronezh, the head of the local administration signed a decree abolishing the export of nineteen types of industrial products and sixteen types of food products.[2]

On the other hand, regionalization also has helped to consolidate areas that already were closely connected economically and geographically. An important example is the process underway in Siberia. In January 1993 the first plenary meeting of the Siberian Council for Foreign Economic Activities, which represented the most active of the nineteen provinces participating in the "Siberian Agreement," gathered in Novosibirsk.[3] In February members' demands were repeated during a new meeting in Omsk, in the presence of Russian Prime Minister Viktor Chernomyrdin. These demands included assertions of full political and economic autonomy.[4] During the constitutional crisis of September 1993, the "Siberian Agreement" issued an ultimatum to Yeltsin: if he did not agree to simultaneous elections of president and parliament under the control of a body consisting of representatives of the regions, they threatened to block movement along the Trans-Siberian Railroad.[5]

The decaying economy often forced regional leaders to take risks. They ignored the central authorities, whom they often perceived as a hindrance to their efforts, and they also paid little attention to the needs of their neighbors. In some areas, regional authorities began to print their own "currency," valid for payments within the borders of a certain territory or even within certain enterprises.[6]

Another reason for the growth of separatism was the center's refusal to perform its governing and coordinating functions. In deciding to move abruptly to a self-regulating, free market economy, the Gaidar government virtually abdicated responsibility for managing the transition period and for cushioning the blow. Thus, during the winter of 1992-1993 there was a catastrophic lack of fuel in many regions of Russia, and power stations were operating at the limit of their capacities. But local authorities were forced to look for fuel themselves, or to take other emergency measures without any hope for help from the center. Local authorities resorted to extreme measures, cutting off power supplies to enterprises, turning off all public lighting, reducing heat to houses, and confiscating oil intended for shipment to Magadan and Kamchatka.[7] Similarly, during the same period the transport of essential cargoes to many northern regions was desperately behind schedule because of the encroaching winter, but the center did not provide relief or send in ice-breaking ships.[8] Instead, the government insisted that necessary resources be purchased by local authorities, without help from the center.[9]

Nor has the situation changed fundamentally under Chernomyrdin. As a result of the government's refusal to advance subsidized credits, shipment of supplies, especially of fuel, has been cut by over half. In September 1993, when regular navigation in the north had ended for the season, the director of the Nizhnekamsk Oil Refinery warned that he had not managed to send the northerners even the oil for which they had paid, since they did not have money to pay for the transportation.[10]

Considerable friction has arisen over the issue of taxation. In reaction to the central government's absenteeism, in July 1992 the presidents of Sakha, Tatarstan, and Bashkortostan declared that in place of the two-channel taxation system they would implement a one-channel system in which each region would determine the amount of money it paid for the services of the center. In the view of local authorities, Moscow always extracted the lion's share of profits for the exploration of natural resources and gave back almost nothing.[11] This situation has now been sharply altered. Increasingly, Moscow is forced to offer various concessions to localities in order to obtain the taxes required by federal law. For example, in August 1992 the center proposed to return to the

Tatar authorities all duties for 2.7 billion tons of exported oil in exchange for 2 billion rubles of taxes that were being held up by the authorities in Tatarstan. A spontaneous redistribution of tax payments between the local and central budgets also took place in other regions. In April 1992 only 49 percent of taxes on profits were paid to the federal budget, while 51 percent were paid to the local budgets.[12] As of April 1993, according to Minister of Finance Boris Fedorov, the center was receiving only about 40 percent of its designated tax revenues.[13] By September 1993, thirty-six regions, including many ethnically Russian ones, had partly or completely stopped making payments into the central budget.[14] Obviously Moscow no longer controls the local situation with regard to collecting taxes. Indeed, after studying the 1993 Russian budget, the Supreme Economic Council of the Russian parliament concluded that the process of "individualization of tax payments" was "accelerating the disintegration of Russia."[15]

Other tensions have arisen between central and regional authorities over the issue of privatization. One source of friction has been the use of official vouchers. The authorities of Chechnia have declared the official Russian vouchers (privatization checks) invalid within their territory, and Tatarstan has decided to issue its own vouchers, good only for Tatarstan's citizens. The Saratov province unilaterally declared a rate of exchange for vouchers of $1 for 20 "voucher rubles," and Bashkortostan supported the Saratov authorities.[16]

The key dispute, however, is over who is the original owner of enterprises, especially the mining and drilling enterprises. The problem is being resolved through the transformation of federal property into republican, provincial, or municipal property through agreements with the center, followed by the issue of stocks.[17] For example, Tatarstan announced that stock in the giant KAMAZ truck factory (which, according to law, was the property of the central government) was to become the property of the republic. Bashkortostan suspended Yeltsin's decrees on privatization of the local fuel industry and on assignment of enterprises to newly created central agencies.[18]

The center has practically no levers of control in the regions, while the regions are discovering new ways of pressuring the central structures. For example, when the Ivanovo textile factories faced a cotton shortage in the summer of 1992, the local authorities demanded either oil and wood to use as barter, or payment in accordance with international cotton prices, and the Gaidar regime was forced to accede.[19] In this way the two-channel system of interdependence between the center and the periphery is being replaced by one-sided dependence of the center. The substitution of Viktor Chernomyrdin for Gaidar changed practically nothing in this regard. Governmental reform programs may appear acceptable on paper, but it is unclear who is prepared to carry them out.[20] As a result the crisis has become more severe, and the regions are shedding their old assumptions of central responsibility.

Regional Disintegration

History repeats itself in many ways. The decay of the Russian economy after the Russian Revolution, caused by nationalization and aggravated by the civil war, resulted in the emergence of new independent states that formerly were part of the Russian empire, such as Poland, Finland, the Baltic republics, the Ukraine, and the Caucasian republics. Siberia, the northern Caucasus region, and the Volga region also became independent, while the Far Eastern Republic existed as an independent state until 1921 and even established diplomatic relations with Russia. Interestingly, it is in these same regions that separatist tendencies have become especially powerful since the demise of the USSR.

The Northern Caucasus

The Northern Caucasian nationalities are not numerous enough to oppose Russia, and are divided by internal rivalries.[21] However, these rivalries are a powder keg that could set off a nationwide explosion in Russia. Given the extent to which Russian society is already strained by political disorder, almost any new collision could cause civil war.

Regional disintegration in the south of Russia is different from disintegration in the other territories of the former empire. The memories of earlier Caucasian wars are still alive here, and a sense of imperialism fosters a comparatively conservative position on the part of the local Russian population, especially the Cossacks. More than the other Russian-speaking regions, Cossack regions gravitate toward Moscow, in opposition to the local, formerly colonized peoples, including more than 100 Muslim nationalities. After the emergence of the USSR, most of these nationalities remained on Russian territory; Abkhazia and part of Ossetia came under the jurisdiction of Georgia; and the Lezgin lands were split by the new border between Russia and Azerbaijan. Yet despite these formal demarcations, the peoples of this region continued to consider themselves a single multinational northern Caucasian group. It is true that occasionally bitter conflicts have arisen between them in the past. Now, however, faced with a threat from outside—either from Christian Russia and Georgia, or from Muslim Iran—they have banded together.[22]

One additional destabilizing factor in nationality relations is a kaleidoscopic change of roles between the "oppressors" and "oppressed." This problem is not specifically a Caucasian one, but in the Caucasus it has taken on the most developed form. The situation in Georgia is the clearest example of how dominant nationalities can precipitate disintegration. From the beginning, the calls by Georgia for independence from Russian oppression were accompanied by a refusal to concede autonomy, even cultural autonomy, for those northern Caucasian nationalities living in Georgia, including Abkhazians, Ossetians,

and Adzharians. When Georgia declared its independence it began a virtual
colonial war against the local population. Yet the picture is complicated by
the fact that North Ossetia has been waging its own campaign against the
Ingush, who had previously returned to the county adjoining the city of
Vladikavkaz, where they had lived before being deported by Stalin. In this
conflict, Moscow has tried to act from a position of strength, playing the
Ossetians and Ingush against each other, while deploying force to insulate the
conflict and prevent further escalation.[23] Yet should the conflict widen, no
amount of troops would keep the situation under control.[24]

The Volga Region

The Volga-Urals region is one of the new centers emerging in Russia. It
appears likely that it will include a union of Tatarstan, Bashkortostan,
Chuvashia, and the Marii-El Republic. The prospects for successful consolidation of the Volga lands around Kazan and Samara are strengthened by nearly
one thousand years of different ethnic groups (including Russians) living side
by side, which has produced a mutually interpenetrating culture. Yet it is also
quite possible that two separate regions, those of the Volga and the Urals, may
emerge here instead. The amorphous "Greater Volga" agreement might be
transformed into a new union, with Nizhnii Novgorod or Ulianovsk as its
capital. A "South Urals Republic," with its capital in Yeltsin's home town of
Ekaterinburg (formerly Sverdlovsk), has already been proclaimed. It may play
an important role as a link between the "European" Russians and the "Asian"
Siberians.[25]

Tatarstan is a key trouble spot, not only for this region but for the Russian
Federation in general. Although the Tatars make up only 4 percent of the total
population of the Russian Federation, they are the second most numerous nationality in Russia (after the Russians themselves), and are concentrated in the
Volga area and adjoining regions to the east of St. Petersburg and Moscow and
to the west of the Ural Mountains. In addition to the issues of taxation, local
vouchers, quotas, and "nationalization" of capital stocks referred to above, the
region also has demanded control over its natural resources. Tatarstan has rejected government requests to maintain oil production at previous levels, citing its own "national interests."[26]

Beyond its defiance of central decrees, Tatarstan has been able to assert its
own autonomy in a highly visible and relatively successful manner. With a
relatively well developed industry and agriculture, Kazan is becoming a new
center of gravity for the Volga region, and the leaders of the nationalist movements of Bashkortostan, Marii-El, Tatarstan, and Chuvashia have signed a
declaration for the creation of a Volga-Urals Confederation.[27] In this way the
greater Volga region, especially Tatarstan, could become a focal point for the
disintegration of Russia.

The precise nature of the relationship between Tatarstan and the Russian Federation remains unclear. In November 1992 the Supreme Soviet of Tatarstan approved a new republic constitution, which, despite pressure from Moscow, amounted to a *de facto* declaration of independence, and in many respects contradicted both the Russian Constitution and the Federal Treaty.[28] In January 1993, Yeltsin met with Tatar President Shaimiev to initial an intergovernmental treaty, according to which Tatarstan agreed to "associate membership" in the Russian Federation. Taxation, privatization, foreign trade, foreign affairs, and military conscription would become the prerogative of Tatarstan.[29] In return for such concessions, the region's leadership generally expressed qualified support for Yeltsin in his confrontation with the former Russian parliament.[30]

Marii-El, Udmurtia, and Chuvashia so far have taken less strident positions than Tatarstan (or Bashkortostan, for that matter). For example, Eduard Kubarev, the chairman of the Supreme Soviet of Chuvashia, declared publicly that he was satisfied with the "calm" relations with the center. To a large extent this is due to the fact that the Chuvashian economy depends on numerous linkages to the Russian economy.[31]

The Siberian-Transbaikal Region

This region includes Tuva, Buriatia, Khakassia, as well as the Ust-Ordyn, Buriat, and Agin-Buriat national districts. In this area, as elsewhere, the combination of political and economic crisis may lead to full separatism. It appears, however, that only Tuva is capable of attaining true autonomy, and in any case Tuva's separatism does not constitute a threat to Russia, or even a threat to regional stability.[32] Tuva was always a fairly separate region, and with no industry it has no influence on the development of neighboring regions. The possible secession of Tuva would not be noticed by most Russians, as was the case with annexation in 1944.

The Northern Belt

The Northern Belt is a chain of former and current autonomous regions, from the Komi and Nentsi autonomous provinces in the West, to the Chukotka Autonomous Province and Koriak Autonomous Republic in the east. While developments in this area may exacerbate instability throughout Russia, they are not a primary cause of instability. There does appear to be considerable popular involvement in Siberian and Far Eastern separatist movements, which in turn has been aggravated by the contradictory economic policy of the center. Furthermore, Yeltsin's announcement of a half-hearted transfer of federal property to the local level, which denied private ownership, only intensified separatist tendencies.[33]

It is impossible to consider the future destiny of the non-Russian autonomous provinces of Siberia, Transbaikal, and the Russian Northern Belt apart from that of the other regions. Most of the non-Russian provinces are parts of a single whole; and in contrast to republics in the European part of Russia, the titular nationalities in these areas are minorities of their populations. This is especially true of the Far North, where non-Russian provinces were created not for economic reasons but to demonstrate the triumph of Stalin's nationality policy. The nomadic native populations encounter twentieth-century realities only when gas and oil pipelines cross the migration routes of the deer herds they follow. Regions where oil, gas, nickel, copper and other minerals have been found are governed by local minions, whose aim is to extract the natural resources and return to Russia. They are unconcerned with the fate of the native populations or the existence of ecological problems; they tend to use the central authorities to acquire extra profits. In return, the center uses them much like a "Trojan horse" in an effort to preserve its power in the regions. The Northern Lands, or rather their leaders, vacillate between the other regions and the center, depending on who seems to have the upper hand and can promise them short-term benefits.

The Federal Treaty and the New Russian Constitution

The fate of power in Russia is being decided not on the surface, in Moscow, or within the central political institutions. As Grigorii Iavlinskii has said, "When the governor of the Nizhnii Novgorod region, Boris Nemtsov, signs the Federal Treaty with [Speaker of the former Russian parliament] Ruslan Khasbulatov, I ask myself: who represents Russia? I cannot understand, which of the two really is joining the Federation?"[34]

The current situation is highly unstable. How long it lasts depends on the policy of the center, and on the extent to which it is perceived to be able to serve the regions. The growing dependence of the center on the periphery revealed itself in the Federal Treaty signed in the spring of 1992. Despite his best efforts, Yeltsin was unable to persuade the representatives of the autonomous republics to delegate greater powers to him. Moreover, the insurgent Republic of Chechnia proclaimed that after its declaration of independence, the Federal Treaty was not its concern. In contrast, Tatarstan has chosen the "Ukrainian variant." It has refused to sign the treaty, but has left the door open for negotiations to decide what share of power Kazan would delegate to Moscow, and what share of power Moscow would cede to Kazan. The Tatarstan leadership has justified its demands on the basis of its referendum on independence. Likewise, the Bashkortostan and Sakha republics reserved for themselves a special economic status that would allow them to control their natural and productive resources. Exactly how power between them and the center will be divided is the subject of a special agreement intended to be en-shrined by treaty, but this signing has been postponed indefinitely. Yet in es-sence, the positions of Bashkortostan and Sakha do not differ much from that of Tatarstan.

The native Russian provinces that signed the treaty also have received im-portant concessions. Indeed, this has been a source of political conflicts, as native Russian provinces have claimed broader rights, similar to those granted to the autonomous republics. As the result of a compromise, they, too, were granted permission to establish local constitutions. But because of the press-ing circumstances the conditions attached to this right were never fully stipu-lated. In order not to lose everything, Yeltsin was forced to make concessions, while at the same time warning that local demands might become more un-yielding, and that negotiations might drag on fruitlessly as a result.

By the end of 1992 it was obvious that the Federal Treaty only weakened the unity of the Russian state. The regions selectively endorsed the articles that enhanced their rights, and virtually ignored those pertaining to the power of the center. The Russian authorities now look very much like the hare from one of the popular anecdotes of Gorbachev period. The hare runs around a railway station, shouting, "Give me your suitcase! Give me your suitcase!" No one replies. "Give me your suitcase, or what happened yesterday will happen again!" the hare cries in desperation. "What happened yesterday?" asks a passerby. "Nobody gave me a suitcase yesterday either," the hare wails.

Once again, the specter of the "war of laws" that paralyzed the Soviet Union in 1989-1991 stands before the country. At that time Yeltsin demon-strated to Gorbachev that he held the trump card. Now, using almost the same language, leaders of autonomous republics are addressing the Russian presi-dent. Keeping in mind the Federal Treaty's guarantee of their right to pass local constitutions, the regions have tried to squeeze as much as possible from the center before the new Russian Constitution is adopted. Thus, the first step on the road to total regionalization was the elevation of the status of the Rus-sian regions to the status enjoyed by the autonomous non-Russian republics. As Vladimir Shiriaev, vice chairman of the Arkhangelsk provincial soviet, stated, "The republics got greater political and economic rights and the prov-inces were cheated of their share." After this statement the soviet passed a bill arrogating to itself the right "to block activities which have been established by the supreme organs of state power, if these activities are contrary to the in-terests of the local population."[35] The same applies to the issue of designating plenipotentiaries. Advocates of secession from Russia considered the decision of the Arkhangelsk soviet a major step toward the creation of a "Pomor'e Re-public."

Similar instances spring to mind. The extraordinary session of the Stavropol provincial soviet held in November 1992 resulted in a demand that the Russian Supreme Soviet give the province the same rights as the autonomous republics. The local authorities have demanded the right to dispose of their own budgets by themselves and to control tax payments.[36] To cite another example, since the beginning of 1992 St. Petersburg has sought to attain the status of a "free city" and the right to control its own revenues.

As a result of such developments, in October 1992 Yeltsin was forced to openly recognize his dependence on the regions. Hoping to receive support from local leaders in his struggle against the parliament, and accompanied by the Moscow leadership, he visited a meeting of the heads of the regional administrations, and announced that the center of reform was shifting to the regions. In fact this was a forced acknowledgment, because the real tempo of the economic reforms was to a great extent determined not in the center, but in the localities, and it depended not only on objective factors, but also on the will and whims of the local authorities. At the same time, Yeltsin suggested that local governments take on more responsibility for social welfare.[37] Although good in theory, under conditions of political instability this change was extremely dangerous for the center, since it was forced to loosen its grip on its last remaining economic levers, along with its ability to influence the processes taking place in the country. Yeltsin had to accept a new redistribution of tax payments in favor of the regions, and to increase to 30 percent their share in export operations conducted in hard currency. Also, he signed a special agreement creating a Federation Council for the purpose of resolving political, economic, and social problems.[38] According to the plans of Yeltsin's advisers, this institution was intended to counterbalance the parliament's authority and to bolster the president's. In actuality the council inevitably weakened presidential power, and paved the way for centrifugal tendencies.

Already by the end of 1992, Oleg Rumiantsev, the former chairman of the Parliament's Constitutional Commission, declared that Tatarstan's constitution and those of Bashkortostan and Sakha contained twenty-nine articles that contradicted Federal Russian laws.[39] Not to mention the fact that, according to Rumiantsev, "Moscow itself is in the front rank of those 'states within the State,' which do not feel bound to observe Russian laws."[40]

The struggle over the Constitution of the Russian Federation has flared up with new force. Supporters of the "statist" line demand a unitary state, reject local autonomy, and call for the reestablishment of a strictly territorial governmental hierarchy. This is the position of St. Petersburg's mayor, Aleksandr Sobchak, who admittedly has limited his demands for self-governance to St. Petersburg. Sergei Stankevich and the other prominent statist figures would agree, if worse comes to worst, with the idea of a "firm" federation that would allow the peoples of Russia a certain diversity of cultural autonomy. On the other hand, the regional "realists," foreseeing the coming battles over the new Constitution, passed a bill during the seventh Congress of People's Deputies that declared the Federal Treaty an integral part of the future Constitution. And at the first meeting of the Constitutional Commission in 1993,

Rumiantsev declared that "powerful forces" were attempting to transform the Russian Federation into an amorphous confederation.[41] Defiant assertions of autonomy elsewhere, such as in Cheliabinsk and Kalmykia, became increasingly common during 1993.

In the fall of 1993, the process reached a new stage. Yeltsin created the Council of the Federation as a semi-official precursor to the upper chamber of the future new Russian parliament, intending that it should act as a counterweight to the Supreme Soviet. This in fact meant that real power had decisively passed into the hands of the regions. Despite Yeltsin's efforts to curtail their influence after dissolving the Supreme Soviet, the council provides the regions with a powerful institutional base. The challenge that they will be able to mount to the power of the president will be incomparably more effective than that posed by the central legislature.

Regionalization on Russia's Road to Market

The process of reform is taking various shapes depending on particular economic, cultural, and political factors in each locality. As a result, the center's consolidating role is increasingly diminished. If Moscow cannot soon find its place within the reforming Russia, its significance will eventually be lost.

Most likely, Moscow will try to institute a policy based on pressure. Such a policy can lead only to the growth of centrifugal tendencies and mutual suspicion and, finally, the determination to secede at any price. In other words, it would repeat the scenario of the disintegration of the Council for Mutual Economic Assistance and of the Soviet Union itself, when, especially in the former case, old economic relations were sacrificed to political interests.

The tendency toward regionalization, which accompanies the fundamental change of the economic system, may reveal a deeper, fairly stable pattern. Perhaps the process of reforming major, relatively well-developed countries or conglomerates of closely connected countries such as the Soviet Union and Russia, China, the United States, or the European Community differs from the process of reforming comparatively small countries. Because of their vast territories, economies of the former type of country have a "closed" character and require the presence of all elements of technological productivity, from mining and drilling to the manufacture of consumer goods. Reform inevitably results in a breakup of stable economic relations, and it may take decades to recreate them.

Accordingly, it may be that regionalization is an appropriate response during a period of total transformation from a centralized economy into a free market one, especially in a situation where the need for transformation has been declared, but private property and economic competition have not yet been introduced. As a result, the formerly closed system disintegrates into a group of quasi-independent, open or partly open sub-systems of a smaller scale. The system's metamorphosis results in new linkages between economic partners, and leads to the emergence of geographically closer and more stable centers of economic orientation. This process may develop peacefully, without revolutionary, violent fragmentation, while preserving the existence of a sovereign, formally unified state. It is scarcely possible that the transformation will result in a reestablishment of traditional structures. More likely, the regions will attain true independence or create mutually advantageous interregional economic and political unions. A model might be Canada, itself a member of the British Commonwealth of Nations, or the United States.

The factors that would affect regional disintegration include the following:

— the presence of natural resources that might be sold for hard currency;
— the relative strength of ethnic and "national patriotic" orientations;
— the existence of other centers of economic and social activity outside of Moscow;
— interregional interdependence and collective self-sufficiency;
— geographic distance between regions and the center;
— the political ambitions of regional leaders.

The boundary of regional separatism is roughly marked by the course of the Volga River to Nizhnii Novgorod and then on to the Ural Mountains in the north. In the south, this borderline disappears somewhere in the Stavropol-Krasnodar plain, where wheat, corn and sunflowers are grown. To the west lies the heartland of historic Russia with its sixteenth century borders. Virtually the entire area is poor in minerals (with the notable exception of iron ore deposits in Kursk). Historically, these lands are closely connected, and are now becoming integrated into a single industrial and agricultural region.

To the east of the Volga River, especially beyond the Ural Mountains, the situation is entirely different. The colonized territories are dominated by transplanted Russians who refer to themselves as Siberians and who have traditionally stood in opposition to the central authorities in Moscow. Accordingly, the idea of self-governance apart from the rest of Russia receives strong support here. New regional sub-centers have already begun to emerge in Siberia, uniting provinces rich in natural resources (oil, gold, diamonds, wood, nonferrous metals) with industrial and agricultural areas.

None of the regions that are demanding economic autonomy has experienced severe ethnic frictions with Moscow. Certainly, ethnic particularism exists in this area, especially in the Volga region, but it has not had an important impact on politics. For example, while the Russian population in Tatarstan was commemorating the 400th anniversary of the capture of Kazan by Ivan the Terrible, the Tatar community was celebrating the memory of its ancestors, who defended the fortress, and no outbursts of ethnic antagonism occurred.

While it is possible to find examples to the contrary, they are not typical of the situation in general. The *minimedzhilis* (a self-elected parliament) in Kazan rejects any compromises with Moscow and has branded both Tatarstan's Supreme Soviet and President Shaimiev "proteges of the colonialists." But as long as Kazan does not dominate negotiations with Moscow, ethnic extremism is unlikely to intensify.

To the east of the Volga, the growth of independence and regionalization are quite heterogeneous processes. On the one hand, the president of "independent" Tatarstan negotiates with Russian President Boris Yeltsin on future relations with Russia, while on the other hand, the heads of the provincial legislatures of Krasnoiarsk and Omsk have challenged the center without making any definite moves.

Farther to the east, the "Siberian Agreement" also includes a heterogeneous mix of regions, with various political and economic leanings. Western Siberia gravitates toward the agricultural Novosibirsk province as a center; the Krasnoiarsk and Altai provinces waver between the Far East and Siberia. Chita and Khabarovsk have not yet tilted clearly in any direction, and are big and rich enough not to require a union with the neighboring provinces. On one hand, it seems unlikely that such an unwieldy conglomerate can survive. Siberia is too wide, diverse, and divided a country to have a united government over its territory. On the other hand, if the "Siberian Agreement" produces a loose coordinating body rather than a body that tries to become artificially centralized, it may prove to be viable. Finally, the Sakha Republic and the Far Eastern territories (including the Pomor'e and Magadan-Kamchatka regions), and Sakhalin Island, which was the first to demand economic freedoms, each have the potential to become relatively autonomous, separate regions.[42] Once the squabble over the Kuril Islands is settled, Sakhalin may well conclude an economic agreement with Japan or another country on the Pacific rim.[43]

Regionalization Inside the Regions

The process of regionalization is developing in two directions. On the one hand, the regions are uniting into new groups (Greater Volga, the Siberian Agreement, the South Urals Republic, etc.). On the other hand, the process of fragmentation has not subsided, and the regional authorities are coming to be viewed by some elements in the sub-regions as new, miniature "centers" whose demands must be resisted.

This process is especially typical of provinces rich in minerals, which do not want to share their profits with the regional authorities. By the summer of 1992, for example, the Dolgano-Nenetskii Autonomous District had declared its independence from the Krasnoiarsk region and announced its intention to establish direct links with Moscow.[44] In the city of Norilsk, the hub for nickel mining and processing, local politicians asserted that the sale of its natural resources could transform Norilsk into a "northern Kuwait."[45] Their arguments were essentially the same as those of the Krasnoiarsk authorities when the latter demanded independence from Moscow: both cited high taxes and the absence of requisite help by the center. By the end of 1992, at the session of the District Soviet, the authorities of Norilsk, Snezhnegorsk, Talnakh, and Kaerkan had demanded autonomy.[46] The Altai Republic and Tuva provide other examples of regionalization within a region.

Possible Scenarios

If a nationalist dictatorship comes to power, the central authorities would almost certainly try to establish a united government over the entire territory of Russia, and eventually over the entire territory of the former Soviet Union. Any attempt to achieve the latter goal would be doomed to failure, however, since it would inevitably cause war with Ukraine, the Baltic states, and the Caucasian republics, while at the same time offending world opinion. On the other hand, the prospects for successful establishment of a united government within the confines of Russia itself depend on the following:

1) Distribution of power between the central and local authorities. If the center remains politically fragmented, the localities will simply pay no attention to its decrees. As discussed above, this has already happened to a significant degree, and local authorities have grown bolder in their defiance. For example, in February 1993 the head of the administration in Ulianovsk refused to grant landing permission to a division of troops returning to Russia from Azerbaijan.[47]

2) The position of local army commanders, and their assessment of the balance of power between Moscow and the local authorities. For example, if Lieutenant-General Lebed, commander of the Fourteenth Russian Army, had not supported the separatist Dnestr Republic in Moldova, it surely would have been defeated. Conceivably, a similar situation might transpire within the Russian Federation.

3) The ability of Moscow to take firm punitive measures and to use rapid deployment forces. The fact that the key posts of defense minister and deputy defense minister are held by generals (Pavel Grachev and Boris Gromov, respectively) who participated in the Afghan War suggests that the center may be receptive to such an approach.

4) The resoluteness of local civil authorities, and the popular will to oppose the center.

The political struggle between Yeltsin and the parliament has greatly strengthened centrifugal forces in Russia. Despite Yeltsin's military victory, the broader questions of governance and institutional formation are still unresolved. Should the struggle between executive and legislature—or any other factional struggle—continue in its recent form, it would probably spell the end of Great Russia and possibly any Russia at all. Connections with the center would continue to erode and the regions would quicken their efforts to unite into new groupings such as the "Greater Volga," the "Siberian Agreement," and the "South Urals Republic." In this case the regions could try to reestablish the old pan-Russian economic structure, but one based on new principles, perhaps similar to those of the European Community. An institution such as a Federation Council representing the heads of regional governments might arise to resolve common problems (as advocated by Novgorod's Boris Nemtsov).[48] Yet it seems rather more likely that as the result of the enormous space of the country and the heterogeneity of its economic development, many regions would be driven to align with neighboring systems, such as those of China, Japan, the Pacific Rim, Asia, or even the United States.

Another and especially grim possibility must be considered. If the center tries to impose order on the regions and the regions are unable to repulse this attempt, a new and possibly quite bloody standoff could arise.[49] The conflict between center and periphery would be mirrored by conflict at the local level between supporters and opponents of integration. While such a civil war might not be so murderous as the Yugoslav tragedy, it would seriously weaken all sides. The economy would collapse utterly, and the regions—including the central European region of Russia—would probably disintegrate into new subregions corresponding to the current administrative divisions. These subregions themselves could easily come to blows in the context of uncertainty and resource scarcity, resulting in growing impoverishment. In such a scenario of self-reinforcing disintegration the entire expanse of Northern Eurasia could devolve into a hopeless state of underdevelopment.

Of course, it is also possible that Yeltsin will succeed in implementing a new constitution, as called for in the aftermath of the military clash in Moscow in September and October, 1993. And yet it remains unclear just how solid, or how conditional, Yeltsin's support actually is in the regions. Certainly in Karelia or Sakha his support is much firmer than in Tatarstan, not to mention Chechnia, which supported Yeltsin purely out of opposition to the more centrist Supreme Soviet. And of course Yeltsin himself may be replaced as president in the foreseeable future. Thus the key political issue remains undecided: is there an emerging consensus in favor of a "new" centralized presidency; or a "new" centralized parliamentary regime; or (most likely) a weak federation in which the president and parliament would have largely decorative functions? At present, as under Gorbachev earlier, the formula "strong center, strong regions" in practice indicates the rise of the latter.

Notes

1. Report of the Russian State Statistical Committee for 1992, *Ekonomicheskaia gazeta*, no. 4, January 1993.

2. *Izvestiia*, December 7, 1992.

3. The Siberian Agreement includes the Khakassia, Tuva, Khabarovsk, Novosibirsk, Tomsk, Omsk, Kemerovo and Chita regions. *Nezavisimaia gazeta*, January 14, 1993.

4. Moscow TV, evening news, February 20, 1993.

5. Moscow TV September 30, 1993.

6. G. Iavlinskii, in *Literaturnaia gazeta*, October 28, 1993.

7. Moscow TV, evening news, December 28, 1992.

8. Mikhail Nikolaev, President of the Sakha (Iakutiia) Republic, "Nuzhen li Sever Rossii?" *Nezavisimaia gazeta*, June 23, 1992.

9. Interview with Gaidar, Moscow TV, evening news, July 22, 1992.

10. Moscow TV, September 20, 1993.

11. Nikolaev, "Nuzhen li Sever Rossii?"

12. Prognoz Ekspertnogo Tsentra RSPP, "Edinstvo reformy i reforma edinstva," Moscow, July 1992.

13. *Izvestiia*, April 13, 1993

14. Moscow TV, September 15, 1993.

15. *Izvestiia*, January 4, 1993. According to one report, 55 of the 89 oblasts and republics are subsidized by the center, although details are unavailable since divulging them is against the interests of both the center and the localities. "Chto govoriat v Parizhe o Rossiiskom biudzhete," *Izvestiia*, April 15, 1993, p.4.

16. Ibid.

17. There were many government decisions in August and September on the assumption of federal property to the local authorities: in the Rostov and Sverdlovsk (Ekaterinburg) regions, in Karelia, in Marii-El and in Shakhovskoi District of the Moscow region.

18. "Eks-avtonomii obediniaiutsia v Soiuze," *Nezavisimaia gazeta*, December 18, 1992.

19. When the center failed to deliver, the local authorities held up transfer of 800 billion rubles which had been allocated for tax payments. Ultimately the money was transferred, but the episode revealed how little recourse Moscow already had. *New York Times*, January 8, 1993.

20. "O finansovo-ekonomicheskoi politike Rossii," *Izvestiia*, January 26, 1993.

21. See "Dezintegratsiia Rossii?", Report of the Council on Foreign and Defense Policy, *Nezavisimaia gazeta*, December 10, 1992.

22. See Kamaludin Gadzhiev, "Geopoliticheskie perspektivy Kavkaza v strategii Rossii," *Mirovaia ekonomika i mezhdunarodnye otnosheniia* 2 (1993) pp. 20-37.

23. Deputy Prime Minister Khizha, then the official Russian representative in Ingushetia, stated, "First of all we should with all our strength help our army. . .to overcome the "Tbilisi syndrome". . .We need our army to understand that now it fulfills its duties for our people." *Krasnaia zvezda*, October 18, 1992.

24. Tensions between the center and Ingushetia have been exacerbated since the

election of new Ingush President Ruslan Aushev. "Ingushetia nastaivaet na vyvode rossiiskoi armii," *Nezavisimaia gazeta,* March 25, 1993, pp. 1-2.

25. *Kommersant-Daily,* September 25, 1993, in FBIS-SOV-93-185, September 27, 1993, p.20.

26. The Supreme Soviet of Tatarstan decided to produce only 23,727,000 tons of oil instead of 29 million tons as under previous "agreements" with Moscow, and to increase annual oil exports from 5 million to 10 million tons. The republic would keep 10 million tons for further processing at the Nizhnekamskneftekhim complex, while the rest would be processed into fuel exclusively for Tatarstan's needs. *Nezavisimaia gazeta,* December 31, 1992.

27. "Konfederatsiia kak sredstvo ot khaosa," *Nezavisimaia gazeta,* December 12, 1992. This possibility was raised again during the September-October confrontation between the central organs, with Tatar leaders inviting Udmurtia to join the others in a Volga Union. *Izvestiia,* September 22, 1993, p. 2, in FBIS-SOV-93-186, September 28, 1993, p. 30. Another emerging center of this region is Samara. See "Povolzhe i Ural podderzhivaiut politiku Rossii," *Izvestiia,* March 2, 1993, p.2.

28. *Nezavisimaia gazeta,* December 1, 1992.

29. "Dogovor o provedenii referenduma", *Nezavisimaia gazeta,* January 23, 1993; also *Izvestiia,* September 29, 1993, in FBIS-SOV-93-189, October 1, 1993, p. 22.

30. "Kazan' i Ufa protiv referenduma," *Nezavisimaia gazeta,* December 31, 1992.

31. *Nezavisimaia gazeta,* December 31, 1992.

32. "Dezintegratsiia Rossii?" op. cit.

33. Ibid.

34. "Pogranichnaia situatsiia," *Literaturnaia gazeta,* no. 44, October 28, 1992.

35. *Izvestiia,* January 26, 1993.

36. "Nepovinovenie v provintsiiakh," *Moskovskie novosti,* no. 48, 1992.

37. Yeltsin interview, Moscow TV, evening news, October 14, 1992.

38. *Nezavisimaia gazeta,* November 16, 1992.

39. Moscow TV, Evening News Program, December 24, 1992.

40. *Nezavisimaia gazeta,* December 5, 1992.

41. Moscow TV, Evening News Program, January 8, 1993.

42. "Pogranichnaia situatsiia," *Literaturnaia gazeta,* October 28 & November 4, 1992; "Sakhalin Goes to Market," *Asia Inc.* 3 (September 1992), pp. 37-38; "Gubernator o prezidente," *Nezavisimaia gazeta,* January 15, 1993.

43. "Fedorovka," *Literaturnaia gazeta,* February 22, 1992.

44. "Severnyi peredel," *Izvestiia,* July 1992.

45. "Metallicheskii rok," *Literaturnaia gazeta,* January 13, 1993.

46. *Izvestiia,* December 25, 1992.

47. The division eventually landed in Smolensk instead. Moscow TV evening news, February 9, 1993.

48. *Nezavisimaia gazeta,* April 15, 1993. However, at least some regions (including Tartarstan and Bashkortostan) have already expressed opposition to this scheme, preferring instead to maintain the existing Council of Heads of Republics. See *Nezavisimaia gazeta,* April 1, 1993, pp. 1, 3.

49. On the possibility and some of the factors relevant to it, see *Sotsialnaia i sotsialno-politicheskaia situatsiia v Rossii: sostoianie i prognoz* (Moscow: Institute of Socio-Political Research, 1993), pp. 22-26.

7

The Russian Military in the 1990s: Disintegration or Renewal?

John Lepingwell

The Russian military faces a number of challenges in the 1990s, and its success or failure in meeting them will determine the military's future, and also the stability of Russian domestic politics and relations with the "near abroad" states, referring to the former Soviet republics, including the Baltic states. Russia has inherited the bulk of the Soviet military and with it many of the old imperial obligations, entanglements, and ambitions of the Soviet Union. In dealing with this legacy, Russia faces several challenges: (1) withdrawing large forces deployed outside its borders, particularly those in the "near abroad"; (2) restructuring and reducing the existing military over the next few years; and (3) reequipping the military to modern standards. These three challenges have come about during a period of unprecedented economic and political instability within Russia that threatens to deteriorate into chaos. Further complicating the problem is the fact that a new, robust system of civilian control over the military has not yet been fully developed.

As a result of these challenges, the Russian military faces the alternatives of renewal or disintegration. The renewal planned by the Ministry of Defense would result in a smaller, more professional, and better-armed military force that is able to protect Russia's interests both within and outside its borders. Yet many social and economic factors are hastening the trend toward disintegration. Regionalism, corruption, and declining morale are corroding military professionalism and weakening discipline within the military. If the trend is toward disintegration, then the stability of Russian civil-military relations may well be threatened. Unless the Russian military and civilian leadership proves adept at understanding and countering these disintegrative factors, the Russian military may rot from within and become a force capable of only opposing the civilian leadership or fighting border wars, but not providing security against foreign foes. This chapter examines the challenges now facing the Russian military, and then turns to the question of whether and how these challenges can be met.

Remnants of Empire

Perhaps the most immediate problem facing the Russian military is the need to rapidly repatriate units deployed in Germany and throughout the former Soviet Union. While this process has proceeded relatively smoothly so far, there have been troubling developments in some areas.[1]

The magnitude of the task of repatriation is daunting. Between 250,000 and 400,000 Russian troops were deployed outside Russia at the beginning of 1993.[2] The political situations in which these forces found themselves varied strikingly. The situation is stable for the forces deployed in Germany, but their future when they return home is uncertain. The forces deployed in the former Soviet Union, however, face the task of either conducting the troop withdrawal within a hostile political environment, or maintaining the forces in situations ranging from stable to armed conflict. Thus, the two cases are worth dealing with separately.

The bulk of the force that is being repatriated is in Germany, where the once-mighty Western Group of Forces (WGF) is now a rapidly dwindling force incapable of fulfilling any meaningful combat role. While the Russian minister of defense had criticized the Soviet Union's agreement to pull the WGF out of Germany so rapidly, he acceded in December 1992 to a speed-up in the planned withdrawal, and the last troops are now scheduled to leave in September 1994.[3]

While redeploying all these forces is within the logistical capability of the Russian military, the problem of how to provide them with new bases and housing facilities is still unsolved. The Russian Ministry of Defense claims that some 106,000 officers and their families are without proper housing, and estimates that this number could increase substantially as the withdrawal continues.[4] The German government is providing funding for the construction of apartments for troops being withdrawn from Germany, but some of the construction is taking place in Ukraine and Belarus, while the total number of apartments provided will reportedly meet only half the demand.[5] The reluctance of local civil authorities to make troop housing a high priority has contributed to growing tension in some regions. One airborne division, redeployed from Azerbaijan to Ulianovsk, reportedly arrived in armored vehicles at the city council in order to emphasize its demands that appropriate housing be provided.[6] While this appears to be an extreme case, the housing shortage, combined with declining living conditions, is resulting in declining morale and growing tensions. This trend is likely to persist as the withdrawal of troops continues.

A different problem is posed by the Russian forces deployed in the now independent republics of the former Soviet Union. When the Soviet Union collapsed in 1991-1992, there was some hope that a unified, or at least joint, military structure could be created under the Commonwealth of Independent States (CIS). Since Ukraine in particular was intent on forming its own military, however, this plan never materialized, and the CIS joint command has become little more than a relatively powerless coordinating body. Ukraine, Belarus, and Kazakhstan assumed direct control of the former Soviet military forces on their territory (with the exception of strategic forces) but Russia assumed direct control in spring of 1992 of former Soviet military forces in the Baltic states, Armenia, Azerbaijan, Georgia, part of Moldova, and some of the Central Asian states.[7] In these near abroad states the Russian military faces a far more complex problem than in Germany. In several of these states Russian forces have become deeply involved in internal conflicts, and in some cases have even been inciting them. We will briefly survey the status of these forces in order to understand the diversity of the problems facing them.

The Baltic States

Well over half of the Soviet forces deployed in the Baltic States in 1991 have already been withdrawn.[8] Although there have been repeated threats by the Russian government to halt the withdrawal, it has continued quietly. The last Russian troops left Lithuania on August 31, 1993, and only a few thousand remain in Estonia. However, perhaps 16,000 to 18,000 Russian troops remained in Latvia in mid-1993, due in part to a Russian-Latvian dispute over the rights of the Russian minority in Latvia. While the forces remaining in Latvia are in part intended to exert implicit pressure upon the Latvian government, they appear to have little significant combat role. Russia, and the Ministry of Defense in particular, appears to have recognized that the position of the forces in the Baltic States is increasingly untenable.[9] The forces there are much reduced in size, have little opportunity for combat training, and are despised by the local populations. While they remain a potentially great bargaining chip for Russia in connection with the minority rights issue, there are other potential means of influence available to Russia in its dealings with the Baltic States.

The Caucasus

Since Armenia is locked in a conflict with Azerbaijan over the Nagorno-Karabakh region and there are ongoing tensions with its neighbor, Turkey, the Russian forces in Armenia are seen as guarantors of Armenian security. Armenia has therefore been negotiating an agreement that would maintain some of the Russian forces, as a hedge against outside intervention.[10] Indeed, Azerbaijan has complained that Russian troops have been fighting alongside Armenian forces in and around Nagorno-Karabakh.[11] In contrast to Armenia, the Azerbaijani government was pleased to see the last Russian forces leave in May 1993, in part because memories of the use of Russian troops in Baku in January 1990 were still fresh, and because the Russian equipment could be used by Azerbaijani forces fighting in Nagorno-Karabakh.[12]

The status of the Russian forces in Georgia has varied as the political and military situation in that troubled country has worsened. There have been repeated accusations that Russian troops have supported the Abkhazian separatist forces with training, material, and even personnel. As a result, there have been calls for the rapid withdrawal of Russian troops. In February 1993 a Russian-Georgian agreement on withdrawal was signed.[13] But after the breakdown of the Russian-mediated cease-fire in Abkhazia in September 1993 and the seizure of the city of Sukhumi by Abkhazian troops, the Georgian position changed. Acknowledging that Georgia was dependent upon CIS, especially Russian, assistance, Georgian leader Eduard Shevardnadze signed an agreement giving Russian forces extensive rights in Georgia, and leasing the naval base at Poti to Russia.[14] It appears that nearly 20,000 Russian troops now in Georgia will remain in place indefinitely.

Moldova

The Soviet forces in Moldova were split in half by the breakup of the Soviet Union. The Fourteenth Army, located in the self-proclaimed "Dnestr Republic" on the east bank of the Dnestr, came under the jurisdiction of the Russian republic, while those forces on the west bank were claimed by Moldova.[15] The Fourteenth Army has since become one of the most prominent political forces in the area, and its commander, Lieutenant General Aleksandr Lebed, has played an unprecedented role in exacerbating tensions between the Russian and Moldovan sides. Lebed has repeatedly stated that the Fourteenth Army would not be withdrawn because most of the enlisted personnel are from the region, but that the army might be disbanded instead.[16] In the latter case, however, it would be immediately reconstituted as the military force of the "Dnestr Republic." The Fourteenth Army thus functions as both a local militia and army, even though it formally remains subordinate to the Russian Ministry of Defense.

The Central Asian States

In Central Asia the Russian military presence has been of mixed importance. During the civil war in Tajikistan the 201st Motorized Rifle Division

(MRD) played a key role by tacitly supporting the conservative forces that won the war. Consequently, relations between the 201st MRD and the Tajik government are good and the division will remain there. The 201st MRD plays a dual role in Tajikistan. It consciously and explicitly considers itself the guarantor of the security of the Russian minority (between 200,000 and 400,000 people) in Tajikistan, and it acts as a guarantor of stability for the newly reinstalled government. Like the Fourteenth Army in Moldova, the 201st MRD is to start recruiting more local residents (presumably with a special emphasis on the Russian-speaking minority). It is also to assist with the training and equipping of an indigenous Tajik military.

The status of former Soviet forces in the other Central Asian states is somewhat less clear. All of the forces stationed in those states have a very large (roughly 90 percent) proportion of Slavic, primarily Russian, officers. For example, there are some 15,000 troops under joint Russian-Turkmen command in Turkmenistan, along with an additional 45,000 troops, most of which are commanded by Russian officers.[17] On the other hand, in Uzbekistan, the government moved quickly to extend control over the Soviet forces on its territory, and some 8,000 former Soviet troops in Kyrgyzstan appear to have been subordinated to the Kyrgyz government, at least for the time being.[18] Yet Russian influence remains significant even in those cases where the forces are not formally Russian, since these states are dependent upon Russian personnel and equipment for their security. Thus, while Russia may have to withdraw only some of the units in the Central Asian states, it may also have to accommodate an influx of former officers from these units if they choose to return to Russia.

This summary shows that the role of the Russian military varies widely, from supporting the government of the host state (Tajikistan) to leading the armed opposition to it (Moldova). Furthermore, it assumes that some of the Russian troops based in the Caucasus and Central Asia are to be withdrawn. Given Russia's geopolitical interests in these regions, however, some Russian forces may remain there indefinitely.

The primary question of interest here, however, is the extent to which the status of these forces influences civil-military relations in Russia proper. Clearly, the return of these forces to inadequate facilities within Russia may cause increased discontent within the military. But beyond this immediate effect, it is likely that the Ministry of Defense will find itself unable to cope with the decision-making problems posed by the continued presence of Russian troops in the near abroad. Commanders in the area may well have their own priorities and policies. If central attention and control of these forces weakens, they may become increasingly involved in local politics, as commanders become tied to local civilians and others for the support and maintenance of the forces. As is argued below, the problems posed by the increasing corruption within the officer corps may further aggravate this problem.

The forces situated in the near abroad thus pose a control problem for

Moscow. Central control may weaken, and this, in turn, may lead to important policy decisions being taken by local commanders, depending on their view of Russia's (or their own) interests. This loss of control could further diminish the coherence of Russian policies, and render the Russian military an even less precise tool of foreign policy than it is now. Furthermore, if senior officers in the forces become used to involvement in local politics, this attitude may be retained if they move to senior leadership positions within the Russian military command in Moscow. If this occurs, one more barrier to military involvement in Russian domestic politics may be weakened.

Restructuring the Military

At the same time that the Russian military is repatriating its troops from abroad it is restructuring and reducing its forces at home.[19] From a force of over 2 million men in early 1992, the military is expected to shrink to approximately 1.5 million by 1995. This force reduction will require the retirement of at least 40,000 to 50,000 officers per year until 1995, although Lt. Gen. Viktor Samoilov, Russian deputy chief of staff for personnel, has claimed that up to 600,000 officers will have to leave by that time.[20] This fact, combined with deteriorating living conditions for servicemen throughout the Russian military (discussed further below), appears to have resulted in significant morale problems in the officer corps.

Contributing to the morale problem within the military is the absence of a clear threat. Where previously the enemy could be clearly identified as the West, this is no longer the case. Indeed, some conservative officers complain that the West has won the ideological struggle without having fired a shot. But apart from this minority view, there is the general problem of defining the threat to Russian security, a necessary first step if military restructuring is to take place on a rational basis.

The first attempt to redefine the threat, the draft Russian military doctrine published in mid-1992, was a compromise document that seemed to provide little concrete basis for force planning. It identified two quite different threats: a continuing threat from NATO, made even more difficult to counter after the collapse of the Warsaw Pact and the Soviet Union, and a newly emerging threat on the borders of Russia, where the defense of Russian minorities and the need to mount "peacekeeping" operations were identified as the most likely contingencies.[21] The forces required for these two contingencies would appear to vary significantly. In the first case, sophisticated forces and command-and-control systems, combined with extensive use of air power would be required. In the second case, much lighter, mobile forces would be necessary, and they would not need such sophisticated command and support systems. While both forces could be included within one military structure, it is not clear which contingency will be given priority in force planning. Debate and approval of a revised draft doctrine was repeatedly postponed during 1993 before finally being approved in early November, and many details remain unclear.

Despite the doctrinal uncertainty, the Ministry of Defense has proposed a plan to restructure the Russian forces that will lighten the force mix by reducing its emphasis on armor and artillery. A heavy capability will be provided by the relatively modern forces being withdrawn from the Western Group of Forces, while the light capability will be based on the existing airborne forces, with perhaps some other forces being restructured for mobile use.[22]

The process of reducing the size of the Russian military may be complicated, paradoxically enough, by the declining conscription rate. The Russian military leadership has complained of large draft shortfalls, with a subsequent drop in manning levels throughout the military. To a large extent this is due to the Law on Military Service, passed in February 1993, which included provisions exempting a large proportion of youths from the draft, provisions to which the Ministry of Defense had strenuously objected.[23] As a result, some sources report that units are on average manned at only about 60 percent of their authorized levels.[24] While at first glance this would seem to hasten the force reduction, in fact it threatens to create a hollow army, with officers being left to close old facilities and eliminate surplus equipment. In many cases, officers faced with seriously inadequate forces may abandon their efforts at combat training altogether.

In an attempt to solve this problem, a volunteer-service system is slowly being introduced. It is planned that by the year 2000, half of the Russian forces will be conscripts and the other half will be volunteers.[25] Over the short term, however, it appears that the number of volunteers will be quite small, and the military will remain dependent upon conscripts. But not only is the quantity of draftees falling, the quality is declining as well. The draft results indicate that the lowest rate of conscription or enlistment is, and will be, from the best educated segments of the urban population. Conscripts and recruits are therefore more likely to be predominantly from rural backgrounds, or less-educated (or lower-class) social groups. Not only might these youths be less qualified, but they also might be more likely to espouse conservative and authoritarian viewpoints than their educated urban counterparts. Similarly, volunteers may be more inclined to support such conservative viewpoints than the population as a whole. The trend toward rural conscripts and volunteers could lead to an increasing divergence in political views between civilian and military personnel that could undermine civil-military relations.

At the same time that the personnel resources of the Russian military are diminishing, there is also increasing concern about the technological level of its arms. The Soviet military watched the Persian Gulf war closely, and the Russian military has inherited its concern that Russian forces run the risk of finding themselves at a substantial qualitative disadvantage. Russian military leaders have complained that the most modern Soviet combat equipment was located in the western military districts of the Soviet Union, which are now in Ukraine. Russia, in turn, inherited lower-readiness divisions with older equipment.[26] The equipment of the Western Group of Forces, the best-equipped of all the Soviet forces, is being redeployed in Russia, and this will help to modernize some of the Russian forces. Nevertheless, even the equipment from the WGF is beginning to age, and will need modernization if Russia is to maintain rough technological parity with the West. Defense Minister Pavel Grachev has warned that unless Russia maintains its military research and development efforts and begins to increase production of high-technology weaponry in the next few years, it will fall hopelessly behind the West.

This modernization is hampered, however, by the extremely difficult budget situation in Russia. In 1992, funding for defense procurement dropped by 67 percent from its 1991 level, and the defense budget had been reduced in previous years as well.[27] Thus, the amount of new weaponry being purchased for the Russian army is proportionally much less than that for the Soviet army in its heyday. Furthermore, given the extremely uncertain economic situation in the country, it is unclear whether the quality level of Russian research and development can be maintained, let alone increased. Even if research and development funding remains relatively stable, it is likely that some of the best researchers may be lured into the private sector (or even out of the country). The increasing difficulty of ensuring supplies of necessary research equipment is also likely to contribute to an overall decline in the quality of the research and development being performed in Russia.

Russia also faces the problem of disposing of its old, surplus military equipment, much of which must be destroyed under the terms of the Conventional Forces in Europe (CFE) treaty signed in November 1990. Not only must thousands of tanks and armored combat vehicles be destroyed by 1995, but the CFE treaty also limits Russian deployments in the so-called "flank" area, which includes the Leningrad (now St. Petersburg) and North Caucasus military districts. Since the military now considers these to be front-line districts that must be built up, Russia has attempted to get the CFE treaty restrictions modified, despite strong objections from the other parties to the treaty.[28]

Even in the best of times, the restructuring that the Russian military leadership is proposing would be an exceedingly difficult, perhaps unprecedented, task. The number of problems that must be solved concurrently is large, and much uncertainty remains in the plans. The task is made all the more daunting by the fact that it is taking place in a state where the political and economic structures are also undergoing widespread changes and where the bases of civil-military relations are still being created.

Having thus surveyed the challenges facing the Russian military, it is necessary to place them in a broader context. How will the ongoing political and economic factors in Russia influence the success or failure of the restructuring? Is the Russian system of civil-military relations sufficiently stable and robust to manage this transition, or is military involvement, and perhaps intervention, in domestic politics likely?

The Uncertain Future of Russian Civil-Military Relations

Despite the turbulent political events of 1992-1993, Russian civil-military relations have been surprisingly stable. While they have been strained at times, some of the worst-case scenarios that had been feared have not come to pass. During the crucial test of military loyalty to President Yeltsin in October 1993, the military demonstrated its support. Even so, the October crisis both underlined the potential political role of the military and focused attention on strains within the military. Over the longer term, the stability of Russian civil-military relations may again be tested by crises, and trends within the military may erode some of the support now enjoyed by President Yeltsin.

The restructuring of the Russian military is taking place in a strikingly different political, social, and economic situation than the one that existed only a few years ago. The Soviet military, until the last years of the Gorbachev period, led a privileged existence: officers were held in high esteem, and the many high-ranking officers had access to a range of perquisites and benefits. Even more important, there was a fundamental agreement between the civilian and military leadership over the crucial importance of military power to the state, and the role of that power in Soviet foreign policy. While there have been some changes in the leadership of the new Russian Ministry of Defense, the bulk of the military remains suspended between the Soviet past and the increasingly uncertain democratic present.

Two fundamental factors determine the stability of Russian civil-military relations: the professionalism or politicization of the military, and the legitimate authority of the government.[29] Disturbingly, current trends suggest that both of these bases of stability may be undergoing erosion.

Professionalism or Politicization?

The Soviet military was always a relatively autonomous organization, and was never deeply involved in politics at the local or regional levels. This autonomy was an important factor in civil-military relations, for it allowed the military to devote more time to its professional concerns, and to develop a significant level of professionalism. In recent years, however, this professionalism has been threatened by a number of trends.

One threat to military professionalism is the sense of disorientation that has affected many Russian servicemen in the wake of the collapse of the Soviet

Union. The Russian military must be able to define its purpose in order to retain its organizational integrity and mission, and to indoctrinate its troops. Defining the Russian military as a force that is intended to engage in border conflicts and peacekeeping operations requires a significant reorientation of purpose for many officers.

Accompanying this loss of mission has been a substantial drop in prestige and privilege. The Soviet officer corps was held in relatively high esteem, and while an officer's life was not an easy one, it did carry with it some security, prestige, and an ample wage. Now, all of these aspects of the officer's life are either under threat or have already disappeared. While opinion polls still show that the public rates the military highly as an institution, the prestige level of service appears to have dropped.[30] Furthermore, despite repeated pay increases, officers' wages may not have kept pace with the rapid rate of inflation.[31] Officers remain stationed in garrisons where the standard of living is dropping and where the military may no longer be getting any priority in its supplies. The net result is a rapid drop in the standard of living for officers and their families, at a rate that might be greater than that for the population as a whole. For those officers who are likely to be retired or discharged into a society where the economy is in shambles, the prospect is even grimmer.[32]

So far, this disorientation and sense of anger at the loss of privilege and benefits does not appear to have been translated into politicization or political mobilization of the military. Instead, a trend towards apathy, distrust in politicians, and concern with personal welfare may be developing within the military as well as within the civilian population. During the October constitutional crisis, calls to arms by the conservative Russian Officers' Union met with little response, suggesting that while there might be some sympathy for its position, there is not enough to cause officers to revolt. Nevertheless, the officer corps tends to be both conservative and nationalistic, and in searching for a new orientation for the Russian military there is a strong tendency to appeal to Russian "patriotism." This form of nationalism evokes the Russian imperial past, and, as Shenfield discusses in Chapter 1, this could provide a basis for supporting strong central power at home and a tough policy abroad.

The Issue of Legitimacy

One of the keys to stability of civil-military relations is the legitimacy of the government as perceived by the population as a whole, and especially as perceived by the military.[33] One of the principal reasons for the failure of the August 1991 coup attempt was the existence of a strong, democratically-elected president (and parliament) in Russia. Similarly, the military's decision to support Yeltsin in October 1993 was partly based on the perception that the president enjoyed greater legitimacy and popular support than the parliament and Vice President Aleksandr Rutskoi.

According to the Constitution, the president is commander-in-chief of the armed forces. Yet, in both the March 1993 and October 1993 constitutional crises, the military attempted to adopt a position of political neutrality. In March there was great speculation as to whether the military would support Yeltsin against the parliament if he chose to dissolve it or if he tried to use the military to enforce his decrees. Similarly, in the October crisis it was uncertain whether the military would decide to support Rutskoi after he proclaimed himself president. Rutskoi, an Air Force officer, certainly had great appeal within the officer corps, although he had damaged his relations with the senior military leadership through his allegations of corruption against Grachev and other generals.

The military's profession of neutrality in these crises appears to have reflected a real desire to stay out of political intrigues. In part this may have been motivated by a fear that direct participation in the political struggle might have exposed rifts within the military and precipitated a split in the ranks, one that could conceivably have led to open conflict and even civil war. The fact that the military decided to intervene only after there had been violent conflict in Moscow suggests that its neutral position was difficult to change.[34] But while noting the military's neutrality, it is also important to point out the limits of this neutrality. During both crises, it was made clear that Grachev remained a loyal member of the cabinet, and he provided symbolic and political support to Yeltsin. The terms of neutrality excluded the use of force, but allowed Grachev a fair amount of political latitude.

Indeed, while the military did finally support Yeltsin in his decision to storm the parliament building, it did so reluctantly. Had Yeltsin ordered the military to take armed action without a previous provocation, the result would likely have been quite different. As it is, the Russian military crossed the Rubicon in October 1993: it chose sides in a political conflict and determined the outcome by force.[35] While such an action may not whet the military's appetite for further intervention in domestic politics, it contributes to an erosion of restraints on both civilian and military leaders concerning the use of the military in politics. In many other states, politicians eventually have come to regret the initial decision to enlist the military in the resolution of political conflicts.

Over the short term the Russian military may well demand its fair recompense for supporting Yeltsin on October 3 and 4. It will almost certainly insist on a further tightening of the laws on conscription, so as to lessen the draft shortfalls. It may also call for a tougher Russian policy toward the near abroad, as well as increases in the military budget. Such measures are likely to be limited, however, and do not represent a qualitative change in the nature of civil-military interaction.

Yet, as Smyth observes in Chapter 3, the long-term legitimacy and stability of the regime is still open to question. New elections to a more representative parliament may help to reduce the tensions between the executive and legislative branches, and a newly formed Constitutional Court may provide an important balancing role. At the same time, continuing uncertainty over the new Constitution, and the increasing tensions that are likely to result as economic and social reforms continue, may serve to weaken the standing of even these new, more democratic institutions. This set of trends, combined with disintegrative trends within the military, may eventually weaken civilian control over the military.

Disintegrative Trends: Corruption and Regionalism

Given the economic difficulties being experienced by the officer corps due to the current economic reforms, the temptation to offer military services and goods on the open market is enormous. Apart from potential economic losses (or gains) inflicted on the country, military corruption tends to erode the barriers between military and civilian actors and politics.[36] If the corruption involves civilian politicians or bureaucrats, it threatens to suck the military into politics and to give it a strong incentive for maintaining corrupt local politicians. In turn, this may erode central control of the military and contribute to its regionalization and disintegration, as it becomes beholden to regional bosses rather than its commanders in Moscow.

While such a trend is obviously rather difficult to quantify, since it is by its very nature hard to observe, it appears to be well-established and growing.[37] As Rudenshiold and Barnes point out in Chapter 2, regional leaders throughout Russia have taken advantage of the political struggles in Moscow to accumulate power and establish their own political machines. Indeed, in areas where military forces are stationed, accommodation between the regional leadership and the local military commander may actually have some positive consequences. The military may benefit from government assistance in improving living conditions, while the civilian economy (or the racketeers) may benefit from access to military resources. The increasing influence and power of organized crime rings, both regionally and nationwide, suggests that the military may also find it beneficial to deal directly with racketeers. Thus, there is a strong possibility that corruption may take on a systemic aspect, as organized crime, local government, and local military forces join in mutually beneficial criminal alliances. Clearly, such a development would have an extremely negative impact on the established system of control.

In addition to corruption, other factors may also facilitate the development of regional identities within the Russian military. While the official policy continues to allow conscripts to be sent anywhere within Russia to perform their service, there appears to be growing support for a proposed regulation that would require conscripts to serve within a given distance (perhaps 1,000 kilometers) of their home. Republics and provinces within Russia may push for such a regionally based recruitment system, just as the Soviet republics did before the collapse of the USSR.[38]

If a move toward local recruitment does take place it could have a mixed effect on Russian civil-military relations. On the one hand, the formation of regional loyalties and closer ties to the local population may help reduce the likelihood of military intervention, since officers and conscripts may be less likely to act against people from their own region. By the same token, however, it might reduce the utility of regular army units in the suppression of local or regional armed conflicts.

At the same time that regionalism may be growing in some units of the Russian military, the military is increasingly being called upon to fulfill internal security functions. While so far most of these "internal security" missions have been outside Russia in Tajikistan, Georgia, and Moldova, forces have recently been deployed in Russia as well, most notably between the Chechen and Ingush. This mission could be quite detrimental to military professionalism, as counter-insurgency warfare is a different kind of threat than that for which the Russian military has been prepared. Studies of other militaries have noted that the development of a strong emphasis on counter-insurgency or internal security missions has eroded professionalism and encouraged military intervention in civilian affairs.[39]

Of greatest concern, though, is the question of whether the identification of military units with certain regions would strengthen the disintegrative tendencies already visible within the Russian Federation. If local leaders feel that they have little to fear from the central government, since it cannot enforce its decisions either through legal means or by force, they might feel their freedom of action to be increased in a wide range of areas. While it appears unlikely, for example, that predominantly Russian portions of the Russian Federation (Iakutia, the Far East) will secede, as Khrushchev argues in Chapter 6, such actions cannot be ruled out. It remains more likely, however, that devolution of power to the regions would severely weaken the ability of a reformist, non-authoritarian government in Moscow to implement its program. Furthermore, the apparent loss of military control, coupled with a fear of separatist tendencies, might contribute substantially to the very sort of constitutional crisis that could precipitate military involvement in Russian politics. The presence of military formations with regional loyalties would then become an issue of great importance.

Civilian Oversight of the Military

The system of civilian control that Russia inherited from the Soviet Union features a prominent role for the uniformed military in most security policy decision-making structures. Not only is the military well-placed to influence security policy decisions, there is also a relative lack of civilian control of defense budgets, military operations, and force deployment. The result is that while civilian oversight may be slowly increasing over time, civilian structures that can fully counterbalance military organizations, especially in the more technical areas, have not yet appeared.

While many reformers advocated the appointment of a civilian defense minister when the Russian military was created, the appointment of Gen. Pavel Grachev as defense minister in May 1993 appeared to represent a setback for those seeking to limit the military's influence. Although a civilian, Andrei Kokoshin, was appointed first deputy defense minister, his primary task is liaison with the defense industry, and there have been no further attempts to appoint civilians to high positions, or to create a civilian Ministry of Defense structure similar to that in many Western countries. While Grachev has suggested that a civilian defense minister could be appointed in 1995, once most of the military reforms have been implemented, the defense minister would still be almost wholly dependent on the military for advice and analysis.[40] Furthermore, the existing organizational structure gives control over forces, as well as almost all operational planning, to the chief of the General Staff. A civilian defense minister would therefore have to contend with a very powerful subordinate.

The Russian defense minister is directly responsible to the president on most issues, since primary control over the military is vested in the executive branch. Coordination of security policy is accomplished through the Security Council, a body composed of leading figures from the executive branch.[41] While great attention has been paid to the Security Council's role, it seems highly unlikely that the Council *per se* has significant powers, or that it dictates policy to the military. The Security Council may instead provide an important vehicle for the military to represent its interests in discussions of security issues, and may function as the main forum at which military and civilian approaches to these issues are debated.

Parliamentary mechanisms for military oversight were not well developed before the October crisis, and did not play a major role in promoting effective civilian control over the military. The Committee on State Security and Defense was understaffed and had a large number of members with direct ties to the military-industrial complex. The parliament appears to have spent relatively little time on military issues, and its oversight of such key documents as the defense budget was comparatively superficial. There is no reason to suppose that the new bicameral legislature will be much different in this respect.

It should be noted that while the military does have a substantial degree of autonomy in terms of policies affecting its own forces, its influence in other areas is less certain. The recent hardening of Russian attitudes towards the West does not necessarily indicate a substantial increase in military influence. As Blum observes in Chapter 8, the change instead appears to be an accommodation to strong conservative forces, perhaps coupled with a more realist approach to foreign policy priorities on the part of the foreign ministry.

Summary and Conclusions

Many of the trends discussed above suggest that the potential for instability in Russian civil-military relations will not disappear over the next few years. Over the short term, however, the prospects for stability in civil-military relations look rather good. There are several reasons for making this assertion.

First, the scenario that held out the most danger of military intervention against the democratic government has been played out. The military's decision to side with Yeltsin against the Supreme Soviet was uncertain until the last moment. Rutskoi's removal from power eliminated the last alternative leader who might have been able to rouse sufficient support within the military to stage a coup.

Second, while the use of the military in civilian politics sets a dangerous precedent, the impact of this precedent may be mitigated by judicious moves on the president's part. If Yeltsin recognizes that the military must not again be allowed into the political arena, he may be able to build more stable civil-military relations. The danger, however, is that Yeltsin will seek to rely upon the military again in political crises, thereby turning an exceptional event into a routine one. This could, in turn, lead to a dangerous erosion in civil-military relations that might eventually backfire on Yeltsin.

Third, in the aftermath of the October events, the executive branch may again give greater attention (and funding) to the military. While such a move may cause alarm in other states concerned about Russia's military might, support for the military leadership's restructuring program might also help to slow or halt some of the negative trends discussed above. The result may be a more capable, professional army that might pose less of a threat domestically, but more of a threat to Russia's neighbors.

In the near term, then, the prospects for direct military intervention appear to be relatively low. Over the long term, however, more troubling trends that are more difficult to offset may cause greater instability within the military. Corruption and regionalism could contribute to the weakening of central control. In turn, increased demands by the regions on the central government could precipitate a constitutional crisis. In this case a dilemma could arise: high military commanders with primary allegiance to Moscow and concerns about the possible disintegration of the Russian Federation could support a move to establish a strong, possibly authoritarian centralized power structure. Commanders of units with strong regional ties could, however, choose to support regional demands for greater autonomy. While such a confrontation would not necessarily lead to conflict, the military could again find itself the key arbiter in a crucial political struggle.

In sum, the splitting of the military along geographical or regional lines, rather than purely political ones, may be a source of future instability in Russian civil-military relations. Such a scenario can be forestalled only by a national accord on a new Constitution and the creation of a fully legitimate government in Moscow. Only through such an accord will it be possible to avert future constitutional crises, with their inherent threat of military involvement. But while a constitutional agreement might slow and reduce the threat of regional affiliations within the military, it will need to be complemented by successful economic policies. Economic reforms and improvements in the military's standard of living are essential if corruption within the military is to be reduced. Thus, ultimately, instability in civil-military relations can be prevented only by a resolution of Russia's broader political impasse. Until such a resolution is found, there remains the danger of the military being brought in to solve political problems by force.

Notes

1. Parts of this section are based on John W.R. Lepingwell, "Is the Military Disintegrating from Within?" *RFE/RL Research Report,* no. 25, June 18, 1993, pp. 9-16.

2. Russian Defense Minister Pavel Grachev has claimed that 400,000 Russian troops have to be repatriated. Interfax, November 28, 1992. This may include forces that are likely to remain in place, however, such as those in Central Asia, and it may include family members as well. The lower figure is from the Russian Defense Ministry, which notes that these forces are to be redeployed from the Western Group of Forces, Poland, the Baltic States, the Transcaucasus, and Moldova. Interfax, December 3, 1992.

3. ITAR-TASS, December 16, 1992. The last Russian troops left Poland on September 17, the fifty-fourth anniversary of the Soviet invasion, thus completing the withdrawal from all Eastern European countries other than Germany. Reuters, September 17, 1993.

4. Interfax, December 3, 1992. Grachev noted the problem of providing housing for returning servicemen in an interview on Russian TV, February 28, 1993.

5. *Trud*, May 14, 1993.

6. *Krasnaia zvezda*, February 9, 1993, p. 3. For a more detailed discussion of this case see Stephen Foye, "Russia's Defense Establishment in Disarray," *RFE/RL Research Report*, no. 36, September 10, 1993, pp. 49-54.

7. "Text of Decree on Defense Ministry Released," ITAR-TASS, as reported in FBIS-SOV, May 17, 1992, p. 31. Forces in the "Dnestr Republic" were taken under Russian jurisdiction in April. See "Decree on Troops Stationed in Moldova Issued," ITAR-TASS, April 1, 1992, in FBIS-SOV, April 1, 1992, p. 27. Forces stationed outside the former USSR had been placed under Russian jurisdiction in March 1992. "Decree on Jurisdiction of Troops Released," ITAR-TASS, March 10, 1992, in FBIS-SOV, March 10, 1992, pp. 20-21.

8. In 1991 there were over 100,000 Soviet troops stationed in the Baltic states.

By late 1992 there were an estimated 50,000 Russian troops, and by September 1993 this figure had dropped to about 14,000 to 16,000 in Latvia and 4,500 in Estonia. See Dzintra Bungs, "Progress on Withdrawal from the Baltic States," *RFE/RL Research Report*, no. 25, June 18, 1993, pp. 50-59, and Baltic News Service, September 9, 1993, and September 2, 1993.

9. For a detailed discussion of the military's position on the withdrawal see Stephen Foye, "Russian Politics Complicates Baltic Troop Withdrawal," *RFE/RL Research Report*, no. 46, November 20, 1992, pp. 30-35.

10. See "Details of Delegation's Armenia Visit Reported," *Pravda*, May 26, 1992, p. 1, in FBIS-SOV, May 28, 1992, p. 25. Two divisions are to remain in Armenia, according to "Former Soviet Troops Continue Withdrawal," ITAR-TASS, June 13, 1992, in FBIS-SOV, June 15, 1992, p. 58.

11. Interfax, February 18, 1993.

12. See *Krasnaia zvezda*, May 27, 1992, p. 2; Russian TV, May 26, 1993. For details on the Russian withdrawal from Azerbaijan see Elizabeth Fuller, "Paramilitary Forces Dominate Fighting in Transcaucasus," *RFE/RL Research Report*, no. 25, June 18, 1993, pp. 79-80.

13. Reuters, February 4, 1993.

14. ITAR-TASS, October 9, 1993.

15. For a more detailed discussion of the role of the Fourteenth Army in Moldova, see Vladimir Socor, "The Fourteenth Army in Moldova: There to Stay?" *RFE/RL Research Report* 2, no. 25, June 18, 1993, pp. 42-49.

16. *RFE/RL Daily Report*, November 17, 1992, November 24, 1992, November 27, 1992, Interfax February 1, 1993.

17. *Nezavisimaia gazeta*, June 16, 1992, p. 3. Interfax April 22, 1993.

18. *Krasnaia zvezda*, May 20, 1993., p. 2.

19. This section is in part based upon John W.R. Lepingwell, "Restructuring the Russian Military," Stephen Wegren, "Private Farming and Agrarian Reform in Russia," *Problems of Communism*, no. 3, May-June 1992, pp. 107-121. *RFE/RL Research Report* 2, no. 25, June 18, 1993, pp. 17-24.

20. Reuters, November 16, 1992. The most recent, and one of the more detailed, expositions of the military reform plan was published in *Rossiiskie vesti*, January 4, 1993, p. 4.

21. The doctrine was published in a special edition of the Russian military journal *Voennaia mysl* in mid-1992. For a discussion of the implications of the doctrine see Scott McMichael, "Russia's New Military Doctrine," *RFE/RL Research Report*, no. 40, October 9, 1992, pp. 45-50.

22. See Grachev's comments in *Rossiiskie vesti*, January 4, 1993 p. 4 and *Rossiiskie vesti*, March 6, 1993, p. 2.

23. *RFE/RL Daily Report*, February 15, 1993.

24. Interfax, December 14, 1992. *RFE/RL Daily Report*, March 2, 1993. Later reports indicate the staffing level may have declined even further. See Stephen Foye, "Rebuilding the Russian Armed Forces: Rhetoric and Realities," *RFE/RL Research Report* 2, no. 30, July 23, 1993, pp. 49-57.

25. *Rossiiskie vesti*, November 4, 1992, p. 2.

26. *Krasnaia zvezda*, October 3, 1992.

27. It is extremely difficult to compare defense budgets over time. It is clear,

however, that productivity in the defense sector has declined drastically in the last few years. For information on the 1992 Russian defense budget and plans for 1993 see Interfax, October 8, 1992 and October 13, 1992.

28. *The New York Times*, October 7, 1993.

29. I make this argument in more detail in "Soviet Civil-Military Relations and the August Coup," *World Politics* 44, No. 4, July 1992, pp. 539-572.

30. Poll results showing high public confidence in the military may be found in Mark Rhodes, "Political Attitudes in Russia," *RFE/RL Research Report* 2, no. 3, January 15, 1993, pp. 42-44.

31. In an interview on Russian television on February 28, 1993, General Grachev noted that servicemen's salaries had been increased seven-fold in 1992 and another 2.3 times in 1993. The increases were episodic, however, and probably did not fully compensate for the rate of inflation, which saw price increases of somewhere between 15- and 20-fold. See S.S. Solovev and S. Ianin, "Naskolko zashchishchen zashchitnik Otechestva," *Armiia*, no. 19, 1993, pp. 17-19.

32. There are some retraining programs available for Russian officers that are intended to ease their transition into the civilian economy, but these appear to be inadequate to meet the demand for them. See ITAR-TASS, February 4, 1993.

33. For arguments to this effect see Lepingwell, "Soviet Civil-Military Relations," pp. 559-561.

34. For a discussion of the military's role see Stephen Foye, "Confrontation in Moscow: The Army Backs Yeltsin...For Now," *RFE/RL Research Report* 2, no. 42, October 22, 1993.

35. This was an almost unprecedented development in twentieth century Russian history. Yet in the context of extreme political instability, the military may be a decisive player in domestic affairs (as the experience of Latin America shows), and therefore its disposition is likely to be a critical factor in the future.

36. Lepingwell, "The Soviet Military and the August Coup," p. 571.

37. See Victor Yasmann, "Corruption in Russia: A Threat to Democracy?" *RFE/RL Research Report* 2, no. 10, March 5, 1993, pp. 15-18, especially pp. 16-17.

38. *Krasnaia zvezda*, March 16, 1993, p. 2; *Izvestiia*, February 10, 1993, p. 1.

39. Lepingwell, "Soviet Civil-Military Relations," pp. 550-552.

40. *RFE/RL Daily Report*, February 8, 1993.

41. The legislative branch was represented on the Security Council by Sergei Filatov, the first deputy speaker of the Supreme Soviet who later joined the executive branch. There appears to have been no representative of the legislative branch up to the time of its dissolution in October.

8

Disintegration and Russian Foreign Policy

Douglas W. Blum

The purpose of this chapter is to move closer to understanding some of the problems and prospects for Russian foreign policy during this uncertain period by considering the interaction between domestic and foreign policy. In particular, it asks how the opposing forces of consolidation and disintegration affect foreign policy, and how foreign policy affects them.

As a first step, the relationship between domestic stability and foreign policy will be explored by examining several developments central to Russia's prospects for consolidation or disintegration: ethnic or national separatism, Islamic fundamentalism, territorial claims by outside states, and purely territorial (non-ethnic) assertions of political-economic independence. The purpose is to highlight some of the ways these factors affect foreign policy calculations. Second, in order to uncover the nature of Russian foreign policy and its influence on domestic cohesiveness, this chapter will examine divergent elite perspectives on international politics, and will consider their implications for state behavior.

Types of Disintegration and Foreign Policy

Ethnic or National Separatism

The most visible and widespread challenge to the integrity of the Russian federation arises from the passionate claims of local ethnic minorities who are now asserting their long-suppressed identities. Some groups located wholly within the Russian federation have demanded full autonomy (for example, Bashkortostan) or even outright independence (Chechnia). In other cases groups are based partly or largely outside Russia, and this poses the danger of conflict between Russian and outside nationalities. Obvious examples include Transcaucasia, with numerous Turkic groups that look to Turkey for aid and political guidance; or Buriatia and Tuva, with their orientations toward Mongolia.[1] Such conflicts have the potential to exacerbate tensions between Russia and other former Soviet republics, as in the case of Lezgin demands for a united Lezgistan that would include Dagestan as well as part of northern Azerbaijan.[2]

Similar dangers lurk throughout the CIS. To take a hypothetical situation, pan-Azeri agitation in Azerbaijan might inflame ethnic brethren across the borders in Iran and in Central Asian republics, which, in turn, could lead to unrest within Russia. In such an eventuality Iran, Turkey, or both could conceivably become involved.[3] A similar problem is raised by the independent foreign policy being pursued by Chechnia, as well as by Tatarstan and Bashkortostan, all of which have close political ties with Turkey. On one hand, it is true that Chechens and Ingush are not ethnic Turks. On the other hand, they have close political affinities with Turkey, and there are important ethnic links between Turkey and Turkic groups such as the Kumyks, Adygeians, Karachais, and others. Despite the fact that Turkey's presence is valued as a counterweight to radical Islam, the prospect of Ankara's looming hegemony in the south is disquieting for Moscow.

The short-term implications for Russian consolidation are unclear. At least in comparison to Chechnia, Tatarstan has been relatively circumspect so far, gingerly exploring its options on the diplomatic front. Yet while Tartarstan's President Mintimer Shaimiev won points for coordinating his visit to Ankara with the authorities in Moscow, there was a predictably sharp reaction to Tatarstan's recognition of the "Turkish Republic of North Cyprus," which, in view of its implications for Russian disintegration, drew criticism even from the liberal press for "failing to consider all the complexities of the problem."[4] Or, to take a related issue, there has been significant trilateral co-operation between Kazakhstan, Tatarstan, and Bashkortostan, including the signing of a formal protocol.[5] Under conditions of rapid disintegration, and depending on prevailing attitudes in the Russian government, it is conceivable that such relations might lead to serious tensions between Moscow and Alma-Ata. Additional examples of pro-Turkic or other irredentist elements might be offered as well.[6] In response, the Yeltsin regime has adopted an increasingly forceful approach. As the examples of Abkhazia and North Ossetia show, separatist movements may be instrumentally useful for Moscow up to a point. The disastrous collapse of Georgian control over Abkhazia forced the Shevardnadze regime into accepting Russian interference and precipitated Georgia's entrance into the CIS and the new Economic Union, as well as acceptance of Russian troops stationed on Georgian soil. Indeed, it appears that certain elements within the Russian military (and in the former parliament) lent active support to the separatists, perhaps hoping to revive the Soviet

Union in fact if not in name.[7] On the other hand, the Abkhazian precedent is not a happy one from the standpoint of Russian disintegration, and the central government cannot endorse armed separatism in the "near abroad" without legitimizing similar tendencies at home. Consequently, the official position of the Russian government has followed an uneasy mix of policies: using the separatist movements to pressure Georgia while at the same time trying to place limits on the rebels' demands, and resisting their requests for incorporation in the Russian Federation.[8]

As in the case of Russo-Georgian relations, ethnic separatism may affect, and be affected by, bilateral diplomatic ties. Germany is an example of the paradoxical implications of close diplomatic relations, as in the case of the German government's financial support for fellow nationals remaining in Russia who wish to resettle the Volga region and reclaim autonomous status. To some extent, compliance with German wishes is a form of quid pro quo for generous economic and political assistance.[9] Furthermore, the Bonn government has encouraged Germans to remain in Russia, and has not endorsed any extreme separatist demands. Some Russians worry that this poses a problem by inviting other states to exert similar pressures, and by reinforcing the legitimacy of claims based on ethnic particularism, something which many Russians resent.[10]

While ethnic particularism on the whole may bode ill for Russian national unity, in some instances it may be considered tactically advantageous from the standpoint of preserving Russian administrative and territorial integrity, at least temporarily. On the one hand there is a danger of spiraling regional conflict that might involve outside powers, but on the other hand there is the prospect of manipulating nationalist or irredentist sentiment in order to deflect separatist tendencies and channel them against other states. Thus, North Ossetian separatism has been restrained due to military hostilities with Ingushetia, which raise North Ossetia's need for Russian military aid. As already discussed, Russia has an interest in maintaining North Ossetian dependence *vis-a-vis* the conflict with Georgia over South Ossetia, and this provides a rationale for backing North Ossetian rather than Ingush claims to Prigorodnyi district. At the same time, however, Russia has an interest in not allowing separatism to get out of hand in the form of a Greater Ossetia, either independent or united with the Russian Federation. As a result, official policy has reflected an attempt to play both sides off against each other, thereby promoting their reliance on the center.[11] The same is true of the conflict between Chechnia and Dagestan over the Aukhovskii district. The central government's support for Dagestan is directed against Chechnia, but it is also instrumental in terms of diverting separatism within Dagestan itself. Similar complexities routinely affect calculations about how to advance Russian regional interests while promoting domestic consolidation.[12]

Islamic Fundamentalism

The specter of Islam has been raised time and again in debates over Russian foreign policy and national disintegration. In part this is a long-standing and somewhat irrational anxiety, and the existence of splits between extremists and moderates within the Islamic movement are often overlooked. In fact, Islam often appears to be a vehicle for expressing nationalist sentiment and cultural particularism, rather than a driving force behind disintegration.[13] Islam has played a subsidiary and largely symbolic role in Tatarstan's secessionism. For example, one demonstration of Tatar sovereignty was construction of the largest mosque in Russia. Furthermore, the president of Chechnia, Gen. Dzhokar Dudaev, has been unsuccessful in his efforts to use Islam for his own political purposes.[14] The overriding issue appears to be ethnic rather than religious affiliation, as demonstrated by the alliance between Christian Abkhazians and Muslim Mountain Peoples against Christian Georgians. On the other hand, the Islamic factor is clearly a wild card in southern Central Asia, where the civil unrest in Tajikistan threatens the stability of other former Soviet republics. The role of Islamic Renaissance Party and other Islamic groups in this conflict causes consternation in Russia, both from the standpoint of national disintegration and the foreign policy dilemmas it creates.[15]

To some degree Russia's relations with all its southern neighbors are affected by the interaction between Islam, outside influence-mongering, and domestic stability. Afghanistan and perhaps Iraq are considered the main state supporters of fundamentalism. Iran's influence is felt, even though most Muslims in Russia and the CIS are Sunni Muslims. In addition, Pakistan, Turkey, and Saudi Arabia have been actively involved in supporting different elements within the variegated Islamic movement, each for its own purposes. Such outside involvements are variously regarded as a challenge to Russia's position, or as posing a danger of destabilization in Central Asia.[16]

Official Russian policy has attempted to establish balanced, normalized relations with all the important regional players, partly in hopes of gaining some leverage on the Islamic question. Particular efforts to strengthen relations with Turkey, which is seen as a major and potentially moderating force within the Islamic movement, have been aimed partly at this issue. Russia has also played an extensive role in attempting to secure the southern borders of the CIS, including preventing arms from flowing across the Afghan border and spearheading implementation of a collective security mechanism for stabilizing the situation in Tajikistan.[17]

Territorial Claims by Outside Powers

A third category of trends that threatens Russian prospects for consolidation is territorial demands by foreign states for control of land lying within

Russian federation borders. This involves disintegration in the most literal sense, and if existing challenges are multiplied, this could become a severely destabilizing development from Europe to the Far East. So far, the most troublesome disputes concern the so-called "northern territories" (the Kuril Islands and Sakhalin) and Kaliningrad.

In the case of the Kuril Islands, a dispute dating to the end of World War II has been a stubborn irritant in bilateral relations, despite repeated efforts by Gorbachev and Yeltsin to reopen negotiations. Important differences exist among Russian political circles regarding how best to respond, with some observers favoring concessions and others taking an adamant stand. Yeltsin cancelled his planned state visit to Japan in September 1992 amid rising nationalist opposition to concessions on this issue. Plans to reschedule the visit arose only after the Group of Seven meeting in mid-April 1993, at which the Japanese yielded to pressure from the United States and Western Europe and committed substantial aid to Russia. Still, the visit in October 1993 produced no breakthroughs. In the interim, due to the ongoing deadlock, Russia explored diplomatic alternatives to Japan. One result has been a perceptible shift toward South Korea, and to a significant extent toward China as well.[18]

Kaliningrad has been the object of Lithuanian demands for immediate withdrawal of Russian troops, as well as cession of territory, and there are forces tending to draw the province out of Russian control and into a zone of Polish-Baltic economic activity. Furthermore, some Russian observers have expressed fears about possible German interests in reacquiring lost territory in what was formerly part of East Prussia, annexed by the USSR in 1945. Such fears have been strengthened by the existence of the Freiheit group, a small but vociferous minority of Russian Germans who have demanded to resettle Kaliningrad. To date, however, the German government has been willing to work toward a mutually acceptable arrangement that would allow open access and flow of trade.[19]

Despite numerous other territories that might in the future be subject to outside claims, there are no other major controversies now. One less hotly contested area is Karelia, which became Russian territory during World War II as an outcome of the Molotov-Ribbentrop protocol. Although the Finnish government has not pressed this issue, it has been raised at the official level and could conceivably become more urgent in the future.[20]

Finally, a special case concerns the Crimean Peninsula, which has not officially been part of the Russian Federation since 1954, when Khrushchev transferred it to the Ukrainian republic. Its disposition as Russian or Ukrainian territory is currently a topic of bitter dispute, and to some Russians involves the question of national patrimony. And, at some point the Chinese government might become interested in reviewing the "unequal treaties" of the mid-nineteenth century.

Non-Ethnic Assertions of Territorial Sovereignty

The general economic collapse has spawned myriad local calls for sovereignty, autarky, or outright independence, as well as various alternatives to the ineffectual plans advocated by the central government. The main issues have been discussed by Sergei Khrushchev in Chapter 6 and will not be repeated here, but it is worth highlighting their significance for foreign policy.

The relationship between territorial fragmentation and Russian foreign policy is an indirect one. The key question is whether the center can generate any consistent and workable policy that a given separatist movement might be willing to accept. Any such approach necessarily carries foreign policy corollaries. For example, the implications of shock-therapy marketization include openness to the West and willingness to accept essential elements of the International Monetary Fund plan. While this might ultimately have succeeded enough to allow market-oriented elites such as those in Nizhnii Novgorod to be co-opted, it inflamed separatist passions in many areas where elites favor higher prices than are now allowed for indigenous resources (such as for gas or oil) or freedom from painful social adjustments on the road to market.[21] Thus, for example, the failure of central government to intervene on behalf of beleaguered areas in the north might lead to an independent Far Eastern Association that leans toward the Association of Southeast Asian Nations or Japan, or even China, with obvious import for Moscow's security concerns.

In contrast, local elites who favor gradual or more limited reforms have advocated extensive state subsidies and restrictions on foreign trade and investment. This philosophy became increasingly influential over the past year, and the Yeltsin regime has attempted to negotiate investment deals that would allow the center to reap economic dividends while still catering to local demands.[22] But any scheme involving an intrusive role for central government would generate enormous resistance in other areas, such as Sakha or Tatarstan, which are interested in pursuing the most lucrative foreign contracts free from Moscow's interference. Local resistance to perceived overcentralization could result in closer economic and political ties with outside actors, such as a tighter union between Tatarstan, Bashkortostan, and Chuvashia, which looks to Turkey or other states to the south for aid and investment.

Foreign Policy Orientations

While these basic issues connect domestic disintegration and foreign policy, the question is how they are perceived by important elements of the Russian elite, and what approaches are advocated for managing them. Without recklessly oversimplifying, it is possible to distinguish several distinct ideological orientations in Russia at present: liberal, statist, and national-patriotic.[23] Each is associated with a significantly different approach for dealing with threats to Russia's territorial and political integrity.

As a caveat, it should be noted that in reality these alternative perspectives are not mutually exclusive, and not all individuals are locked into a given world view. Instead, the relative prevalence of one or another perspective reflects the overall mix of values, operational assumptions, and policy priorities within the elite at any time. Despite its shortcomings, this approach may be useful in identifying key themes and assessing their policy relevance.

A second caveat is that Russian President Boris Yeltsin has straddled the political spectrum in a unique manner, and his views are not systematically included in any of the orientations discussed below. While surrounding himself mainly with liberal reformers at the outset, Yeltsin carefully preserved his ability to manipulate different constituencies, and during 1993 he moved toward a centrist position. Furthermore, his own inclinations appear to be a mixture, including primarily liberal approaches to domestic economic reform and openness to the West, along with occasional strikingly hard-line attitudes toward threats to national unity.[24] It is possible that Yeltsin will reemerge as a dominant figure following the dissolution of the obstructionist parliament. Yet given the fluidity of the political situation and the emergence of strong challengers, his personal influence in the future must be considered highly uncertain.

The following section describes the general assumptions and values associated with the liberal, statist, and national-patriotic perspectives on foreign policy, and links them with key themes of domestic disintegration. The question is how proponents of each outlook react to various internal and external developments, and how such developments affect their political viability.

The Liberal Orientation

Until the end of 1992, the official line in Russian foreign policy mirrored the liberal perspective associated with Foreign Minister Andrei Kozyrev and others within the Foreign Ministry and the academic community. This outlook resembles the tenets of classical liberalism, with its emphasis on human rights, the peaceful nature of democracies, the mutual benefits of open borders and interstate cooperation, and the possibility of transforming international affairs through enlightened choice. The liberal orientation in foreign policy is marked by a self-image of Russia as a "normal" great power. This image is fairly restrained; although Russia's place among the leading powers is regarded as a birthright, at the same time the Soviet Union's former arrogance and pretensions to dominance over other states is rejected. Russia is often envisioned as a "guarantor of stability" in Eurasia or as a leading spiritual force capable of galvanizing global cooperation.[25] An example concerns the civil unrest in Tajikistan. As articulated by Foreign Minister Andrei Kozyrev and other liberal figures, Russia's objective has been to restore political stability in Tajikistan and throughout the region rather than engaging in geopolitical jockeying.[26]

Indeed, far from challenging the international order, liberals have expressed a desire to affiliate with the leading states and international institutions, and have suggested that partnership relations might be consolidated with only limited competition and no serious frictions.[27] Finally, another characteristic of liberalism is its negative attitude toward military coercion. In this viewpoint, the use of force aggravates conflicts and makes them less amenable to resolution.[28]

It is possible to identify several important links between liberal foreign policy views and approaches to managing disintegrative trends. One such link is the priority accorded to the principle of national self-determination. Some liberals regard it as an absolute principle, applicable to international as well as domestic politics. This implies the wholesale rejection of force as a response to ethnic or political-economic separatism, despite the unwelcome consequences of separatism in the short term.[29]

Others refuse to elevate the principle of national self-determination to an absolute value, or they place limits on its applicability to domestic politics. This translates into somewhat greater willingness to use force in extreme cases, particularly if geographically or economically critical areas are involved.[30] Yet short of the truly extreme, liberals are willing to accept substantial decentralization and local autonomy based on ethnic or territorial criteria, within a federal context.[31] There also tends to be a heightened sensitivity to Western concerns about human rights abuses, and this provides an additional reason for not using force.[32]

Liberals accept religious and cultural heterogeneity in Russia, and tend to be sensitive to the desires of outside states and ethnic groups to fashion their own self-identities. Consequently, from the liberal perspective Islam is not considered inherently threatening, but merely part of the diverse cultural mix expressed by the broadly inclusive definition of "Russianness" (*rossiiane*). Likewise, liberal commentators have warned against building a new Russian identity on the basis of Orthodoxy since this would intensify separatist trends among non-Orthodox groups, both at home and throughout the CIS.[33]

Another important linkage between foreign and domestic policy concerns the liberal free-trade orientation in foreign economic relations. This is connected with the assumption that the Group of Seven states will find it in their own interests to help Russia modernize and join the front rank of developed countries. Denying the necessity of painful trade-offs, liberals typically assert that foreign economic openness will bolster Russian economic growth and enhance productivity and competitiveness without jeopardizing national security.[34] While the resulting autonomy granted to local elites may be welcome in some areas, as Khrushchev notes in Chapter 6 it also intensifies the drift toward economic disintegration.

As mentioned, the liberal approach tends to seek compromises in interstate disputes, and this relates to the question of outside territorial claims. The outstanding example is the wrangle with Japan over possession of the Kuril Islands. Liberals have favored the increasingly unpopular idea of shared sovereignty or even gradual removal of Russian control in return for continued access. Association with such policies has done much to discredit liberalism in the eyes of a considerable segment of the populace. For example, Ambassador Lukin was subjected to harsh criticisms for suggesting such an approach, and pressure to avoid any "capitulation" on this issue was the main factor that caused Yeltsin to cancel his official visit in 1992.[35] Similarly, liberals have been optimistic about the prospects for achieving a stable *modus vivendi* with Germany and Lithuania on the status of Kaliningrad.[36]

Finally, it should be noted that a reverse relationship between domestic and foreign policy also exists: trends in the direction of disintegration have helped to discredit the liberal foreign policy line. In particular, the failure to halt centrifugal tendencies by means of accommodation has raised doubts about whether this tactic is advisable in general, either at home or abroad. This is especially true of developments in the immediate periphery, where outcomes feed back directly upon the situation in Russia. Calls for patience, conciliation, and mutual respect have become less attractive to many who feel the need for a strong hand at the helm to defend Russia's interests.

The Statist Perspective

The leading proponents of statism describe themselves as moderates or centrists, and although statism differs from liberalism in important ways, it is certainly not a drastic negation of liberal principles. Statism resonates with traditional realpolitik assumptions about international relations, including the competitive nature of politics, the importance of power, and the legitimacy of spheres of influence. Statists emphasize Russia's self-image as a "great power," and reject the servile obeisance to Western priorities and institutions that they ascribe to the liberal view.[37] Thus, while there is general recognition of the value of Western political and economic support, there is also resentment and geopolitical wariness. As Ramazan Abdulatipov, formerly the chairman of the Supreme Soviet Council of Nationalities, remarked in opposition to the International Monetary Fund program, "It would be better to go hungry for a few days than to lose one's pride and independence for decades."[38] This is linked to the perception that Western powers are attempting to extend their influence into the traditional Russian sphere, and carries the prescription to engage in hardball economic competition.[39]

In keeping with their stridently independent position, statists are not inhibited from taking actions that might evoke righteous indignation abroad, including use of force to ensure the security of Russian borders or for defense of Russian nationals abroad.[40] Also, in contrast to the liberals' aversion to using force, statists emphasize the importance of deterrence and the need to establish resolve.[41] As Sergei Stankevich declared,

> If our partners, while conducting with us peaceful diplomatic negotiations, in parallel continue a ruthless slaughter, and we agree to such a dialogue, very soon we will stop being taken seriously, because with us anything is possible.[42]

As with liberalism, there is an important interconnection between statist foreign policy perspectives and attitudes for dealing with domestic disintegration. Of course, the most direct contrast to liberalism is that the statist outlook demands stricter limits to disintegrative trends. Not only is military power perceived to play a potentially important role in foreign policy, it is also considered a viable option at home.[43] On the other hand there may be a growing willingness to bow to the inevitable and accept full autonomy in certain areas that are considered relatively expendable, such as Chechnia.[44]

Because of such concerns about domestic stabilization, statists are especially sensitive to regional security threats. On the one hand, closer ties with Turkey, Pakistan, Iran, and Afghanistan are welcomed for providing markets, sources of investment, and enhanced legitimacy for the Russian government. On the other hand, there is considerable wariness about the influence of regional powers, which might erode Russia's position and ultimately exacerbate internal disintegration. Perceived meddling in Russia's internal affairs on behalf of ethnic brethren might be expected to bring a sharper reaction from a statist regime, including threats to engage in counter-subversion. A striking example of this came when former Azerbaijani President Abulfaz Elchibei welcomed Tatarstan's declaration of independence by referring to traditional Tatar-Turkic affinities. Stankevich responded angrily in an open letter, warning against Azeri interference in Russian affairs.[45]

Similar concerns are reflected in the "limited sovereignty" approach to the CIS, under which a much tighter form of integration would evolve under the guidance of strengthened central institutions.[46] This approach was reflected in a series of initiatives during mid-1993, aimed at bringing former Soviet republics securely within the Russian sphere of influence. This included indirect military leverage in Azerbaijan and Georgia, in which Russian ability to aid or inhibit armed separatist movements was a key factor in the decision of both states to join the CIS. In addition, the Yeltsin regime used powerful economic leverage (including threats to discontinue trade in oil and gas) to manipulate the CIS member states into accepting a new arrangement according to which a virtually unified economic policy would be anchored by Russian institutions.[47]

In addition to the direct benefits of closer cooperation, statists also anticipate greater control over centrifugal processes within Russia, since in a tighter union Russia would have greater weight in dealings with member states. For example, it might be easier for Russia to persuade Kazakhstan not to interfere in Bashkortostan and Tatarstan, and to exert influence with regard to Russians living in Kazakhstan.[48] For these reasons a number of military and civilian figures have called for a special status for Russia, giving it the right to intervene in local conflicts throughout the area of the former Soviet Union.[49]

However, statists are reluctant to support non-Russian ethnic claims outside Russian borders since this might have unwelcome reverberations at home. This is reflected in the official stand on the conflict between Armenia and Azerbaijan over Nagorno-Karabakh, where, despite Russia's closer ties with Armenia, Moscow has refused to provide unambiguous support. Of course several issues are involved here, including a cautious reluctance to burn bridges with Baku, which has been fruitful since Geidar Aliev's return to power. But a significant factor appears to be concern for the domestic ramifications of supporting Armenian claims. Similarly, there is staunch resistance to the idea of Russia's participating in joint intervention in former Yugoslavia, not least because of the precedent it might set for outside involvement in ethnic disputes within Russia or throughout its sphere of influence.[50] Similarly, the importance of stability in the Middle East for the stability of the Central Asian states and southern Russia leads some to oppose the introduction of disturbing influences of any kind, whether Iraqi expansionism or American intervention.[51]

Finally, statism's strong geopolitical emphasis and perceived need to demonstrate resolve is expressed in a refusal to give up strategic resources or to accede to outside territorial claims. This has been a major point of resistance in the impasse over the Kuril Islands.[52] Moreover, the former Supreme Soviet repudiated the 1954 transfer of the Crimea to Ukraine, and prominent statist figures have been at the forefront of this movement.[53] A skeptical realist sensibility also influences attitudes toward outside states, even those as friendly as Germany, which may be suspected of harboring designs on Russian land.[54]

The National-Patriotic Orientation

Nationalists of various hues and stripes populate the political landscape of Russia, and it is difficult to generalize about the current and prospective influence of nationalism as a whole. Still, it is possible to differentiate a relatively mainstream variant of nationalism, which includes many prominent figures whose views largely fall under the statist rubric, from a more extremist variant. The latter, which will be referred to as national-patriotism, is dealt with here.[55]

The national self-image associated with this outlook is transformational or even messianic, emphasizing the exclusive characteristics of Russia. National-patriotism is often associated with fantasies of a powerful Slavic union led by Russia, and including all of the brethren Slavic peoples of middle Europe. Or, it may stress the rightfully exalted status of "greater Russia," as the embodiment of essential human values, or as the natural core of a Eurasian empire.[56]

Whatever the particular fantasy, there is general agreement that Russia's objectives should be to consolidate and extend its sphere of influence at the expense of its competitors. National-patriots share a strong distrust of all outside actors, including international agencies, and consequently express a preference for unilateral solutions. For example, Aleksandr Sterligov of Russian National Congress has called for massive counter-intervention against peace-keeping troops in Yugoslavia on behalf of Russia's "Slavic brethren."[57] Not uncommonly, such views are combined with xenophobia and projections of anti-Russianism, which is attributed to jealousy or evil. In its most virulent forms this includes a notion of embattled Russia struggling to regain its glorious Slavic empire, while being beseiged from within and without by Western imperialists, Zionists, liberals, and the like.[58] From this standpoint, national-patriots are adamantly opposed to disintegration, which is seen as having both a geopolitical and spiritual dimension. Russia's rightful predominance ought to be asserted, and this calls for a powerful state to which local elites are subordinate and within which minority groups are subsumed.[59] In this view, neither ethnic nor territorial separatism can be tolerated, and foreign economic relations must be tightly regulated.

The strategic assumptions of national-patriotism are overwhelmingly geared to deterrence, and are accompanied by recurrent images of snowballing threats and falling dominoes. The international balance of power is perceived as multipolar and characterized by shifting coalitions. Not surprisingly, many of the most cherished values are linked to military power. The army represents vital defensive might and is at the same time a repository of national virtue, and a bastion of the forceful resolution needed to reassert Russia's imperial sway.[60] In their policy prescriptions, national-patriotic types also tend to recommend heavy reliance on force, with no distinction drawn between its internal or external application. Thus, Commander of the Fourteenth Army Aleksandr Lebed calls for re-annexation of the "Dnestr Republic," and has called for Russians to take up arms against Moldovans in defense; and the National Salvation Front has advocated military intervention against the Baltic states in defense of Russian nationals.[61] In cases such as Chechnia's or Tatarstan's declarations of independence, national-patriots favor military solutions to preserve unity.

While an alliance with the West is virtually ruled out, the possibility of siding with Islamic states has been suggested by some, and national-patriotic and holdover communist figures sharply criticized the American military campaign launched against Iraq in the waning days of the Bush presidency.[62] This interest may be partly the result of anti-Westernism and anti-Semitism, and may partly reflect concerns about sullying Russia's image as a reliable ally by abandoning ties from the Soviet period. Others, however, are much more suspicious or even overtly hostile toward the Islamic movement, viewing it as a powerful rival force and as a danger to Russian Orthodoxy.[63] This latter view carries obvious implications for Islamic fundamentalism as a disintegrative force within Russia, since these individuals favor a strict policy of curbing any ethnic or religious movements that challenge the center's authority.

Conclusion

The preceding examination of Russian foreign policy has revealed some of the complex interconnections between external affairs and the prospects for domestic consolidation. Obviously, diplomatic relations with Ukraine, Lithuania, Germany, Finland, and Japan affect, and are affected by, the existence of territorial disputes. Yet there are important links between foreign policy and other factors related to disintegration as well, including ethnic separatism, Islamic fundamentalism, and local (non-ethnic) assertions of autonomy.

Foreign policy bears on the problems of ethnic separatism and Islamic fundamentalism by influencing relations with states that various groups look to for self-identification and support. Official ties with these external actors affect the avenues available to them for exerting influence on indigenous populations, and this may have an impact on the directions that separatist movements take within Russia. The general foreign policy orientation exerts influence more subtly by its acceptance or rejection of prevailing international institutions and norms that may be applicable to domestic affairs. Finally, foreign policy indirectly influences the pragmatic calculations of local elites concerning the cost-benefit ratio of close relations with the Russian Federation and compliance with central decrees.[64] Liberalism, statism, and national-patriotism offer different perceptions of these issues and propose different ways of dealing with them.

Indeed, as we have seen, general foreign policy orientations are deeply interrelated with assumptions about how to manage disintegrative processes in Russia. The statist orientation perceives a competitive international environment, and prescribes assertiveness and unilateral actions abroad. At the same time its requisite notion of a strong state carries important implications for domestic policy, including subsidization and political latitude for compliant elites, as well as more forceful interventionist attempts to achieve national consolidation if necessary. The liberal view, on the other hand, assumes a more benign image of international politics and a more interdependent notion of great power standing, in which Russia is at once a competitor, collaborator, and co-author of a new international order based on openness and human rights. This is linked to a far more laissez-faire approach to domestic affairs than that envisioned by statists. Finally, the national-patriotic orientation sees a hostile international setting, and places a premium on maintaining allegedly pure Russian values. This leads to calls for radical domestic centralization, coupled with foreign policy balancing or expansionism.

By 1993, the continued drift toward disintegration had contributed to the emergence of statism as the dominant perspective in politics.[65] This has resulted in a more assertive foreign policy line and a less accommodating attitude towards the CIS and the other former Soviet republics, especially in defense of Russian nationals or when the unity of Russia is at stake.[66] In the context of domestic political instability and regional turbulence, this general trend appears likely to continue.

Yet while statism is ascendant now and for the foreseeable future, important ideological challengers are waiting in the wings should it fail. The liberal line has not fallen into eclipse, and its resonance with political views in developed states suggests that it will continue to provide an alternative orientation in the future. Extreme nationalists and holdover communists were greatly overrepresented in the Congress of People's Deputies, and their popular appeal is quite limited. Yet if separatist trends continue and economic stabilization remains elusive, more dangerous forms of social dislocation and ethnic unrest may ensue, and extremist views may become more attractive. Furthermore, if, as Lepingwell warns in Chapter 7, the military breaks apart and local commanders become increasingly independent of central control, it may be impossible for authorities in Moscow to prevent provocative actions leading to regional war. Lack of vigorous economic and political support by the international community may help to discredit even relatively accommodating world views and thereby contribute, at least at the margins, to the likelihood of such developments. In this event a very different pattern of domestic and foreign policy would emerge, with powerful and lingering effects on Russian development and international politics.

Notes

1. "Sudorogi kompromissa," *Nezavisimaia gazeta*, May 7, 1992, p. 3; also Toomas Alatalu, "Tuva - a State Awakens," *Soviet Studies* 44, no. 5, 1992, pp. 881-895. For analysis of these and other examples see *Sotsialno-politicheskaia sitsuatsiia v postsovetskom mire* (Moscow: Tsentr etnopoliticheskikh issledovanii), monthly reports.

2. "Lezginskaia problema obostriaetsia," *Nezavisimaia gazeta*, March 27, 1993, p. 3.

3. "Lidery Kazakhstana i Azerbaidzhana v Moskve," *Nezavisimaia gazeta*, September 7, 1993, pp. 1, 3.

4. "Dikaia diplomatiia," *Nezavisimaia gazeta*, November 18, 1992, p. 4. For an overview of Tatarstan's growing diplomatic and foreign economic agenda, see "Slitno ili razdelno?" *Izvestiia*, March 11, 1993, p. 4.

5. KazTAG-TASS, August 19, 1992.

6. See the report by the Institute of Socio-Political Research, *Sotsialnaia i sotsialno-politicheskaia situatsiia v Rossii: sostoianie i prognoz*, Moscow, 1993, pp. 24-25.

7. T. Goltz, "Letter From Eurasia: The Hidden Russian Hand," *Foreign Policy*, no. 92, Fall 1993, pp. 92-116.

8. Interview with Kozyrev, "Mirotvorchestvo stoit nemalo. No otkaz ot nego eshche dorozhe," *Krasnaia zvezda*, September 1, 1993, p. 3; also see the earlier government statement, "Vooruzhennyi Konflikt v Abkhazii: obrashchenie pravitelstva Rossii," Izvestiia, October 13, 1993, p. 1.

9. "Rossiia i Germaniia dali svet novomu pokoleniiu dogovorov," *Izvestiia*, December 17, 1992, p. 4.

10. L. Pochivalov and O. Prudkov, "Rossiiskie nemtsy: uekhat ili ostatsia," *Literaturnaia gazeta*, no. 51, December 16, 1992, p. 13.

11. *Sotsialno-politicheskaia situatsiia v postsovetskom mire*, esp. pp. 29-32.

12. For a general discussion of this point, see K.S. Gadzhiev, "Geopoliticheskie perspektivy Kavkaza v strategii Rossii," *Mirovaia ekonomika i mezhdunarodnye otnosheniia* 2, 1993, pp. 20-37, esp. 24-25.

13. Ibid, pp. 30-32.

14. On symbolic uses of Islam, see *RFE/RL Research Report*, August 14, 1992, p. 79; and "Muftii, mully, imamy i politika," *Nezavisimaia gazeta*, October 24, 1992, p. 3. I am indebted to Professor Sergei Arutunian of the Russian Institute of Ethnology and Anthropology for discussion of this issue.

15. For a background discussion, see *Afghanistan and Post-Soviet Central Asia: Prospects for Political Evolution and the Role of Islam* (Washington, DC: United States Institute of Peace, 1992).

16. Vladimir Skosyrev, "Islamskie ekstremisty otvergaiut ideiu primireniia i obstrelivaiut aeroport Kabula," *Izvestiia*, Aug 3, 1992, p. 4; "Rossiia osuzhdaet iranskoe vtorzhenie v Azerbaidzhan," *Nezavisimaia gazeta*, September 8, 1993, p. 2.

17. Tsentr etnopoliticheskikh issledovanii, "Sotsialno-politicheskaia situatsiia v postsovetskom mire," May 1993, pp. 29-31.

18. "Moskva smotrit na vostok," *Moskovskie novosti*, no. 31, Aug 2, 1992, p. 12; "Soiuzniki, partnery, sosedi," *Nezavisimaia gazeta*, July 16, 1993, p. 5.

19. "Perspektivy Kaliningrada," *Nezavisimaia gazeta*, December 16, 1993, p. 4; also see M. Hoff and H. Timmerman, "Kaliningrad: Russia's Future Gateway to Europe?" *RFE/RL Report* 2, no. 36, September 10, 1993, pp. 37-43.

20. *Izvestiia*, February 17, 1992, p. 1.

21. "President - za rasshirenie prav rossiiskikh respublikh," *Nezavisimaia gazeta*, October 23, 1992, p. 1.

22. For example, Russian negotiations concerning British exploitation of copper deposits in Chita province, Moscow TV, November 8, 1992, in FBIS-SOV-92-217, pp. 6-7; and see "Kuzbass poluchaet konkretnuiu pomoshch iz Evropy," *Izvestiia*, April

16, 1993, p. 1. On governmental concessions to Sakhalin see ITAR-Tass, December 8, 1992, in FBIS-SOV-92s-237, December 9, 1992, p. 5; and "Siberia: Exiled No Longer," *The Economist*, November 21, 1992, p. 64.

23. In Chapter 1, Shenfield adds an additional, "neo-Soviet" category. I omit it here because the neo-Soviet perspective is not a major factor influencing Russian international conduct and thereby indirectly affecting domestic consolidation. I also focus specifically on foreign policy orientations, whereas Shenfield is primarily concerned with "ideal types" relevant to domestic politics.

24. Thus, following the confrontation with parliament in the fall of 1993, Yeltsin moved to dismiss certain heads of local soviets, and banned opposition parties.

25. Comments by Andrei Kozyrev in "Dumat o svoikh interesakh," *Izvestiia*, October 2, 1991, p. 3; Vladimir Lukin, Russian Ambassador to the United States, "Our Security Predicament," *Foreign Policy* 88, Fall 1992, pp. 57-75.

26. "Moskva pytaetsia pogasit Tadzhikskuiu mezhdousobitsu," *Nezavisimaia gazeta*, November 11, 1992, pp. 1, 3.

27. Kozyrev, "Partiia voiny nastupaet," *Izvestiia*, June 30, 1992, p. 3; and the comments by Deputy Foreign Minister Georgii Mamedov, in "Pozitsiia ministerstva inostrannykh del Rossii," *Pravda*, November 6, 1992, p. 3. On the existence of limited competition, see Lukin's speech at the Foreign Ministry, in *Diplomaticheskii vestnik*, no. 6, March 31, 1992, pp. 36-39, at p. 37; also Petr Aven, former Minister of Foreign Economic Relations under Gaidar, "Vneshne-ekonomicheskie sviazi Rossii: kakimi im byt?" *MEiMO*, July 1992, pp. 44-47.

28. Thus, the liberal outlook tends to be associated with "spiral" rather than "deterrence" assumptions. The classic exposition of the spiral image and the security dilemma is Robert Jervis, "Offense, Defense, and the Security Dilemma," *World Politics* 30, no. 2, January 1978, pp. 186-214. See A. Kozyrev, "Partiia voiny nastupaet," *Izvestiia*, June 30, 1992, p. 3; "A minnoe pole tak veliko," *Rossiiskaia gazeta*, July 25, 1992, p. 7.

29. For example, former First Deputy Foreign Minister Fedor Shelov-Kovediaev, "V kritike vneshnei politiki Rossii my stalkivaemsia s opasnym neprofessionalizmom," *Nezavisimaia gazeta*, July 30, 1992, pp. 1, 5; also Vladimir Stupishin, Russian Ambassador to Armenia, "Pravo natsii na samoopredelenie i territorialnaia tselostnost gosudarstv," *Nezavisimaia gazeta*, August 5, 1992, p. 3.

30. See Sergei Shakhrai's comments in "Raion chrezvychainogo polozheniia," *Izvestiia*, January 10, 1993, p. 5; and Yeltsin's statements in favor of using force in the North Ossetian-Ingushetian conflict. Moscow INTERFAX, November 7, 1992, in FBIS-SOV-92-217, November 9, 1992, p. 34.

31. See the interview with Valentin Tishkov, who resigned as chairman of the State Committee on Nationality Policy in late September 1992 under heavy criticism. "Bezrassudno otdavat vlast odnoi etnicheskoi gruppe," *Nezavisimaia gazeta*, October 24, 1992, p. 3.

32. Kozyrev, "A minnoe pole tak veliko," *Rossiiskaia gazeta*, July 25, 1992, p. 7; and see the statements by Deputy Foreign Minister Vitalii Churkin, in "Rossiia chut ne stala opasnym mezhdunarodnym partnerom," *Izvestiia*, July 23, 1993, p. 2.

33. A. Bogaturov, M. Kozhokin, and K. Pleshakov, "Vneshniaia politika Rossii," *SShA*, October 1992, pp. 27-41; also V. Tishkov, "Dilemmy razvitiia Rossii," *Etnopolis*, no. 1, 1992, pp. 77-85.

34. "Boris Fedorov nadeetsia na rezultativnost Tokiiskoi vstrechi," *Izvestiia*, April 15, 1993, p. 3. See also A. Iu. Davydov, "Vneshniaia zadolzhennost Rossii i sotrudnichestvo s mezhdunarodnymi finansovymi organizatsiiami," *SShA*, October 1992, pp. 47-55; and Elena Volkova, "Vneshniaia politika Rossii: evropeiskii kontekst," *MEiMO*, September 1992, pp. 18-29.

35. For example, see "Chastnyi vizit Burbulisa serezno ozadachil Tokiiskikh obozrevatelei," *Izvestiia*, September 3, 1993, p. 3.

36. "Rossiia - Germaniia: chto dalshe?" *Nezavisimaia gazeta*, November 5, 1992, p. 5.

37. Rutskoi's comments, Radio Rossii, December 2, 1992 in FBIS-SOV-92-232-S, December 3, 1992, p. 14; Khasbulatov's speech at the Foreign Ministry, in *Diplomaticheskii vestnik*, no. 6, March 31, 1992, pp. 30-32, at p. 31; and Natalia Narochnitskaia, chairperson of the International Affairs Committee of the Constitutional-Democratic [Cadet] Party, in "Natsionalnye interesy Rossii," *Mezhdunarodnaia zhizn*, July 1992, pp. 134-144 at p. 140.

38. R. Abdulatipov, "Sokhranit i vozrodit rossiiskuiu federatsiiu," *Etnopolis*, no. 1, July 1992, pp. 5-15 at p. 9. Also "Rossiia raschitivaet na pomoshch MVF, no ne soglasna sledovat vsem trebovaniiam fonda," *Izvestiia*, July 6, 1992, p. 1; and "Senat SShA predostavit Rossii pomoshch," *Izvestiia*, October 1, 1992, p. 1, 5.

39. Elgiz Pozdniakov, "We Must Rebuild What We Have Destroyed with Our Own Hands," *International Affairs*, nos. 4-5, April-May, 1992, pp. 129-136. See also the views of former Minister of Foreign Economic Relations, "Sergei Glazev: uspekh zavisit ot realizatsii preimushestv Rossiiskikh predpriatii," *Nezavisimaia gazeta*, September 9, 1993, pp. 1, 4.

40. Interview with Nikolai Travkin, Interfax December 21, 1992, in FBIS-SOV-92-246, December 22, p. 24; interview with late Chief of Staff Viktor Dubynin, "Mirotvorcheskie sily obkhodiatsia nam v kopeechky," *Izvestiia*, September 1, 1992, p. 3; and "S Kozyrevym - bez kozyrei?" *Komsomolskaia pravda*, September 3, 1992, p. 3.

41. See statement by the General Staff, "Genshtab: ostanovit sokrashenie voisk na iuzhnykh kurilakh," *Nezavisimaia gazeta*, July 30, 1992, p. 1 and 3.

42. Stankevich was referring to the Trans-Dnestr crisis, but intended his argument to apply broadly. S. Stankevich, "Poka nikomu ne udavalos polnostiu iskliuchit silu iz arsenala politiki," *Izvestiia*, July 7, 1992, p. 3; and see idem, "Formula stabilizatsii v `goriachikh tochkakh'," *Rossiiskaia gazeta*, July 28, 1992, p. 1.

43. Former Minister of Security Viktor Barannikov, Radio Rossii, December 10, 1992, in FBIS-SOV-92-240-S, December 14, 1992, pp. 26-31; Ramazan Abdulatipov, "Vrazhda opasna dlia Otechestva," *Narodnyi deputat*, no. 4, 1993, pp. 11-13; Aleksandr Vladislavlev and Sergei Karaganov, "Tiazhkii krest Rossii," *Nezavisimaia gazeta*, November 17, 1992, p. 5.

44. The Republic of Chechnia attained *de facto* recognition by the Russian Congress of People's Deputies. ITAR-TASS, January 14.

45. *Rossiia*, no. 47, November 18-24, 1992, p. 1, in FBIS-SOV-92-227, November 24, 1992, p. 15.

46. Comments by former Chief of the CIS joint command Marshall Shaposhnikov, Radio Rossii, December 11, 1992, in FBIS-SOV-92-240-S, December

14, 1992, pp. 24-26; and at a conference sponsored by the CIS military command, ITAR-TASS, April 5, 1993, from *RFE/RL News Briefs*, April 5-8, 1993, p. 6.

47. "SNG stanovitsia ekonomicheskim soiuzom po tipu konfederatsii," *Nezavisimaia gazeta*, September 8, 1993, p. 1; "Neftianye dolgi staviat pod ugrozu ekonomicheskii suverenitet respublik," *Finansovye Izvestiia*, September 10-16, 1993, p. 1. For a representative statist assessment, see "Ustupki, konechno, delaiutsia. No ne Moskve-zdravomu smyslu," *Krasnaia zvezda*, September 11, 1993, p. 2.

48. "Predprinimateli SNG priniali obrashchenie k glavam gosudarstv Sodruzhestva," *Izvestiia*, October 7, 1992, p. 2; "Kak vybiratsia iz krizisa - vmeste ili porozn? Nastaet pora opredeliatsia," *Krasnaia zvezda*, December 17, 1992, p. 1. On the need for closer military cooperation see Shaposhnikov, "Voennye aspekty kollektivnoi bezopasnosti," *Izvestiia*, July 3, 1992, pp. 1-2. Thanks to Stephen Shenfield for discussion on this point.

49. Interview with Adranik Migranian, member of Presidential Advisory Council, July 1993; also Lt. Gen. Leonid Ivashov, Secretary of CIS Council of Defense Ministers, in *Krasnaia zvezda*, November 24, 1992, p.2; and for a general discussion by Roman Solchanyk, "Back to the USSR?" *Harriman Institute Forum* 6, no. 3, November 1992. As noted above, Kozyrev's own statements in 1993 reflected the government's drift in the statist direction.

50. S. Stankevich, "Formula stabilizatsii v `goriachikh tochkakh'," *Rossiiskaia gazeta*, July 28, 1992, p. 1; "Moskva prizyvaet Serbov poiti na ustupki," *Izvestiia*, April 21, 1993. Russia also abstained during a UN vote for sanctions against Serbia, held on April 17.

51. "Novye puti vo vneshnei politike," *Nezavisimaia gazeta*, October 24, 1992, p. 4; "Esli na Blizhnem Vostoke nachnetsia `kholodnaia voina'," *Rossiiskaia gazeta*, July 28, 1992, p. 7.

52. "Parliament rekomenduet presidentu ogranichitsia," *Nezavisimaia gazeta*, August 26, 1992, p. 2.

53. "Postanovlenie Verkhovnogo Soveta Rossiiskoi Federatsii," *Diplomaticheskii vestnik*, no. 12, June 30, 1992, p. 5; author's interviews in the Supreme Soviet Subcommittee on International Affairs, July 1993.

54. Igor Orlik, "Rossiia i vostochnaia evropa: problemy i perspektivy," *Mezhdunarodnaia zhizn*, July 1992, pp. 27-35 at p. 33.

55. This includes Aleksandr Zhirinovskii, individuals affiliated with the National Salvation Front and the Russian National Congress, the umbrella Pamiat organization, and elements of the military establishment such as the Officer's Union. All of these organizations were officially banned by Yeltsin in October 1993.

56. Gennadi Ziuganov, "Evraziia - sudba i vyzov," *Pravda*, December 24, 1992, pp. 1-2; "Rossiiskoe narodnoe sobranie: politicheskie printsipy i blizhaishie zadachi," *Obozrevatel*, February, 1992, p. 16 and 11-17.

57. Interfax, December 21, 1992, in FBIS-GOV-92-246, December 22, 1992, p. 18.

58. "Russkie idut!" *Narodnaia pravda*, June-July 1992, p. 6; E. Volodin, "Pauza?" *Sovetskaia Rossiia*, November 14, 1992, p. 5; Aleksandr Varenik, "Klevetniki Rossii," *Den*, no. 35, August 30-September 5, 1992, p. 2.

59. Comments by Viktor Aksiuchits, Iurii Bokan, Mikhail Astafiev, and Valerii Khomiakov, "Tupiki: gde zhe vykhod?" *Vozrozhdenie*, no.1, 1992, pp. 18-20 and 45.

Also Viktor Alksnis, "Za rodinu, za SSSR!" *Den*, no. 52, December 27-31, 1992, p. 1. Compare Oleg Rumiantsev's comments, quoted in "Est o chem podumat," *Rossiiskaia gazeta*, December 2, 1992, p. 2.

60. Not surprisingly, such views have found support within the military itself. "Esli khotim rastit nastoiashchikh soldat, nado preodolet `dukhovnyi vakuum'" *Krasnaia zvezda*, December 4, 1992, p. 1.

61. Interview with Lebed in *Izvestiia*, February 26, 1993, p. 5; on the National Salvation Front, INTERFAX, October 24 and 26, 1992.

62. "Palestinskoe soprotivlenie," *Den*, no. 31, August 2-8, 1992, p. 3. "Russia Urges the Security Council to Reconvene on the Iraq Fighting," *New York Times*, January 19, 1993, p. A7.

63. Eduard Volodin, "Vyzov bezdny," *Sovetskaia Rossiia*, August 22, 1992. p. 1.

64. See the report of the Expert Institute of the Russian Union of Industrialists and Entrepreneurs, "Edinstvo reformy i reforma edinstva," Moscow, July 1992.

65. See Kozyrev's warning about the implications of the new trend in his mock-serious speech to the December meeting of the CSCE in Stockholm. "`Shokovaia terapiia' Andreia Kozyreva," *Izvestiia*, December 15, 1992, p. 6. The new orientation led to a change in the official line regarding sanctions against Serbia. See the statements by Ambartsumov on Belgrade TV, December 16, 1992 in FBIS-SOV-92-243, December 17, 1992, p. 23, and by First Deputy Foreign Minister Anatolii Adamishin, Interfax, December 17, in FBIS-SOV-92-244, December 18, 1992, p. 49.

66. Yeltsin issued a decree calling for "more active" steps to protect the rights of Russians abroad. ITAR-TASS, December 1, 1992, in FBIS-SOV-92-232, December 2, 1992, p. 7. Note also that the treaty signed with Hungary in November focused on the need to safeguard human rights and counter "aggressive nationalism." ITAR-TASS, November 11, 1992; and see Kozyrev's comments on Budapest TV, November 11, 1992, in FBIS-SOV-92-219, November 12, 1992, p. 27.

Conclusion:
Is Disintegration Inevitable,
and Why Should We Care?

Douglas W. Blum

Post-Soviet Russia has experienced a short but already tumultuous history. Its very legitimacy as a self-defined, sovereign state has been brought into question as its social and political fabric has threatened to give way. To some extent, this is the unavoidable result of the collapse of empire and the wrenching separation of its parts. Added to this is the change in the international distribution of power, and the difficult process of learning the new rules of the geopolitical game. But in large measure the stormy nature of Russia's post-Soviet passage is due to internal sources of instability, including inter-ethnic tensions, religious intolerance, national chauvinism, economic dislocation, and a lack of fully legitimate political institutions. The preceding essays have addressed a number of these themes in an attempt to understand the forces shaping Russian political development today.

The problem of forging a coherent and widely accepted ideology will be a key factor in determining the outcome of Russia's struggle to become consolidated. In the absence of any shared self-identity, it obviously will be extraordinarily difficult to attain social cohesion or political legitimacy. Moreover, the kind of self-identity and vision of society that does emerge will have an important bearing on the course of reform and its prospects for success.

In Russia now there is no available revolutionary ideology capable of galvanizing mass support. Liberal democracy lacks deep indigenous roots, and in any case may be unable to provide the kind of guidance needed in the present period of turbulence. Other possible sources of identity, such as traditional communitarianism, Orthodoxy, and Russian exceptionalism, all appear too limited in scope, given the heterogeneity of the population. Similarly, the Tsarist legacy has very restricted appeal, and efforts to reimpose it would cause mass political, religious, and ethnic tensions. Shenfield suggests that the most likely basis for ideological consensus is historical. But the uneven, often con-

tradictory nature of Russian history invites a ragtag assortment of symbols and
allegiances, reflecting the most diverse aspects of Russian political culture. In
this context it is unclear that any viable form of self-identification can soon
emerge to provide social and political cohesion.

Other possibilities exist, of course. The lack of democratic traditions
coupled with extreme instability could result in a recrudescence of Tsarist and
Soviet tendencies in political culture. This could well lead to the emergence of
a new prevailing ideology that combines several elements, such as patrimonial
state interference, Orthodoxy, and pan-Slavic nationalism, none of which
would be able to provide an attractive enough platform by itself. In conditions
of serious social dislocation, a hybrid ideology might become quite attractive.
Yet it remains doubtful that such an ideology would provide the basis for lasting social cohesion.

Another, more optimistic, possibility is that a democratic ideology may
gradually emerge and become institutionalized. The Russian parliament could
potentially play a key role in this process. As Smyth argues, the parliament
provides a central, highly visible forum within which particularistic and general concerns could be reconciled and a shared identity formed. In this way it
could be instrumental for integrating the divergent interests of local elites. Yet
in practice, there is a critical need to establish a responsive electoral system,
disciplined parties, enforceable property rights, and consistent rules. Deep political cleavages may exist but, as the examples of Italy and Israel show, this
need not preclude a stable polity. The development of well-institutionalized
parliamentary mechanisms and procedural norms can play an important stabilizing role.

The prospects of such developments coming to pass are difficult to gauge.
Smyth points out that the autonomy and relative political standing of parliament is determined to a considerable extent by the interaction between parliament and other leading actors. In the recent past the parliament and executive
have pursued confrontational strategies, each attempting to capture or undermine the other. This conflict may be resolved with the emergence of a new
bicameral legislature, but whether this is a temporary or permanent resolution
will depend on the ability of key actors and interests to overcome a collective
action problem of cooperation, to reach an institutional accommodation that
goes beyond personalities and power plays, and to fashion a clear understanding of respective roles and prerogatives.

If parliament were to emerge preponderant, there would probably be a net
increase in social tension, since this would eliminate the mediating role the
executive is capable of playing. Furthermore, it seems probable that Yeltsin's
surprisingly strong showing in the April 1993 referendum, and the public support for his dissolution of the Supreme Soviet in the fall of the year, reflected a
widespread sentiment in favor of a strong executive to bring Russia out of its
crisis.[1] On the other hand, as Rudenshiold and Barnes as well as Khrushchev

argue, a preponderant executive alone would not be sufficient to ensure consolidation, and might well inflame the conflict between the center and the localities.[2] Rather, a representative system, including a strong executive and clear separation of powers, might be ideally suited to resolving Russia's current malaise, if only it could be attained. Unfortunately, the longstanding deadlock damaged parliament's institutional legitimacy, and served to exacerbate various disintegrative tendencies.[3] Yet, as Smyth observes, if the crisis is ultimately resolved by the emergence of a robust legislative framework balanced by executive and judicial authority, this would represent an important step on the road to consolidation.

Of course, the structural issue is only one part of the overall problem. There is still a host of practical questions regarding how to find a way out of the current crisis. One influential approach (broadly represented by the Civic Union) involves maintaining the integrity of Russia; slowing down privatization and marketization; resisting increased prices; providing social guarantees; and offering assistance to state enterprises in danger of bankruptcy. If such an alternative were implemented consistently it might provide a basis for consolidation. This would depend, however, on its ability to achieve economic stabilization at the macro level, including increased productivity and successful management of state debt, budgetary deficit, money supply, and basic services.

Unfortunately, as Spagat's chapter attests, there exists a combination of structural and infrastructural deficiencies that will be extremely difficult to remedy. Labor and capital productivity provide two keys to Russia's future economic stabilization, and each would be enhanced by competitive pressures and rewards. But in the absence of market conditions, and given the prevailing political priorities, inefficient firms are rewarded while efficient ones are punished. This underscores the lack of rational guidelines for investment decisions, and the lack of credit markets to fund such investments in any case.

While new, stricter guidelines for bankruptcy have been introduced, and a tentative agreement has been reached to curb credits and limit growth of the money supply, it remains uncertain whether such measures will be enforced. As Spagat suggests, unless such actions are taken it will be hard to improve or even maintain the stock of existing human and physical capital.

Another problem that has not been adequately addressed is the demands of organized labor. In Cook's view, there remains an entrenched (neo-Soviet and statist) mentality based on the notion of a "social contract" that is very difficult to dislodge. Mounting unemployment and a general decline in living standards will certainly create enormous popular pressure to expand social welfare programs.[4] Under the multi-party system there will be electoral incentives for political actors to avoid painful adjustment measures in their approach to labor-management relations.

At the same time, labor has become independently organized, and the corporatist approach of the tripartite mechanism has broken down. This poses a major challenge for any reformist government, since labor's successes in organizing make it a significant constituency, which would be politically advantageous to co-opt. On the other hand, doing so might be antithetical to reform, and full employment and wage subsidies would contribute to inflation (especially under conditions of falling productivity). And as Cook also points out, although the leaders of some of the independent unions favor reform, often the rank and file do not. It seems likely that only by pressing ahead with marketization will it be possible to galvanize the economy and destroy the vestiges of the paternalistic alliance between labor and management. Notwithstanding the social and ideological problems this poses, such developments may be necessary for consolidation at the national level.

The emergence of a functional domestic economy is crucial for the prospects of consolidation as well. A productive economy could provide rational incentives for policy alignment at the regional level, including payment of taxes and acceptance of federal regulation, rather than defiant and ultimately inefficient autarky. The paradox of Russian economic policy coordination is that increased regional participation is essential for stabilization, but this participation is unlikely to be forthcoming unless stabilization occurs. In many respects this, too, involves a collective action problem. Local elites might be more willing to cooperate if simultaneous cooperation by other localities could be assured, but the erosion of legitimate central authority makes this more doubtful.

As Khrushchev shows, critical shortages and production problems create a vicious cycle of political and economic decay at the local level. As the technological level of enterprises declines, they become less able to achieve profitability, and their markets become more restricted. Not surprisingly, in the general atmosphere of scarcity and uncertainty, inter-regional disputes have broken out over transportation, access to resources, and contract fulfillment. In contrast to the Soviet period, when central authorities stepped in to break through bottlenecks and to ensure the provision of critical supplies, under Yeltsin the center began to delegate more responsibility to the localities. This fostered a process that has now gained massive momentum and cannot be easily contained. Such frictions may be intensified by local ethnic conflicts, which may themselves be exacerbated by economic hardship, and by the influx of refugees from the former Soviet republics in response to regional upheavals and anti-Russian sentiment.[5]

The growth of local autonomy and civic involvement may play an important role in promoting political stability. Yet at present there are reasons to doubt that the emerging civil society will contribute directly to political consolidation. As Rudenshiold and Barnes observe, local political infrastructures and grass roots party organizations are still very weak. Furthermore, a characteristic aspect of post-Soviet local politics appears to be a reaction against any form of "centrism," even within a single party. This makes it particularly difficult for parties to consolidate and to acquire legitimacy. Finally, the fiasco of parliamentary politics in 1992-1993 contributed to widespread popular cynicism about the political process. This combination of adverse economic conditions, internal squabbles, and mass alienation make it difficult for a stable party system to emerge in Russia. The reformed electoral law and its inclusion of proportional representation from party lists provides a strong impetus for improving party cohesiveness and discipline. But this may not be enough. It remains to be seen how popular attitudes align themselves with elite groupings, and how well organized various competing interests will be.

If multiparty democracy flounders, several other outcomes become correspondingly more likely. One is the tendency for extremist groups to arise, especially in view of the political cultural trends discussed by Shenfield. Another is the intrusion of local "mafias" into the political process, and the displacement of local politics by corruption. A third, and perhaps most probable, outcome for Russia as a whole is the tendency for entrenched local elites to assert themselves and maneuver for political solutions that express a commitment to managerial power (and perhaps social welfare programs). This development might be coupled with considerable local political autonomy on the basis of vested interests and patronage networks.

Thus, two extreme possibilities exist: the reemergence of a strongly centralized state; or the collapse of Russia into numerous ethnic- or territorially-based states, some truly sovereign and others dominated by regional powers. Between these two extremes several other possibilities suggest themselves: a federation allowing considerable devolution of authority; a confederation (which might itself be a transitory stage); or a mixed system, including some areas that are well integrated and others that are only loosely associated with the Russian center.

Prevailing statist attitudes would probably foster efforts to enforce at least a significant degree of territorial and political unity, against the wishes of separatist groups. However, the manifold problems with such solutions make it doubtful that enforced consolidation could work. After dissolving the parliament in the fall of 1993, Yeltsin attempted to pressure the provinces to accept a strong federation, and such an arrangement is envisioned in the new Constitution. Despite executive leverage and legal codification, however, local authorities may simply refuse to comply, and may grow even more defiant. It remains uncertain whether there is popular support for tightly integrated political and economic structures, and it is doubtful that such measures can effectively be imposed by decree. Extreme efforts to override local resistance could undermine not only the executive, but all central political authority.[6] In sum, there seems likely to be a continued trend towards political disintegration in the short run.

The process may take quite different forms in different regions. In some cases local elites have resorted to provocative actions such as withholding taxes; insisting that local taxes be available for local expenditures; or demanding control over natural resources and other commodities capable of generating hard currency. In other areas the tendency has been toward reimposition of paternalistic command controls at the local level, or a mixed approach (such as that espoused by Civic Union). Furthermore, not all regions by any means currently advocate separatism. Of those that do, some favor an autarkic orientation instead of openness to outside economic penetration. Often, regional fragmentation has expressed several disintegrative factors at once. For example, the decisions by Tatarstan and Bashkortostan to withhold taxes were the result of combined ethnic, political, and economic grievances. In the case of the Kurils and Sakhalin, local declarations of sovereignty were not based primarily on economic or nationalist principles, but on defiance of central manipulation and defense of vested interests that would be jeopardized by return of the territories to Japan.[7]

And of course, continued fragmentation is only one possible outcome. Another possibility is political amalgamation or economic integration at the provincial level, conceivably leading to creation of a number of larger, functionally independent, regions. Khrushchev suggests that the resource-rich areas east of the Volga are particularly likely to seek economic (and perhaps political) independence, and to pursue direct ties with foreign trading partners. Indeed, as long as this process is not carried to the point of rupture with the Russian Federation, it is likely to be supported by liberals and statists at the center.[8]

One of the dangers associated with the drift toward disintegration is the emergence of assertive military involvement in domestic politics. Lepingwell is rather optimistic about the short-term prospects for stable civilian-military relations. However, he is more guarded in his assessment of longer-term trends in this area. As he argues, there are immense problems involved in maintaining military professionalism while undergoing large-scale force reduction and reorientation in mission, especially in the context of economic crisis and declining political legitimacy. The prevalence of authoritarian and nationalistic tendencies, the continued intrusion of military officials in the political process, and the weakness of civilian institutions all contribute to the difficulty of constructing stable civil-military relations.

The independent political influence of the military might be significant during this unsettled period, especially if the standard of living for its officer corps continues to decline along with the quantity and quality of its overall human and material resource base. The growing regional role of the military is also relevant here, since, as Lepingwell points out, the military has assumed an increasingly active role in internal security missions. This raises the possibility of *de facto* autonomy on the part of local military commanders, or conceivably an enhanced role of the central military apparatus in filling the void created by the absence of stable state institutions. Coupled with the emergence of a national-patriotic ideology, the result could be a heavily militarized set of institutions and policies. This, in turn, would increase the likelihood of a resort to coercive measures in order to consolidate Russia, or at least to prevent further disintegration. It should also be noted that the process of local militarization does not depend only on the integrity of the Russian Federation's armed forces, but also on the disposition of local political authorities, some of whom may favor developing their own militias in order to assert their independence or to protect against incursions by other armed formations. The emergence of a Cossack military force is only one manifestation of what may become a general trend.[9]

Domestic disintegration also affects foreign policy calculations. As I argue in Chapter 8, there appears to be a logic to this process, such that disintegrative tendencies lead to statist (or harder-line) responses, which lead to foreign policy assertiveness in order to defend Russian interests and to insulate Russia from regional perturbations. This may portend the restoration of the Soviet Union in a new, somewhat truncated form, probably as a more closely intertwined Commonwealth of Independent States in which Russia has the dominant voice. If not managed skillfully, this development might lead to tensions with Russia's neighbors to the south and east, who may be suspected of fishing in the muddy waters of ethnic unrest. Beyond the CIS, relations with the West may tend to be rather competitive, and Russia may not always be counted on to adhere to multilateral security measures and peacekeeping initiatives. Yet the West is likely to remain an important focus of Russian policy, and a partner in resolving many problems in international trade and security.[10] At the same time, Moscow will probably favor a balanced policy according to which relations with the Asian-Pacific Region and Eastern Europe assume roughly equal priority, and in which national interests are pursued instead of overarching supranational ends.[11]

Yet this is only the central government's approach. Independent foreign policies are already being conducted by several autonomous entities within Russia, and the number may grow. It is also certain that regional actors will pursue independent initiatives in foreign economic policy. Whether such developments prove destabilizing or not depends partly on the reaction of the center, and partly on the policies forged by the localities. A significant danger is the emergence of armed local disputes (arising from ethnic, ecological, or economic problems), possibly leading to spiralling military conflicts that could easily cross Russian borders. This is particularly worrisome given the potential devolution of authority to local military commanders, about which Lepingwell speculates, as well as the proliferation of independent militias in newly independent regions such as Chechnia and Tatarstan.[12]

Thus, it may be that stability is more attractive than potential growth, and that paternalistic statism is more attractive than market competition for assuring it. And from a strictly political standpoint, statist solutions offer a vehicle for coalition-building between entrenched local elites, military-industrialists, and nationalists.[13] After all, autarkic institutions and interest groups that survive from the Soviet era have an interest in blocking liberal internationalism, just as Great Russian xenophobes and Orthodox extremists have an interest in stemming the tide of ethnic and cultural diversity.

Yet, as the authors of the preceding chapters have taken care to point out, the political situation in Russia is quite fluid, and significant alternate tendencies may come to the fore in this ever-shifting, extraordinarily complex pattern of political and economic development.

Indeed, in answer to the question of which trend is ascendant—consolidation or disintegration—it is tempting to answer that both are. There seem to be two powerful, partially opposing trends underway. One leads to the imposition of central controls, both to buffer the transition to market and to provide some coherence in the face of chaotic social and political fragmentation. The other is the devolution of political and economic decision-making authority to the local level, given the lack of a cohesive national identity, the vacuum of central political authority, the absence of a properly functioning national market, the collapse of supply and social services, the deficiencies of "national" parties or unifying central institutions, and the pull of local ethnic or other traditional allegiances. In reality, however, these trends are only partially in opposition, and depending on the prevailing ideology and policy agenda they may actually be complementary in certain essential respects.

First, it should be clear that centralization is not equivalent to consolidation. Efforts to impose central control are very likely to be thwarted by breakaway local assertiveness. Yet far from expressing a failure of consolidation, this merely reveals the impossibility of imposing a uniform authoritarian regime without massive use of force (the success of which would be highly doubtful in any case, not to mention financially ruinous). Second, it should also be clear that decentralization is not equivalent to disintegration. The emergence of autonomous regional power and stable, local level political authority are, at least in theory, entirely compatible with the consolidation of functional central institutions.[14] Between the extremes of anarchy and pervasive central governmental regulation there exists quite a large gray area within which post-Soviet Russia may come to rest.

How long will the present course run? Is there a logical endpoint of centrifugal tendencies, at which point centripetal tendencies will begin to assert themselves? Beyond the foreseeable future of continued disintegration, the longer term picture may be quite different.

First, there may exist a deep underlying sense of Russian identity that has not yet become evident due to the more urgent task of completing the process of self-assertion and independence. It may be that after this necessary initial stage has been carried out, the residual elements of commonality will become more pronounced and facilitate some form of renewed association.

In any case, there appears to be a solid foundation for the functional consolidation of Russia. The economic interdependence of much of the former Soviet area remains an inescapable fact. In the absence of truly massive foreign subsidies and joint projects to provide new capital and develop natural resources, the Russian government will be forced to retain traditional foreign economic relationships and attempt to put them on a new cooperative basis.[15] The same holds true within Russia itself. Given the piratical tendencies of some business elites and the dangers posed by short-term profit maximization, certain sectors—such as mining and energy—may benefit from a degree of central regulation.[16] Furthermore, even autarkically inclined or separatist regions will face objective pressures to deal with traditional partners in order to utilize existing resources and compatible technologies.[17] As the example of Western Europe suggests, functional linkages combined with elite interpenetration may lead to closer and more stable cooperation, if not full reintegration. If institutionalized and accompanied by the construction of norms, this process could become self-reinforcing and spill over to other areas; it might even come to take on the larger dimension of identity creation.

Finally, the international context within which such developments unfold will have an important bearing on Russia's prospects for consolidation. For example, an expansion of NATO—whose continued existence is of dubious value in any case—would probably serve to promote coercive actions against domestic sources of Russian disintegration, as well as hegemonic, balancing policies in the former Soviet republics. In contrast, a cooperative, non-threatening West can help strengthen the viability of liberal or moderate statist platforms, while at the same time limiting the appeal of extremist arguments.[18] This, in turn, might help facilitate consolidation, and make Russia a more stable and trustworthy partner for the future. Such outside influences may well have an effect, and it would be a mistake to dismiss them as insignificant.

But it is also important to recognize that much of what counts in terms of the international context goes beyond purposeful state policy. In this broader sense the international environment may also contribute to the long-term consolidation of Russia. The international context suggests that tendencies toward marketization will win out, especially in view of the competitive pressures for scientific-technological innovation. The requirements for integration into the international economy are stringent and the necessary domestic adjustments would be painful, but the benefits it offers are immense and the penalties for remaining isolated are considerable. This in turn offers incentives for efficient forms of domestic cooperation, which strengthens the tendency for interlocking networks to arise. Such developments are further encouraged by the emergence of a global culture and instantaneous communications. This creates increasingly porous boundaries across which people, goods, and services flow, and through which identities become more intermingled. All of these trends offer hope for Russia's future.

Foreign initiatives may also be helpful in reducing the risks of militarization or the creation of internal security dilemmas, which would make Russia more disintegrated and dangerous. A useful overall approach would be the implementation of what Janice Gross Stein terms a "reassurance strategy," which would include arms control, mutual security guarantees, and unilateral steps to alleviate Russian concerns (for example, the elimination of submarine-launched ballistic missiles from American submarines).[19] In addition, the International Atomic Energy Agency and other multilateral mechanisms for monitoring deployments and sharing defense-relevant information could be helpful for the emergence of strong civil institutions and the prevention of preponderant military influence in Russian politics.

International diplomacy also may have a positive influence on the outcome of the struggle between center and periphery. Instead of siding reflexively with Yeltsin or with central institutions *per se*, it will be essential to recognize the inevitability and legitimacy of decentralization, and to tailor policies to regional political realities. In terms of foreign economic aid, one goal would be to assist in the gradual replacement of existing capital stock, and in retraining personnel with skills suitable for a higher level of technological development. Such policies ought to be pursued regardless of the specific effect they might have on the distribution of power between Moscow and various localities.

For these purposes, large-scale financial aid by Western governments and international organizations, such as that announced by the Group of Seven in mid-April 1993, will be essential for years to come. Such assistance will have to cover a broad range of programs, such as export credits, grants for private entrepreneurship, a fund for ruble stabilization, and long-term debt restructuring.[20] This ought to include a two-fold strategy of encouraging outside investment in major projects, as well as subsidizing grass-roots investment in small businesses (along the lines of the Grameen Bank in Bangladesh).[21] It would be a mistake to ignore violations of human rights or democratic norms; there is no obligation to render aid indiscriminately to any and every Russian regime. Yet it is important not to be too rigid. It will be necessary to take the Russian political context into account when formulating standards or imposing sanctions.

The combination of functional interdependence, normative assimilation, and practical aid could help foster the emergence of strong democratic ideologies and institutions in Russia. This will require considerable effort and money, but as others have correctly argued, it must be understood as an investment both in military and demographic security, and in long-term economic growth. Avoiding the anarchic disintegration of Russia would contribute to geopolitical stability even beyond Eurasia, and would make it possible to concentrate on other, increasingly urgent problems of national and international security.

Notes

1. For example, R. Shakurov, "Avtoritarnaia vlast predpochtitelnee bezvlastiia," *Izvestiia*, April 2, 1993, p. 4.

2. One survey found much higher support for the central government versus the parliament among residents of central oblasts and large cities than among inhabitants of small towns and rural villages. "Est vysshii sudiia -- narod," *Izvestiia*, March 27, 1993, p. 4.

3. This leads to the tendency for a "war of laws," as Sergei Khrushchev observes, which reflects an absence of legitimate authority. For example, "Ukaz prezidenta Rossii 'o deiatelnosti ispolnitelnykh organov do preodoleniia krizisa vlasti'," *Izvestiia*, March 25, 1993, p. 1.

4. "Nuzhen novyi kurs sotsialnoi zashchity grazhdan Rossii," *Ekonomika i zhizn*, no. 15, April 1993, pp. 1-2. Unemployment figures are spotty, but as Linda Cook points out, the numbers appear to be growing.

5. For example, according to reports, only about 200,000 Russian speakers remained in Tajikistan by the spring of 1993, down from 495,000 in 1989. Interfax, April 13, 1993.

6. Indeed, some hard-line conservatives hope for this result. See A. Salutskii, "Chto vpered?" *Pravda*, September 25, 1993, p. 2.

7. "Novyi protest Tokio," *Nezavisimaia gazeta*, December 18, 1992, p. 4.

8. Sergei Shakhrai has expressed a vision of the center as a "facilitating force" for interregional connections. "Povolzhe i Ural podderzhivaiut novuiu gosudarstvennuiu natsionalnuiu politiku Rossii," *Izvestiia*, March 27, 1993, p. 4.

9. "Sozdana edinaia organizatsiia kazachikh voisk Rossii," *Izvestiia*, March 27, 1993, p. 4.

10. Yeltsin presented the START II agreement as the "final elimination of military confrontation," while at the same time carefully refuting any notion that Russia wished to form a "closed alliance." Speech to British Parliament, Moscow TV, November 10, 1992, in FBIS-SOV-92-219, November 12, 1992, p. 10.

11. Comments by Deputy Foreign Minister Grigorii Kunadze on Russian relations with the Far East, on Mayak radio, December 5, 1992, in FBIS-SOV-92-236, December 8, pp. 10-11. As one well-known journalist observed, at present "North Ossetia is more important for the fate of Russia than North America." S. Kondrashov, "Orientiry novogo mira," *Izvestiia*, November 30, 1992, p. 7.

12. Ted Hopf warns about a similar danger in the former Soviet context. "Managing Soviet Disintegration: A Demand for Behavioral Regimes," *International Security*, Summer 1992, pp. 44-75.

13. Although this was not generally the case in the past, it may be more likely in the multi-party context of the new parliament. See V. Lipitskii, chairman of the executive committee of Civic Union, "K voprosu o 'smykanii' tsentristov s neprimirimoi oppozitsiei," *Nezavisimaia gazeta*, September 10, 1993, p. 1.

14. High-level recognition of this fact is itself an auspicious development. See E. Pain, "Grozit li Rossii uchast SSSR?" *Literaturnaia gazeta*, June 16, 1993, p. 12.

15. The reformed Economic Union within the CIS reflects this general point. For example, for Russia to quickly develop its own oil and gas industries, its primary hard currency earners, it will require at least in the short term substantial cooperation with former Soviet republics for refineries (Belarus, Latvia, and Ukraine) and new construction (Azerbaijan). See *Neft i gaz vo vneshnei politike Rossii* (Moscow: Russian Foreign Policy Institute, 1992), esp. pp. 46-52. The mutual dependence of Russia upon Ukraine (for transportation to Europe) and of Ukraine upon Russia (for gas and oil) was evidenced by the agreement to maintain supply and concessionary prices, which was not altered by the Massandra accords. "Ukraina budet poluchat Rossiiskii gaz po samym nizkim tsenam," *Izvestiia*, March 18, 1992, p. 1. Nevertheless, as pointed out in Chapter 8 above, Russian has used pressure to garner favorable terms for debt repayment.

16. P. Sergeev, "Toplivno-energeticheskii kompleks Rossii: kak vyiti iz krizisa," *MEiMO*, August 1993, pp. 95-101.

17. Again, shared reliance on the energy industry offers a good example. Witness the formation of a consultative council, bringing together leading figures from the central ministry, regional experts, and representatives of the largest enterprises in the fuel-energy complex. "Regiony privlekaiutsia dlia formirovaniia energeticheskoi politiki," *Finansovye izvestiia*, April 2, 1993, p. II.

18. D. Deudney and J. Ikenberry, "The International Sources of Soviet Change," *International Security* 16, no. 3, Winter 1991/92, 74-118. Jack Snyder's general argument about the risks and benefits of trying to exert influence from outside remains relevant in the post-Soviet context. J. Snyder, "International Leverage on Soviet Domestic Change," *World Politics* 42, no. 1, October 1989, pp. 1-30.

19. Janice Gross Stein, "Reassurance in International Conflict Management," *Political Science Quarterly* 106, no. 3, Fall 1991, pp. 431-452.

20. See the cogent argument by David Lipton, "Reform Endangered," *Foreign Policy*. Spring 1993, pp. 57-78.

21. Plans are underway to create a joint Russian-international organization to provide guarantees to foreign investors. "Finansovye garantii dlia zarubezhnykh interesov," *Izvestiia*, March 11, 1993, p. 1.

About the Book
and Editor

Will Russia continue its process of fragmentation and decay, or will it manage to achieve lasting stability and cohesion? This timely and provocative book examines the chief dilemma facing Russia today, analyzing the factors likely to affect its resolution. Individual chapters focus on ideology and identity, party formation, elite politics, regionalism, labor and economic reform, civil-military relations, and foreign policy. The authors evaluate trends in each area, considering their implications for the disintegration or consolidation of the post-Soviet state.

Douglas W. Blum is associate professor of political science at Providence College.

About the Contributors

N. Catherine Barnes is a program officer with the International Foundation for Electoral Systems.

Douglas W. Blum is an associate professor of political science at Providence College.

Linda J. Cook is an associate professor of political science at Brown University.

Sergei Khrushchev is a visiting research associate at the Center for Foreign Policy Development of the Thomas J. Watson Jr. Institute for International Studies at Brown University.

John Lepingwell is an assistant professor of political science at the University of Illinois, Champaign-Urbana, and is currently a research fellow at Radio Liberty in Munich.

Eric Rudenshiold is a program officer with the International Republican Institute.

Stephen D. Shenfield is a research associate at the Center for Foreign Policy Development of the Thomas J. Watson Jr. Institute for International Studies at Brown University.

Regina A. Smyth is a doctoral candidate in political science at Duke University.

Michael Spagat is an assistant professor of economics at Brown University.

Index